ESSENTIAL MARKETING

ESSENTIAL MARKETING

Tony Proctor

CollinsEducational

An imprint of HarperCollins *Publishers*

Published by
Collins Educational Ltd
77–85 Fulham Palace Road
Hammersmith
London W6 8JB

First published in 1992

British Library Cataloguing
in Publication Data is
available on request from
the British Library.

ISBN 0–00–3276309

Typeset by CG Graphics, Aylesbury, Bucks.
Cover designed by Ridgeway Associates.
Cartoons by John Stuart Clark (Brick).
Printed in Great Britain by Cambridge University Press, Cambridge

Contents

Foreword

Every book in the Collins Essential Series is designed carefully to put you in control of your learning.

When you use this book, you will not only cover the core elements of your course, but you will also benefit from the author's use of modern teaching and learning techniques, with the result that you will make the best possible use of your time.

This book has:

- an introductory section at the beginning of each chapter, which focuses your attention on its contents and which tells you exactly what you will have learned by the end of the chapter. These are your learning objectives

- periodic summaries and reviews which regularly remind you of the content you are covering and so reinforce your learning

- notes in the margin of the text, where the author takes the role of a tutor: picking out key ideas, highlighting and explaining difficult concepts and guiding you to a better understanding of the main text

- frequent activities allowing you to learn from applying the ideas in the text. The results of these activities accumulate to give you a full set of notes on the subject

- suggestions for further reading that will help you to develop a broader understanding of the subject – this is always worth extra marks in the exam, as well as being more satisfying

- advice on study skills which gives you valuable suggestions for making the best use of your study time and improving your learning.

Learning is not easy: nobody learns without effort. However, if you use this book effectively, you will not only succeed in your course and assessment, but you will also enjoy the experience of learning.

Preface

Getting organized for study

Find out at the start of your course:

- how long it is, in hours per week and in total
- what homework and course work will you have to do
- what organization arranges for your assessment. What is the content of the syllabus? Is there a document laying this out? Get a photocopy. What knowledge and skills will you be assessed on? Is there a document specifying these? Get a photocopy. How are you going to be assessed? If by examination, what is the date of the examination? If by course work assignments, when will you be briefed on these and what are the final deadlines?

Place

Identify a location at home which is your study place and nothing else. Just a table will do. With practice you will reach a point where the act of sitting in that chair, at that table triggers the work response in you. This will not happen if you choose to work on the settee where you usually watch TV.

Time

- draw up a calendar of crucial dates for your course of study: term dates, assignment deadlines, examination dates. Make this the very first page of your notes
- how will you fit study around your other commitments? You cannot simply add a course on to an already over-full life. You will have to re-organize your life to make time for study and make better use of any time you fritter away now
- at what time of day do you work most effectively – not prefer to work – work more effectively. Experiment
- for how long can you study effectively at a stretch. Practise and test your learning until you know the answer to this question. For most people the answer is 'about an hour'. Then they need at least a short break
- private study for two hours everyday is much more effective than a ten-hour stint on Sunday
- for each period of study, set yourself realistic objectives. In this book every chapter starts with a set of targets or **objectives**. Use the chapter objectives to phase your study
- plan your study sessions and their objectives a week in advance. Things may not go exactly to plan, but at least you will know

what you have to do to make up for lost time
- when you have finished a chapter look at the chapter objectives again. Have you learned what you were supposed to learn?

Equipment

The minimum you will need is:

- A4 sized paper, brought in a pad with holes ready-punched
- an A4 ring-binder file, so you can store your work properly. File dividers are useful
- card index cards – if you want to make an index of key terms and key concepts. You can find or make a cardboard box to keep them in
- for this course a scrapbook, or plastic wallets would be useful for storing real-life examples of adverts, promotional materials marketing news, product launches and so on
- a pen you find it easy to write with
- your textbook(s).

Making and storing notes

Activities:

This book is written so that your responses to the activities in it will accumulate to give you a good set of notes on the most important aspects of marketing. But they will only be good notes if you can retrieve them for later use. This means:

- that you should head your answers so that you will know later what they were responses to. For example the first activity in this book asks you to:
  'Make a list of organizations . . . and categorize them according to whether you think they are production, product, sales, marketing or marketing (societal) oriented in their approach to business'
  an appropriate heading for this would be 'Business organizations: different orientations'
- that you store them properly

Key terms:

In order to respond adequately to the activity above, you will have to know the meaning of certain terms. For example, 'production orientation' or 'product orientation'. The best way to store information on key terms, key concepts, and sources of information is using card index cards. Take care in making decisions about classifying your cards. This isn't just a chore. You will learn a great deal about the subject by trying to decide whether, for example, to file 'production orientation' under 'P' for 'production' or under 'B' for 'business orientation – production' or somewhere else. The last objective for each chapter is a listing of the most important terms.

The marketing concept and the nature of marketing management

 You will see this sign where I have suggested an activity for you to carry out. Sometimes it will be an investigation, sometimes an essay, sometimes something else.

Introduction

Marketing can be viewed as both a functional aspect of a business and a business philosophy. Both of these viewpoints are explored in this first chapter. Over time, firms have adopted various **business orientations** and these are considered along with their implications for how firms perceive the marketplace. This chapter also draws the clear distinction between **selling** and **marketing**.

Finding a way of making a product or service different from that of competitors is seen as a key aspect of marketing strategy in both consumer and industrial markets. It is usually referred to as creating a competitive differential.

Marketing is part of the management process. It involves planning and taking decisions. The chapter ends by indicating that an organizational structure is required that will make it easy to implement marketing decisions and plans.

DEFINITIONS OF MARKETING

▶ Numerous definitions of marketing can be found in Malcolm McDonald and John Leppard's book *The Marketing Audit*, Butterworth Heinemann 1991 pp. 4–5.

There have been many definitions of marketing over the years and the definitions have changed with time. The important point in any definition of marketing is that it should make a clear reference to identifying and satisfying customer needs and to the building of support mechanisms upon this principle. The following definition meets this requirement:

> The activity that can keep in constant touch with an organization's consumers, read their needs and build a programme of communications to express the organization's purpose and means of satisfying them.

▶ The Chartered Institute of Marketing, Moor Hall, Cookham, Berks.

The official definition offered by the Chartered Institute of Marketing is somewhat shorter but also contains the same basic ideas:

> . . . the management process responsible for identifying, anticipating and satisfying consumer requirements efficiently and profitably.

What is a market?
A market is a collection of people sharing a common want or need and who are motivated to enter into exchange processes to satisfy the need or want.

Evolution of the marketing concept

The **marketing concept** is an approach to business that stresses achieving business goals through customer satisfaction. Businesses adopting the concept produce goods and services for which there is an identified customer demand. By paying attention to customers' requirements an organization can put itself into a better position to supply wanted goods and services. In so doing, provided it charges a reasonable price and other things are in order, it should make a profit. Under these circumstances the company is said to be **marketing oriented**.

Firms adopt a variety of approaches to business. One way of classifying these approaches is to categorize them as adopting one or other of the following orientations or concepts:
- production orientation (concept)
- product orientation (concept)

Needs, wants and demands

We experience **needs** when we are deprived of some basic satisfaction. In order to satisfy these needs we develop **wants**. **Demands** are wants for specific products or services together with an ability and willingness to purchase them. For example:

We are hungry – needs
We want food to satisfy our hunger – wants
We have just enough money to purchase fish and chips and decide that this is the best way to spend our money to solve the hunger problem – demands

- selling orientation (concept)
- marketing orientation (concept)
- societal (marketing) orientation (concept)

We shall look at each of these orientations in turn.

The production orientation

Production orientation places an emphasis on finding a cheaper way to produce goods so that cost savings can be passed on to consumers who will benefit as a result.

A good example of production orientation is to be found in the invention of movable type. Gutenberg's creation of movable type for printing made it possible for books to be produced much more cheaply than had previously been possible. The saving in cost was passed on to the user or consumer and many people were able to own books for the first time. Technology brought about the production concept.

► Historically, technology and the production concept together brought about many benefits to society. The harnessing of steam power to industry made it possible to mass-produce many products at a cheap price to the consumer.

An example of production orientation

Volkswagen Beetle
In 1936 Adolf Hitler opened the first factory for the manufacture of Germany's 'People's car', the Volkswagen. It was designed by Ferdinand Porsche and was intended for mass production at popular prices. The idea was to put the nation on wheels, doing for Germany what Henry Ford had done for the USA.

While production orientation does work in the consumer's interest it only goes a small part of the way towards what nowadays we call 'marketing orientation'. Production orientation still exists in some firms. Such firms assume that people will buy their products because they are cheaply priced. This may be true where the demand for a product exceeds the supply and customers are more interested in obtaining the product than in its finer details. As in the case of the Gutenberg press it may also work where a product's costs are unduly high and a price reduction would expand the market. Unfortunately, in adopting a production orientation stance opportunities may be missed since such enterprises are not really sensitive to customer wants and needs.

Product orientation

Product orientation rests on the belief that if someone builds a better product then everyone will rush to the factory gates to buy it. It leads to a preoccupation with the product or service rather than the need and ignores what the consumer requires.

One of the consequences of the Industrial Revolution was the development of large size firms in the nineteenth century and the growth of business competition. Some firms began to recognize the need for advertising and other forms of promotion. One outcome of competition was that firms began to concentrate on producing a better product in order to gain a competitive edge in the marketplace. This is now referred to as product orientation and like production orientation it persists in some firms to this day.

▶ Alfred Bird, the British half of General Foods as it is now known, was famous for its advertisements in the latter half of the nineteenth century. The first pictorial advertisements appeared in 1880 and the firm along with T. B. Browne set the pattern of advertising through agencies.

▶ An American called Emerson is credited with originating this advice. Several firms have tried to do just this – one product was a laser mousetrap which failed.

▶ Over-engineering is a very important problem. If customers expect a certain quality for a given price and everyone else recognizes the price-quality 'pitch' it is pointless for a firm to offer more quality for the same price unless it gains a sustainable competitive advantage.

Product concept or orientation

If you build a better mousetrap the world will beat a path to your door to buy it.

An example of product orientation
Over- engineering

At the end of the Second World War a large armaments manufacturing company based in the UK and accustomed to working to precise tolerances in manufacturing its products carried on this tradition into the peace time production of industrial products.

These products were much better than competitors' because they were engineered to tighter specifications. However, the cost of working to such high standards forced up the costs of production. The users of the products only required them to be manufactured to lower tolerance specifications and since competitors were supplying products to the lower specifications at the same price, the ex-armaments firm had difficulty in making any profit at all.

Product orientation contrasts with production orientation. The latter is based on the idea that if you can bring down the **price** of a product then this will lead to customer satisfaction. The former is formed on the notion that providing a **better** product will lead to customer satisfaction. If the customer is primarily interested in a cheaper or a better product then one or other of these approaches may work. However, neither addresses the important question of what the customer really wants.

Sales orientation

Competition increased during the early part of the twentieth century. Following the depressions of the 1920s and early 1930s most firms came to realize that they had to actively **sell** a product if they were going to survive.

This kind of approach to business assumes that people will want to buy a product or service that a firm or other organization can supply. It assumes that it is only necessary to inform people about the product, persuade them that it is a product which they require and make it available for them to purchase.

A **sales orientation** approach is often characteristic of firms with over-capacity problems. The approach involves firms selling what they can produce rather than what the market really wants. A sales orientation approach takes the product and the market as given and assumes that a good salesperson can sell anything. However, it overlooks the crucial point that if one starts with consumer wants and needs and produces a product to meet those needs then the task of selling is made easier. In addition it ignores the argument that by starting with the consumers' wants and needs it is less likely that opportunities in the marketplace will be missed.

▶ Over-capacity arises when firms have increased their production capacity to meet real or anticipated demand only to find that the demand is either not sustained or never experienced.

Marketing orientation

Marketing orientation focuses on the consumer and how the organization can satisfy consumer wants and needs and make a profit in doing so. The argument is that such an approach enables the enterprise to identify opportunities that exist in the marketplace.

There are four considerations that have to be examined in detail when adopting a marketing orientation. These are:

- the market
- the customer
- the marketing team
- making a profit (or achieving some other company defined objective)

The implication of marketing orientation is that markets need to be tightly defined and marketing programmes tailored to suit the needs of each target market. This, it is argued, is likely to lead to satisfied customers.

A satisfied customer (or better still one who is more than satisfied) is likely to remain a customer, recommend others to buy from the same source, be less tempted to buy competing products and services and be prepared to buy other products from the same source.

People in an organization's marketing department have to work together towards shared marketing goals and have to share this viewpoint with other departments in an organization. The purpose of marketing is to help an organization reach its stated goals.

Marketing orientation

Customer satisfaction is the key to success

► T. Levitt proposes that the purpose of a business is to create and
keep a customer. Firms adopting a
societal orientation do not pursue
profit as a primary objective. It is
purely a business requirement. T.
Levitt, *The Marketing Imagination*,
New York: Free Press, 1983, p. 6.

However, achieving customer satisfaction is not enough in itself. A
builder who gives away free houses to people will more than
likely create considerable customer satisfaction. However, such an
approach will not generate any income for the builder. Similarly, if
an organization fails to meet financial targets, even though it creates customer satisfaction, it may not survive for very long.

Societal orientation

The most recent form of business orientation, the **societal orientation**, builds upon the marketing orientation. It grows out of the
concern for **consumerism** – that is the need to act in the best interests of the consumer. It is argued that long-term consumer satisfaction can best be achieved if firms and other organizations provide
goods and services which are of good quality, are safe to use and
and do not damage or destroy the environment in which we live.
Consumers may want bright white writing paper because it looks
and 'feels' clean. Such paper, however, may contain harmful
chemicals which can under some circumstances, endanger people's health. A firm may wish to produce and market a paper
which is safe since this is in society's best interests. Unfortunately
such paper is grey in colour because it does not contain the harmful chemicals. In the short run the consumer may not be satisfied
with the product because the paper is not white and may even
continue to buy white paper even though it is harmful. Indeed the
consumer may have to be educated to see the benefits of a new
product.

 Make a list of organizations with which you are familiar.
Categorize them according to whether you think they are

The societal marketing concept

a) Orientation towards the customer

One should start with the customer and develop products that satisfy customer needs and wants. In so doing one should be able to develop volume sales and enjoy a comfortable level of profits.

b) Corporate culture

The organizational ethos and structure has to be such that it is possible fully to implement the marketing concept. This means that there should be staff in the organization who see their jobs as being marketing. However, having 'marketing' in a job title is not the only indication of being marketing oriented. All members of the organization who come into contact with customers or clients should see it as part of their role to adopt a marketing oriented approach to business.

c) The long-term interests of the customer

The organization should be seen to be working to serve the long-term needs of the buyer and society as a whole.

production, product, sales, marketing or societal oriented in their approach to business.

Can you explain why they appear to adopt a particular orientation to business?

Connie's Coiffure

Connie runs a ladies' hairdressing salon in Denton, near Manchester. Her clientele comes from a mixture of social backgrounds and includes women from newer, private houses out towards Haughton Green and women from a number of nearby council estates. They vary in age from twelve to eighty and business is brisk and busy.

Recently, Connie opened a new salon in Reddish, a few miles away from her main premises. The business caters for a similar clientele. She initially hired one hairdresser to operate the business. The business is not doing well, however, and she is considering closing the Reddish shop.

The hairdresser she has put into the salon is a young woman who has only just moved into the district. She has worked previously for a salon in Croydon on the south side of London and has supplied good references. Some of the younger customers of the Denton salon, who work in the local factories and shops, say that their friends who have used the Reddish salon have found the hairdresser 'stuck-up' and 'a bit posh'.

How would you analyse this problem in terms of business orientation and in particular the marketing concept?

Marketing versus selling

In some people's minds marketing and selling are the same thing. However, selling emphasizes the needs of the seller whereas marketing spotlights the needs of the buyer. Selling concentrates on getting money for a product or service that an organization has created. Marketing on the other hand aims to satisfy customer needs through the product.

> **Marketing versus selling**
> John, 'I'm in selling – I sell what I'm told.'
> Phil, 'I'm in marketing – I tell you what to sell.'

Marketing is concerned with strategy. A firm's strategy may be to increase its sales and profits by selling more of what it currently produces to existing customers. Alternatively, it may be to achieve growth by getting people who currently buy other firms' products or services to buy from it instead. There are many different strategies that can be used. In order to implement strategy, marketing makes use of **tactics**. The tactics are to do with: pricing, distribution, the product and **promotion** (including selling). We refer to these tactical decision areas as the elements of the marketing mix. From this we can see that selling is a component of marketing.

A channel of information and an influence on behaviour

Marketing identifies needs and wants and provides the means of satisfying them. In order to do this it has to obtain information from customers in the marketplace about their needs and wants. The **information-gathering mechanism** takes the form of specially commissioned **market research** studies and marketing information systems.

An organization also has to inform prospective customers that it has the means of satisfying their wants and needs. This it does through the mechanism of the **promotional mix** – advertising, personal selling, sales promotion and public relations. In addition, because most firms are in competition with one another they have to use marketing communications to inform the market that their product is superior to that of competitors.

Within the framework outlined, we can readily appreciate that marketing employs channels of communication both to discover consumer wants and needs and to influence behaviour. We will see just how this occurs in the chapters on consumer behaviour and marketing communications.

▶ Peter Drucker, *Management Tasks, Responsibilities and Practices*, Harper and Row, 1974, p. 64, has argued that the aim of marketing is to know and understand the customer so well that the product or service will sell itself.

▶ Strategy is what firms use to accomplish their business objectives.

▶ See Chapter 2 for a full discussion of the marketing mix.

▶ Marketing involves channels of communication between sellers and purchasers: conveying information about what the customers want to the firm, and conveying information about what the firm provides to the customers.

MARKETING MANAGEMENT

Marketing management is about putting the marketing concept into practice. It involves finding out what customers want or need and feeding this back through the organization so that goods or services can be produced which will satisfy these wants and needs. It involves making decisions about pricing, distribution and promotion. It also involves determining how the organization's objectives can be satisfied in terms of seeking out and exploiting opportunities in the market. The task of management entails getting jobs done through people. It includes planning actions, organizing people to implement actions, coordinating efforts to achieve plans, controlling the plan so that it achieves its objectives, and appraising performance.

► Marketing planning is discussed in detail in Chapter 6.

Planning entails setting objectives and targets that have to be achieved in the future. The plans which are created then become the blueprints for future actions and inform people in the organization where they are going and what they have to achieve within a given period of time. As we shall see later in the book, the marketing plan is linked with other plans in the firm. In the case of a manufacturing firm, for example, the other plans relate to production, finance and personnel. All of these are part of what is called a **corporate plan**.

Planning is a formalized process in big firms but may appear to be casual or even nonexistent in smaller firms. The latter often say they are too busy keeping up with current orders to have the time to write down formal marketing plans. That is not to say, of course, that such firms do not have any marketing plans.

The purpose of organizing is to produce efficient working relationships between people along with a sense of cooperation and purpose. All of these are necessary to make it easier to accomplish goals and objectives that have been set in the marketing plan. Marketing management also involves having to deal with other organizations. For example, a firm may decide to advertise its products. In such a case it has to liaise with an advertising agency that will design and place advertisements on its behalf. At the same time it has to get its salespeople and its distributors to work together so that they will support any advertising campaigns that are launched. This means that marketing management has to coordinate the activities of various departments within the organization along with those of other organizations. Co-ordination is a very important aspect of marketing management activity.

Having plans and circulating them around to everyone who is concerned with their implementation is not enough. Left to their own devices people are apt to set about doing things in their own particular way and at their own speed. Indeed, some things may not get done at all. Organizations try to get round the problems that this can create by exercising control. **Control** implies keeping

► Management includes planning actions, organizing people to implement actions, coordinating efforts to achieve plans, controlling the plan so that it achieves objectives, and appraising performance.

everyone and everything on the planned route towards achieving set objectives.

Achievement of a single objective is not sufficient in itself. For example, a firm could set itself the target of increasing its share of the market from thirty-eight per cent to forty per cent within twelve months of the initial planning date. In order to achieve this target it would realize that it would be necessary to increase marketing expenditure. Targets for increased marketing expenditure would therefore have to be set at the same time. However, if the firm subsequently incurred fifty per cent more marketing expenditure than it had planned in achieving the forty per cent market share then it would be difficult to view control in this instance as being effective. Marketing plans involve the setting of multiple objectives which must include cost and resource utilization constraints.

► Objectives might be to attain a certain increase in market share and to maintain profitability at its current level while so doing.

Appraisal involves assessing what has been achieved and how well it has been achieved. Appraisal will produce information which can be used to help prevent the same kind of problems arising time and time again. For example, if the target was to sell forty thousand pairs of black tights through vending machines in the West End of London over a six month period and only twenty thousand pairs were sold, appraisal amounts to accounting for this fact. It may be that vandalism to vending machines contributed to the shortfall in sales. In such an event, taking into account damage to the machines, profitability on this form of distribution would be lower than expected. Clearly, if vandal-proof machines could be installed this would alleviate the problem, but of course it would add to the investment costs. All this information would be pertinent to future marketing plans relating to the product and the actual targets, if any, that were set.

Marketing decisions

► Marketing decisions concern the 4 P's of the marketing mix: product, place, promotion and price.

Marketing management involves making decisions. An important decision involves determining what mix of products to offer because this has an impact on the profitability of a profit-oriented organization (this is discussed in detail in Chapter 10). The kind of decisions that marketing management has to make relate to what are known as the 'Four P's of the marketing mix'. These are:

- product
- price
- promotion
- place

► Chapters 11 and 12 examine product and new product decisions respectively.

Product decisions include those concerning the introduction of new products or the withdrawal of existing products. They also involve modifying products, positioning products and branding products.

► Chapter 13 examines pricing decisions

Price decisions comprise setting prices relative to competitors' prices which also involves setting margins and discounts.

Promotion decisions can be categorized under the headings of advertising, personal selling, sales promotion and publicity.

► Chapter 15 discusses advertising and Chapter 16 examines selling.

Place or **distribution** decisions involve choosing what is the best way to get the product or the service to the customer.

► Chapter 14 looks at distribution decisions.

Consumer and industrial marketing

Consumer goods are those goods which are bought by or on behalf of the ultimate user. That is ordinary people in the street like ourselves. Clothes and food are examples of consumer goods. Most of the marketing which we see every day relates to consumer goods. We see advertisements in the newspapers, commercials on television, merchandising aids in supermarkets, shop-window displays, price deals in all kinds of shops and occasionally commercial travellers or salespeople calling on retailers. Consumer goods marketing is a sophisticated business backed up by private marketing research companies and advertising agencies which undertake considerable volumes of work for consumer goods companies. Some companies spend millions of pounds each year on marketing activities.

Industrial goods are goods supplied to industry for use in the production of other goods. They may themselves be intermediate goods not destined for use by the final consumer. Industrial goods include plant and equipment, raw materials and many different kinds of services. Marketing applies just as much to industrial goods as it does to consumer goods. We shall be exploring how industrial buyers differ from consumers in Chapter 7. We should note here, however, some of the key differences in terms of marketing management emphasis when dealing with industrial buyers rather than consumers.

There are fewer industrial buyers than there are consumers and the buying process can be more complex. The nature of the marketing mix with respect to industrial markets can be substantially different to that directed at consumer markets.

► Consumer goods are goods bought by the ultimate consumer. Industrial goods are used in the production of other goods.

Meeting competition – searching for a differential advantage

Competition is a feature of many if not most aspects of business and commerce. Firms compete with one another for business and some do very well while others are less successful. Ultimately, it is those firms that are best able to satisfy consumer wants and needs which are most likely to do well when the market is competitive. As a consequence, a firm would do well to work towards producing a strongly **differentiated product**. That is not to say that 'me too' strategies will not work. However, firms which try to achieve strong product differentiation do have a better chance of being competitive and being successful.

► Many IBM 'clone' microcomputer firms have enjoyed success by a 'me too' strategy.

Marketing consumer goods requires a different marketing mix from that required for marketing industrial goods

There are many more potential customers for consumer goods than there are for industrial goods. This has an influence on the methods of marketing communication that are most apt to reach the respective audiences.

Large numbers of consumers, often making rapid regular buying decisions in retail outlets, encourage consumer goods firms to use advertising of one form or another. It is usually the cheapest and most effective way of giving information out to potential customers.

Advertising is important to producers of industrial goods and firms make use of advertising in trade journals to bring their product to the attention of the industrial buyer. However, there is a much greater emphasis on personal selling in industrial marketing. Technical representatives or teams of marketing specialists with technical know-how are often used to call on prospective buyers.

Differentiation

A product or service is made up of basic features and added values.

Basic features
components, ingredients, performance.

Added values
image, service, styling, support.

Differentiation is achieved through making the added values more attractive to the customer.

► Rather than product or service features the firm should look at the benefits it is providing to the user. Differentiation may be achieved by offering customers benefits which are different to those obtainable from competing products or services.

► Differentiation is achieved through making the added values more attractive to the customer.

Differentiation is accomplished by users perceiving that there are specific benefits attached to a particular company's product or service when it is compared to competitors' offerings. We can visualize a product as comprising of a set of basic features – components, ingredients, performance – and a set of added values – image, service, styling, support. We can achieve product differentiation through the added values. The more attractive the firm can make the added values the more differentiated from competitive offerings the product becomes.

A differential advantage

'He wants a Rainbow 99 with a rocket sticking out of it. A small, plain cornet will NOT do thank you.'

 Watch some advertisements on television or alternatively have a look through a magazine of your own choosing and see if you can identify some of the ways in which firms are trying to persuade viewers or readers that their products are superior to those of competitors.

MARKETING ORGANIZATION

A suitable organization structure has to be in place to enable marketing plans and decisions to be put in to operation. Marketing is one of the tasks of a business. It is not surprising therefore that it should lend itself quite well to a task-based or functional type of organization structure. A typical functional marketing structure is shown below:

▶ Other functional aspects of a business include production, personnel and finance. Functional aspects of marketing include marketing research, advertising, sales, and distribution.

A battery manufacturer

The marketing director coordinates, controls and appraises the activities of all the people below his or her level in the organization structure. Each one of the four people who reports directly to the marketing director has functional responsibility and accountability for a particular aspect of marketing. To each one of them in turn there are other people who have responsibility and accountability.

All organizations have to carry out the same kinds of marketing activities and so all firms adopting a functional marketing organization structure will adopt some variant on the approach outlined above. Precisely who does what in an organization will depend on tradition in the company and the importance the company attaches to that function. In the example above pricing policies may be determined by the marketing director in conjunction with the chief executive and the director of finance. The day-to-day running of the sales force, however, is left to the discretion of the sales manager who is accountable to the marketing director. Similarly, the sales office manager deals with all the paperwork associated with sales to customers. This includes progressing orders and invoicing for payment. The sales office manager is **not** accountable to the sales manager for what he or she does but **is** accountable to the marketing director. If an account is not settled by a customer then responsibility for dealing with the matter may be shared between the company's finance department, its legal department (or else the company secretary) and the sales office.

A functional organizational approach to marketing is often found in manufacturing companies. However, some manufacturing companies find it easier to deal with marketing matters if they adopt a product-based structure. In such a case a product manager takes responsibility for the marketing of a group of products which have much in common with one another. An example organization is shown below:

A pharmaceutical firm

There are other types of marketing organization structures to be found. For example, if the number of sales is extremely large the business may be divided into regions or even countries. The organizational structure created will then reflect this geographical division. A marketing manager may exist for each region or nation.

Another kind of organization structure reflects the situation where a firm sells its goods through different kinds of distribution channel, each one of which is substantially different to the other. Provided that each one of the channels has a high volume of business, firms may choose to organize their marketing activities around individual distribution channels. A marketing manager may then exist for each distribution channel.

► The presence of people with marketing titles will vary with size and type of industry. Different marketing organization structures are found in practice and reflect different situations.

 If you work for a firm see if you can find out where marketing fits into the organization. Try constructing an organization chart. If you do not work for an organization, or as an alternative to the above, try finding out from friends or relations where marketing fits into the firm in which they are employed. They may even be able to produce an organization chart for you, with your help. They may allow you to visit the company and find out for yourself.

If you are a full-time student at a college, find out how the college is organized for marketing.

Yet another commonly encountered structure is to be found where a company carries a number of **branded goods** and where advantages are to be obtained from having a brand manager responsible for dealing with the marketing of a brand (see page 21 for an explanation of branding).

► Goods may be branded. This means that a company will give a product a particular name to distinguish it from competitors' products. Branding encourages consumer loyalty to a product.

CHAPTER SUMMARY

1 Marketing is both a functional aspect of a business and a business philosophy. Over time firms have adopted various business orientations and these have different implications for how firms perceive the marketplace. Two important concepts have evolved, the 'marketing concept' and the 'societal (marketing) concept'. Today the latter is preferred since not only does it stress to the need to satisfy customer wants and needs but it also stresses the need to hold the welfare of the consumer very much in mind.

2 Selling is an integral part of the marketing armoury. It should not be seen as an alternative to marketing nor should it be seen as being independent of marketing. It is part of the marketing mix.

3 Getting a competitive advantage over other firms is a fundamental objective of marketers. A competitive differential can be obtained by augmenting the benefits which are offered to customers in a way which is different to that of competitors.

► Now that you have reached the end of the chapter, turn back to the objectives and make sure you have achieved each of them.

4 Marketing is implemented as part of the management process and involves the planning and the taking of decisions. Suitable organization structures are required to do this. Depending upon a number of circumstances different organizational structures are more appropriate.

2

Dimensions of the product and the elements of the marketing mix

Chapter objectives

By the end of this chapter you should:

▮ understand what is meant by the marketing mix and the variables which influence it

▮ know how the marketing mix variables (the four Ps) – price, product, promotion and place – interrelate with one another

▮ understand how decisions concerning one or other of the marketing mix variables cannot be made without considering the implications for the other variables

▮ know that the product (or service) is a complex entity in itself made up of quality, features, options, style, brand name, packaging, sizes, services, warranties, and returns

▮ know that the price is a complex entity and that there can be several prices for the same goods – taking into account discounts and allowances

▮ know that promotion is a complex entity comprising selling, advertising, sales promotion, etc. And that within each area of promotion there are many and often complex decisions to be made

▮ know that distribution is a complex entity involving channel decisions and physical distribution decisions

▮ be familiar with the following terms as used by marketers: marketing mix, product, price, promotion, distribution, marketing intelligence, marketing research, benefits to the customer, target groups, quality, features, product differentiation, competitive advantage, options, style, brand name, company logo, packaging, legal obligations, warranty, price band, list price, discounts, allowances, credit facilities, selling, advertising, publicity, sales promotion, distribution coverage, inventory management, transportation.

Introduction

This chapter introduces the marketing tools which an organization has at its disposal to influence customers and to compete effectively in the marketplace. The tools are:

- the product (or service)
- the price
- the method of promotion
- the method of distribution (place)

These are commonly referred to as the four Ps of the **marketing mix**. In addition one can argue that there is a fifth element, **marketing intelligence**. The word 'intelligence' covers the ideas of both marketing information and marketing research.

INTERDEPENDENCE OF THE ELEMENTS OF THE MARKETING MIX

The elements of the marketing mix do not work in isolation from one another. A firm that produces a high-quality product would normally expect to market it through up-market retail outlets, charge a premium price for it and promote it through media that has an up-market or 'quality' image.

Making decisions with respect to the elements of the marketing mix is an extremely complex procedure since the elements themselves are complex entities. Here, we will briefly introduce each element in turn and then explore it in greater detail in later chapters.

► Rolex watches are durable and have a high quality image. As a consequence they have a high price tag, are advertised in quality glossy magazines and are sold through exclusive jewellery outlets.

(ACT) Consider each one of the following products and suggest what implications there would be for the four Ps of the marketing mix in every case. In all cases you need to consider the nature of the product itself; the price of the product; the method of promoting the product; and the method of distributing the product. You should pay particular attention to the interdependence of the elements of the marketing mix variables. For example, if you decide that a Rolls Royce is a very exclusive car you have to decide on the implications this will have for the price and the method of promoting and distributing the car.

Rolls Royce cars   ladies' tights
box of matches   bibles
daily newspaper   college scarves
christmas cards   electronic pocket organizer
lap top portable computer   golf clubs
ladies' fashion shoes   shoe polish
men's umbrellas   pop music cassettes

The product (or service)

When marketing a product or a service one should give attention not to the features of the product or the service but to the benefits it creates for the user. It is these benefits which make the product

► In 1991, Forte announced that it was repositioning its restaurant facilities in Posthouse hotels. The new image it wants to create is one of a place where 'fun family eating' can take place.

► Products and services are produced and offered in different forms to meet with different customer wants and needs.

or service attractive to the customer. The firm marketing the product or service has to communicate these benefits to the user, directly or indirectly, in order to persuade the latter to make a purchase.

Tangible goods as the outward signs of success

The fact that someone is the chief executive of a large and very successful commercial enterprise is only evident to those people who have a close association with the person concerned. In a crowd the person may not stand out at all.

On the motorway, however, the person who drives a new Maserati, Rolls Royce, Lamborghini, or some other very expensive car, does stand out as someone who we think must be very successful. The benefits of owning such a prestigious car are reflected in the fact that it represents success and is a symbol which readily conveys signals about that person's status to other people.

People may buy clothes to suit their personality. Through the clothes bought, a person expresses that personality. The benefits here are the ability to express that personality. In another instance, however, the benefits may be of a different nature. We often hear people talking about a suit or a dress being 'practical' for a particular purpose – for example, party-going or wearing for work. People buy clothes for different purposes. This immediately suggests that there will be different target groups of customers based on various notions of the benefits associated with the clothing.

The idea of different target groups, based on the product or service benefits, also applies to consumer durables. For example, manufacturers of washing machines have had to recognize that people have different family sizes. They have catered for this by producing machines of different sizes. This idea also applies to industrial products and services. Agricultural tractor manufacturers have to recognize that farmers use their tractors for different purposes. In vineyards tractors need to be small and have narrow tracks to enable them to move up and down between lines of vines. On the broad farmlands of East Anglia and on the prairies of North America farmers use high-powered tractors to plough large areas of arable land.

The ability of a product or service to produce the kinds of benefits desired by the user is reflected in various attributes. **Product decisions** have to be made about these attributes. When a producer of goods or services makes decisions about 'the product' he or she is making decisions about the following:

- quality
- features
- options
- style

- brand name
- packaging
- sizes
- services
- warranties
- returns.

We will consider each one in turn in the sections below.

 Some of the product decisions mentioned above could be considered part of the promotional mix. Can you say which ones they are?

Quality

Quality is a term that is universally applicable to all products – except perhaps where it is physically impossible to create product differences in quality. Even in such cases, however, producers can still try to promote their products through **hidden** quality differences. Quality is a relative value that we put on things. It relates to our expectations about product performance. Fortunately, large groups of people have common ideas about quality and it is possible to produce and market products that will meet with the perceptions of large groups of customers. Groups of customers sharing a common perception of a particular level of quality form market segments. A firm can direct its promotional messages to these groups of customers provided that it knows how to reach them.

▶ Producers may link their products to 'hidden' benefits – washing powders which may be 'good for the hands', petrol which is 'good for the engine'.

▶ See Chapter 11 for a detailed discussion of product quality.

 Suggest how 'quality' might be defined with respect to the following products or services:

restaurants	fish and chips
public transport	discos
hospital treatment	transatlantic flights
holidays abroad	cars
higher or further education	houses

Features

Features relate to specific characteristics of a product that may make it easier to use for certain purposes. For example, there are front loading washing machines and top loading washing machines. Front loading washing machines usually have a transparent door through which one can observe the process of washing. The advantage of a front loader, however, relates to the ease of loading washing into the machine. It requires less effort to bundle clothes from ground level into a front loader than it does into a top loader. Top loaders, on the other hand, may take up less space in a cramped kitchen. The features of the products have different benefits.

Producers try to make their products appeal to different groups

▶ Packaged holidays have features which have differentiated them from self- catering holidays. The former include travel arrangements to and from the destination and usually include some, if not all, meals.

of customers by building different features into their products which produce different benefits in recognition of the fact that people have different requirements. Like the strategy of product differentiation, it is a means of gaining a competitive advantage in the marketplace.

Options

Options are product features which are not included in the standard product. Producers may consider that it is not worthwhile incorporating certain features into the standard product. It may be that not everyone will want a particular feature. Moreover, since including special features usually involves additional cost, this will push up the price and the customer may be deterred from purchasing. On the other hand, additional groups of customers may be persuaded to buy the product because optional features are available. Therefore the firm can put itself in the position where it obtains the best of both worlds by offering options.

The strategic marketing problem here is to strike a balance between permanent product features and optional extras. The car market is a good illustration of where one finds examples of product features and options in operation. All Volvo cars have built in safety features – for example a tubular cage frame around the passenger compartment and reinforced doors. The specification is standard in all Volvo cars and attempts to satisfy the wants and needs of its target market – the safety conscious motorist. Volvo also provides optional extras for its cars – a sliding roof, variations in engine size, etc.

Style

Style is something that we almost innately seem to understand but which we often have difficulty in describing in words. In the car market it can be the difference between a 1990 model and a 1985 model. It refers to the appearance of the product and in the car market reflects the 'lines of a product'. Style is something that goes out of fashion with the passing of time, though it may very well come into fashion again.

Product 'style' is most applicable to consumer goods, though it can be found in industrial products as well. We associate style mostly with goods such as fashion clothes and motor cars, though, of course, it is equally applicable to holidays, the theatre or cinema, and to many other products. Style relates to the image that the producer wants to be associated with the goods or services. The image of the goods, in turn, has to fit in with the user's self perceptions. The symbolic action that a user puts on the product can be used to good effect by the producer in promotional strategy.

The consumer is extremely **style conscious** and usually likes to be up to date with current styles. Of course, there are always exceptions to this. However, it seems that the number of people who are 'style conscious' is sufficiently large for style to be

▶ Packaged holidays may include options to visit tourist attractions. These are extras that are not included in the price.

▶ We can see clear evidence of style in products that have strong aesthetic appeals – for example mock 'Georgian' or 'Tudor' type houses.

considered an important consideration when making strategic decisions about products.

 Select three of the following products, and study their packaging and television, newspaper/magazine and point of sale promotion. How are they given 'style'? Are essentially the same products differentiated by style to attract different kinds of consumer?

jet airliners
ladies' dresses
gents' suits
chocolates

TV dramas
crisps
microcomputers
buildings

Brand name and logo

Marketing management has two important strategic marketing tools at its disposal in the **brand name** and the **company logo**. The brand name and company logo are economical on promotional space and can sometimes have a very lasting effect. If you ask a person at random in the street to name the major soap powder companies operating in the UK the likelihood is that the person will not be able to tell you. Ask the same person to name a soap powder brand and immediately such brands as Persil and Daz will be recalled.

  The recommendation is that brand names should be short and snappy, and easily remembered. Ideally, brand names should capture the 'spirit' of the product in the name. Logos, on the other hand, should be very distinctive and easily recognized, preferably incorporating the name of the organization. ICI, Ford, Shell and IBM have instantly recognizable logos. Any one of these firms could issue an advertisement incorporating its logo and the company would be identified immediately.

  Branding is a strategy that a firm adopts to ensure that people can always rely on obtaining a particular quality in the products purchased. If a customer purchases an IBM computer then he or she can expect a particular level of performance from that machine – this is guaranteed. Moreover, if the product fails to live up to expectation then the customer knows how to obtain a replacement product. With unbranded goods, one can never be sure of the quality of the product. It is a hit and miss affair. It may be almost impossible to obtain a replacement for an unsatisfactory product or one that fails in use after the lapse of a period of time.

Packaging

For some products the **packaging** is effectively the product. Perhaps the best illustration of this is in the 'box of chocolates'. Not only is the Black Magic brand name, for example, instantly recognized by millions of people but so too is the packaging – the famous black box. Marketing management can use the packaging

A teddy boy

Teddy boys – wearers of clothes that projected images of 'the self' to other people

At the outset of the 1950s decade the 'teenager' as such did not exist. At its close 'teenager' was a word in everyone's vocabulary. Teenagers not only had a name but they had invented their own distinct culture. In the USA young men modelled themselves on James Dean or Marlon Brando. In Britain there were teddy boys.

Teddy boys had a quite distinct uniform. They wore draped jackets with velvet collars, bootlace ties , drainpipe trousers and sideburns. A few, though not many, collected other accoutrements such as flick-knives and bicycle chains for use in inter-gang rivalry.

The 'uniform' itself was reminiscent of what was worn by men in Britain at the turn of the century in what is called the 'Edwardian' era. The diminutive of Edward is of course 'Teddy' and hence the name 'teddy boys'. The turn of the century in Britain saw the birth not only of a new century but also of a new social era. Society was becoming more permissive and tolerant after the Victorian era when a much stricter set of values had been in force.

In the late 1940s Britain was recovering from a world war which had dragged on for six years. From 1945 through to 1955 consumer goods were in relatively short supply and there was rationing of even basic commodities. From the late 1950s the standard of living began to rise and there was increasing affluence.

Teddy boys defined their own wants and needs. They had their suits made bespoke, before clothing manufacturers mass-produced them. They flourished at a historical period when 'youth' became defined as a lucrative market segment. The material basis for this was the post-war economic boom which gave people relatively high disposable incomes.

to play to the perceptions of people. It was indicated above that people often buy clothes and other products because they fit with their self image. Products and their packaging, too, can become extensions of the self. The products people buy can become part of their own 'packaging' and project their preferred self-image to people they meet.

Where products are fairly homogeneous a major way to distinguish one product from another is through the packaging. Interestingly, however, the packaging serves a dual purpose. People buy chocolates as presents for others and through the choice of packaging either display their self-perceptions or their perceptions of the person to whom they are giving the present. Thus we can see that the function of packaging is multi-dimensional and from the marketers point of view presents a plethora of strategic options.

Size

A product does not always come in one size because different consumers clearly have different requirements. An important area for marketing strategy decision making is working out the best combination of sizes to offer and the quantities of each size to produce and market.

Services

Many products are extremely complex and need to be installed on the customer's premises. Moreover, some products require after sales service to ensure that they function properly. The marketing decision here relates to the service facility to offer. Microcomputer dealers offer different forms of maintenance contracts to businesses and individuals who have purchased a system from them. Some customers require a considerable amount of service whereas others are prepared to manage without but expect a lower price for the product. This is an area where firms try hard to gain a competitive advantage.

> ► Even textbooks come in different sizes. Business people do not have much time to read such books. In consequence many books on marketing aimed at this market segment are extremely short. They are often read on aeroplane trips as is witnessed by the relatively large number of such books which can be found in stationery and book sellers at airports.

Domestic appliances

Some domestic appliances can be easily installed by the consumer. This is particularly the case with many electrical goods which are supplied with the electrical connection plug already attached, for example, radios and irons. Others are more difficult to install or can be dangerous if not properly installed.

Installation of televisions may need expert assistance in terms of erecting and fine tuning an aerial. In the case of gas or electrical appliances, such as fires and cookers, care has to be taken to ensure that they are correctly connected to the mains supply. This requires expert knowledge.

Warranties

Customers purchasing a product always need to have some assurance that the product will work. There are legal obligations binding on manufacturers and suppliers to ensure that the goods are reasonably fit for the purpose for which they are intended. A company which sells a second-hand car without an engine to an unsuspecting buyer would clearly breach the law and the customer could sue the vendor for reparation. However, the scope of the law is rather limited and certainly does not extend to cover products that have been in use by the customer for more than a given length of time.

► The difference in product quality between brands of tyres is not obvious to many motorists. Some vendors of tyres however recognize that the guarantee is a key benefit that consumers can readily appreciate.

Tyre Replacement

A motorist who buys a replacement car tyre has a clear expectation that the tyre will last for many thousands of miles. Should the tyre fail, for example the tread come adrift after only a few thousands of miles, then the customer will feel that the supplier should provide some compensation. Some tyre fitting organizations now offer a warranty scheme by which the customer can, in the event of failure, have a replacement tyre fitted at a discounted price. The discounted price reflects the number of miles the failed tyre has covered since it was fitted.

To marketing management the interest here is in specifying the appropriate discount rate in proportion to the number of miles covered. Clearly, the supplying firm does not want to make a loss on its sales of tyres.

► Quality, features, options, style, brand name, packaging, sizes, services, warranties and returns are all decisions that can be made about a product or service to make it suit identified wants and needs.

Returns

Finally, there is the aspect of returns. Faulty products need to be replaced and a producer should develop a policy for dealing with this. By statistical sampling methods one can determine the probability of returns occurring by chance. Where numbers of returns fall outside acceptable limits, action is called for.

The price

Price is a key element in the marketing mix. If customers consider that the price is too high then sales will be stifled. If customers consider the price is too low then sales will also be stifled. In the latter case people may think that the product quality has decreased or that the product is about to become obsolete. There is usually an acceptable band of prices within which consumers will be prepared to buy any given product or service. The task of marketing management is to determine the price which will maximize sales or profits, depending on the current objectives pursued by the organization.

Objectives are likely to differ from time to time and pricing strategy will vary to take account of these shifts in objectives. We will consider the whole question of pricing strategy in Chapter 13. Here, however, we will concentrate on the complexities of the pricing decisions.

 Take a copy of your local evening or weekly newspaper and study the prices of a wide range of consumer goods which you will find advertised in them. Make notes on the range of different prices which are charged for the same items. Can you work out why the prices are different from one another?

List price

There can be several prices charged for the same product. This will vary according to the nature of the purchaser. In the first place there will be a **list price**, which is the price at which the producer offers the product for sale. The marketing department helps to establish this list price. It may be based upon cost plus a desired level of profitability or it may be based on a belief as to what the market will bear. The list price should be high enough to allow discounts to customers which in turn should still allow the firm an adequate profit margin.

Discounts

Discounts from the list price may be given to customers or to distributors who fulfil certain requirements. A customer who orders a large quantity of a product may be given a quantity discount off the price. Another customer who settles accounts early may receive a discount for doing so. Discounts can be given to distributors if they provide the producer with valuable marketing information, or if the customer pays cash for goods , and so on. Discounts are part of the firm's strategic marketing armoury and should be employed to good effect to achieve specific sales and profit objectives. Ensuring that overall profit and sales objectives are met can be a complex affair in large companies and can only be achieved through systematized planning and control.

Allowances

Another dimension to pricing relates to giving **allowances** for a trade-in against a new purchase. When a person buys a new car he or she usually has an old one to dispose of. This can be traded in part exchange and an appropriate allowance off the list price can be given for the traded-in vehicle.

Sometimes a firm may take a product in part exchange and sell it at a nominal price to a third party that specializes in the refurbishing of used products. Domestic appliance retailers may accept a refrigerator or a cooker from a customer in part exchange against a new one. They will resell it for a nominal price to a firm that specializes in rejuvenating old appliances. In these cases the customer benefits in two ways. In the first case he or she gets something for the old product – a psychological boost leading to the belief that he or she has made a good deal. Secondly, the customer has an awkward problem taken off his or her hands – how to dispose of the old product. Allowances often turn thoughts into actions.

Credit

The transaction takes place when money exchanges hands. Sometimes, where industrial goods or high value consumer goods are concerned, the customer might not have the means to purchase the required goods for cash. It is under such circumstances that the vendor can help by providing **credit facilities**. Credit facilities are

Quantifying discounts

Customer: 'Why haven't I got a 25% discount like everyone else?'
Sales assistant: 'Because one drawing pin isn't a bulk purchase.'

► If a producer sells 100 items at £10 and there is £2 profit on each item, then the total profit will be £200. If the price is reduced to £9 (i.e. a discount is given) and sales are then 300 items, then the profit will be 300 x £1 = £300. In this case profits increase. Moreover, if the customer will not buy from the producer unless the price is £9, then the producer stands to lose £300 profit.

► Second-hand car dealers will often welcome a car taken in part exchange since not only will they make a profit on the first car but they will also make a profit on the car that is taken in part exchange.

Price is a strategic tool which can be used by firms to assist in the marketing of goods or services. Discounts, allowances and credit are important adjuncts in specifying price.

not just an adjunct to the pricing mechanism, they are an integral part of it.

 Consider the following:

A taxi driver at Madrid airport charged two tourists £25 for a journey of some six or seven miles to one of Madrid's railway stations at 6.30 a.m. on a public holiday. The recommended price for normal day time hours is around £8 and the price on the airport bus to the city centre was approximately £2.50. Do you think that the taxi driver charged a fair price?

Promotion

▶ Promotion decisions are discussed in Chapter 15.

Selling, advertising, publicity and sales promotion come under the heading of **promotion**. The producer has to put together a mix of promotional activity to help market products or services.

Like product and price, promotion comprises individual decisions that have to be made. The following are illustrative:

Selling
- what specific sales and profit targets, by product and customer, to set for various members of the sales team?
- what kind of sales organization to adopt?
- how to deploy the sales force for maximum effect?
- what kind of incentive scheme to set for sales personnel?

Advertising
- how much to spend on advertising?
- which advertising agency to use?
- what the purpose of the advertising should be?
- qualitative decisions concerning the content of the advertising
- choice of advertising media – TV, journals, newspaper, radio, billboards
- timing of advertisements.

Publicity
- what kind of press release to make
- which media to choose.

Sales promotion
- what kind of point of sale display material to use
- whether to run competitions for distributors or customers.

Like product and price, promotion involves complex decisions. In addition to having to make individual decisions, such as the ones indicated above, decisions also have to be made about the promotional mix. That is, should there be a greater emphasis on personal selling or on advertising? And what about publicity and sales promotion?

Looking at the factors listed above, suggest where the emphasis in the promotional mix should fall for the following products/services

- travel agents
- a local dramatic society
- a used car retailer
- a public house.

► Selling, advertising, sales promotion and publicity together make up the elements of the marketing communications mix.

Distribution or place

Distribution involves making the product or service available to customers. It is important to distinguish between distribution channels and physical distribution. Distribution channels relate to the kind of intermediaries who are to be used in getting the goods to the user. Physical distribution relates to handling of the goods and, in particular, to such things as warehousing, inventory management and transportation.

Without adequate distribution, ultimate sales to the customer are unlikely to be achieved in the quantities expected. Distribution is a vital component of the marketing mix. As is the case with the product, the price and the promotion, place or distribution is a complex decision. The first strategic distribution decision that the firm has to take relates to choosing the appropriate channels of distribution through which to market goods or services. By way of illustration, consider the case of a firm marketing pocket calculators. The decisions would involve identifying how best to bring the product to the market. Several strategies might suggest themselves, for example:

► Distribution decisions are discussed in Chapter 14.

- sell through speciality office supplies shops
- sell through chain stores such as W H Smith and John Menzies
- sell by direct mail
- sell through mail order catalogues.

What the firm has to ask itself is:

- who are the potential customers?
- where would the potential customers normally shop for a pocket calculator?

We will look in later chapters at various distribution channel strategies that firms can adopt.

Coverage

Coverage is an important dimension of distribution strategy. Coverage refers to the potential market that distribution outlets serve. If the firm does not have a distribution outlet for its product in a particular area then it may not be providing full coverage. Of course, it may be providing full coverage through an alternative medium such as direct mail. Distribution coverage and advertising strategy must go hand in hand. There is no point in providing advertising support for a product in an area where there is little or no distribution coverage provided.

Locations

Distributor locations can be vital in ensuring that the market is properly covered. If most people in an area shop for the good or service in an out-of-town location there is little point in going for major distribution locations in a city centre. It also has to be realized that different distributor locations attract different amounts of customer traffic flow.

It may be possible to sell diamond jewellery through a small town jeweller's shop even if this shop is badly located (for example, in a back street). However, there may be insufficient numbers of passers-by to generate the volume sales the producer requires to keep the business viable.

Inventory

Inventory management is another name for stock control. The strategic question is how to maintain the best level of stock to ensure that the firm meets demand in the marketplace. This can be a perplexing strategic problem. Distributors, particularly at the retail level, are obviously not keen on stocking slow moving lines and err on the side of keeping small stocks rather than high stocks. Any firm holding stocks is tying up its cash and probably paying for the holding of the stock twice over by way of loans and rent on storage space. With high interest rates the problem is exacerbated.

The onus is very much on the producer to ensure that the distrubutors have sufficient stock to meet the actual demand. A profit can only be made if the cost of providing additional stock is less than the profit generated from sales of stock. The question of how much stock to hold is closely allied to the level of customer service that the firm wants to provide. The topic is explored in the chapter on distribution.

► See Chapter 14

In recent years the improvements in communications brought about by computer-based management information systems have made it easier for firms to maintain adequate stock levels. It is easiest to do where the producer has some degree of vertical integration, for example it owns its own distribution outlets or exercises direct control over the outlets. Many large retail chains operate on-line systems which enable them to know both their own stock levels and stock levels at other branches. If a store runs out of an item it is often possible to obtain that item for a customer within a few hours from another branch.

Transportation

Finally we will consider transportation. The marketing decisions here involve choosing the best method of transportation to bring goods to the distributors or direct to the customers. This is largely determined by the nature of the product. Perishable products have to be refrigerated and moved quickly. Bulky items with an indefinite life span, for which demand is spasmodic or slow moving, can be transported at a more leisurely pace. The best method of transportation will depend on the circumstances. An important overseas customer needing a vital part of machinery, for example, may be prepared to pay the cost of airfreight to obtain the required part.

Getting the right mixture

Billy Brelsford is wondering what to do about a market research report he has just received from TP Associates regarding his new product the Brelsford Special. The Brelsford Special is a revolutionary spark plug which once fitted to a petrol engine never needs to be replaced. In fact the longer it is in service the more efficient it becomes. Moreover pre-launch technical testing showed an increase in fuel economy of over 300 per cent across all sizes of engine.

Sales of the product have fallen well short of expectations and Billy has an in-tray full of angry letters from dealers asking him to take back stock which they have been unable to sell because of his apparent inability to provide the advertising support at the consumer level.

The market research highlights a lack of consumer awareness of the product, disbelief in claims about the product from those who did know about it and a large proportion of respondents indicating that no spark-plugs could possibly be worth £50 a set (average prices for traditional spark plugs range between £5 and £10 a set).

In addition no-one who had their car serviced by a garage could ever recall their garage mentioning the new product to them at service time. Amongst the DIY enthusiasts many reported seeing the products in DIY stores but indicated that they preferred to 'stick with what was familiar'.

Nearly eighty per cent of the motoring DIY shops that Billy Brelsford had initially approached had agreed to stock the product but most of the garages he had approached had been sceptical about the product's claimed performance and politely refused to stock it. Promotion had been limited to point of sale leaflets explaining in great detail the technical specifications of the product.

Where do you think Billy Brelsford might have gone wrong? What should he do now?

▶ Wedgwood has retail distribution outlets in many large stores throughout the country and every night a computer based at HQ in Staffordshire scans records maintained at distribution outlets. This enables Wedgwood to monitor sales and to dispatch items as and when required.

▶ Place or distribution decisions involve choosing the best channels to use in order to bring the goods to the market. Coverage and location are key factors to be considered. Inventory and transportation are decision areas in physical distribution.

CHAPTER SUMMARY

1 A firm has a number of strategic tools at its disposal to win customers over to its products and services. These are the product, price, promotion and the method of distribution. Together they make up four elements of the marketing mix – the four Ps.

2 Overall it has to be ensured that marketing mix variables set for any product or service complement each other and add to the strategic impact of marketing activity. Marketing mix decisions have to be taken in conjunction with one another.

3 Each one of the four marketing mix variables is a complex entity in itself involving different kinds of decisions. Product decisions involve such things as quality, features, options, style, brand name, packaging, sizes, services, warranties, and returns. Pricing decisions include discounts and allowances. Promotion comprises selling, advertising, sales promotion, etc. Within each area of promotion there are many and often complex decisions to be made. Distribution involves channel decisions and physical distribution decisions. Even managing finished stock level can be thought of as part of the process of distribution.

▶ Now that you have reached the end of the chapter, turn back to the objectives and make sure you have achieved each of them.

3 The marketing environment

Chapter objectives

By the end of this chapter you should:

▌ know how changes in social and cultural values have had an impact on customers' wants and needs in the marketplace and how this has affected the nature of goods on offer

▌ know how political, fiscal and economic policies can effect the demand for products both in home and overseas markets

▌ recognize how changes in technology influence the types of products that are produced and the implications this may have for marketing practice

▌ know the kinds of legislation that have been set up to try to ensure that firms compete fairly in the marketplace and behave in a responsible way towards consumers

▌ know how changes have taken place in establishments for distributing goods over the past thirty years or so and what impact this has had on marketers of consumer products

▌ know what are the main 'green' issues concerning the environment and the kind of steps that firms can take and have taken to keep in line with green policy

▌ understand the ethical issues involved in the marketing of goods and services

▌ know about the different types of consumer protection agencies and consumer watchdog organizations that have been established to monitor that firms and how they act in the interests of the consumer

▌ be familiar with the following terms as used by marketers: cultural values, superstores, green marketing, fast track marketing.

Introduction

The **environment** may be thought of as the surroundings within which a business works. In business literature reference is made both to an internal and an external environment. The former usually refers to the various assets and resources possessed by a firm. That is its workforce, plant and machinery, know-how, financial resources, etc. Financial resources refer to people, institutions and developments, etc., which influence what the organization can do – from the outside.

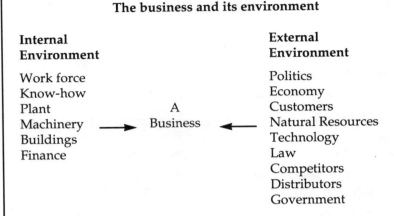

The business and its environment

Internal Environment		External Environment
Work force		Politics
Know-how		Economy
Plant	A	Customers
Machinery	Business	Natural Resources
Buildings		Technology
Finance		Law
		Competitors
		Distributors
		Government

All firms need to take notice of the environment in which they operate and the changes that are likely to take place in it. They are also in a position to influence the environment. Organizations come up with new technological ideas and put them into practice. The new technologies then become part of the environment and influence what other organizations can do.

The firm can exert considerable control over the internal environment but it cannot exert control to the same extent over the external environment. It can only influence it. In this chapter we will be looking at the external environment and how it impinges on the activities of a firm.

CHANGING PATTERNS, CHANGING STRATEGIES

Marketing decisions and plans are made within the context of an ever changing external environment. The nature of the environment and the changes that take place within it present opportunities, threats and constraints to a firm's activities. The nature of the markets themselves change over time requiring entirely different marketing strategies to be adopted for the same products. For example, years ago mass markets existed for many different products. Mass markets are markets in which there is a large volume demand for a standard product. An increase in the standard of living accompanied by customers looking for individualized products led to the replacement of mass markets with highly fragmented markets. These new markets are based upon distinct niches and segments; one of which may still be a sizeable 'value for money' segment.

Other examples of changes in the marketing environment include the introduction of the microchip and the impact it has had on many types of consumer durables, for example, washers, cookers, etc; changes in people's shopping habits as a greater emphasis is put on convenience shopping; the influence of ideas

► Today we see popular production cars on the streets in many different colours but this has not always been the case. Henry Ford is reputed to have said about the model T - 'Give it to them any colour as long as it is black'. This was the colour in the UK until after the end of the Second World War in 1945.

Changes in the marketing environment: holidays

One hundred or so years ago most people tended to work such long hours and had so little in the way of disposable income that they did not really have holidays as we know them. An annual works outing to a local beauty spot or place of interest was the main event of the year. Such trips were made possible largely by the development of the railways. In the first half of the twentieth century an increase in living standards, accompanied by the growth in personalized transport in the shape of the car, led to a considerable increase in the holiday traffic. Resorts all over the UK began to blossom out and infrastructures in the form of the entertainment business, hotel accommodation/guest houses and restaurants developed. Other retail trades also benefited from the expansion.

Since the Second World War many more people have started to take their holidays abroad. Places that people once read about only in geography books have now become as familiar as Blackpool, Brighton and Scarborough. Increasing affluence coupled with big steps forward in the development of air passenger transport have made this possible. Other related growth areas have been travel agency business, an interest in learning languages and the appearance of a large number books or guides on countries and foreign resorts.

► A fundamental dimension to the marketing environment is its dynamic nature and its impact on business practices.

expressed in other countries such as those belonging to the EEC and enacted through the European Parliament; new legislation passed by central government on matters relating to safety, for example, compulsory use of seatbelts in the rear of a car, making it necessary for car manufacturers to fit them as standard to all new cars sold in the UK.

Important aspects of the marketing environment

The most important areas of the market environment are:

● customers
● competitors
● social and cultural values
● political, fiscal, economic and legal policies
● technology
● establishments for distributing goods.

► Customers and competitors and their influence on marketing are considered elsewhere in the book. In this chapter we will look at some changes in social and cultural values and consider the other elements of the marketing environment.

Cultural values

In domestic markets it is common to find that different regions of the country have different buying preference patterns that seem to reflect different cultural and traditional values. Moreover, because our towns and cities are now very cosmopolitan in nature it is quite common to find large ethnic groups living in concentrated urban areas. These groups, too, have distinct cultural values which

► In 1989 ethnic minorities made up less than five per cent of the population of the UK. In the Greater London area, however, the figure was seventeen per cent, in the West Midlands twelve per cent and in West Yorkshire it was eight per cent.

are reflected in their buying preference patterns.

At the level of international marketing, language is an aspect of culture which requires attention in marketing communications. Different levels of educational attainment influence the extent to which written communications can be understood and acted upon. Hence written instructions accompanying a product may be a major problem. This problem is exacerbated by product liability – that is the need to inform the user how to use the product correctly. The manufacturer needs to avoid legal redress resulting from the consequences of a product being misused by customers.

Religious beliefs, both at home and abroad, have a major impact upon consumer attitudes and purchase behaviour. This is often reflected in the kinds of food that people will consume, the drinks they will purchase and even their manner of dress. Even business practices can vary considerably between different areas and countries.

Sleepy afternoons

Siestas are taken in some regions of the world. In the Tuscany region of Italy if you run out of petrol after 2.00 p.m. you may have to wait several hours before you can fill up your petrol tank.

In many parts of Spain shops open in the morning, close during the afternoon – the siesta time – and open again at around 4.30 p.m. until quite late in the evening. As in Italy, the custom is a result of experiences in the warmer parts of the country where in the summer it is much too hot to move around and work in the heat of the afternoon. However, it is worthwhile pointing out that even in Spain's highest city, Avila, the custom is practised in the winter when the climate is not a great deal different to that experienced in the United Kingdom!

Social organization is something which often reflects cultural values. Some cultures respect age and experience while others give it less credence. Some cultures make much more use of the extended family concept than others.

Marketers have to understand cultural values in all aspects of implementing the marketing concept and managing the marketing mix.

Television programmes constitute a service which is made available to all people in the UK. The UK in fact is quite cosmopolitan in nature and is made up of many different cultural and ethnic groups. List down as many different cultural groups as you can. Next, look through a number of back copies of the *Radio Times* or the *TV Times* and find out to what extent programmes are likely to appeal to specific cultural audiences.

Based on your analysis, do you feel that any of the audiences are over represented or under represented?

► Cultural values impact on both consumer behaviour and marketing or business practice.

Political, fiscal and economic policies

Government policies can exert considerable influence over what firms can do and how consumers will react in the marketplace. Legislation over such things as labelling, packaging, advertising and environmentalism all have an impact on business and have to be taken into account when designing packaging and formulating advertising messages.

Adverse government statements about unhealthy foods or ingredients in foods can have a devastating effect upon demand in an industry. In 1990 a salmonella scare relating to eggs seriously damaged UK egg-producers' incomes.

▶ The anti-smoking legislation in the UK has made tobacco companies turn to overseas markets where a less repressive attitude exists.

 Visit the main library in your nearest town or city. Ask to look at back copies of the national newspapers for 1990 (they are usually on microfilm or microfiche). Follow through the course of the salmonella scare on eggs and examine in particular what impact it was reported to have on the egg business.

Governments impose tariffs on certain imported goods to discourage demand for them. Importing firms then have to find ways of getting round the problems that this creates. For example, tariffs on fully assembled goods may be quite high but if firms import the goods as sub-assemblies the tariffs are usually lower. Local people can be employed to assemble the sub-assemblies into finished goods.

▶ The reasons for imposing tariffs or taxes on imports are explored in Chapter 18.

Political instability in a country can also have a marked effect on marketing methods used by exporters in accessing that country's markets. It may be preferable, for example, to sell the licence to manufacture the product to a producer in the country concerned for a once only royalty fee.

Variations in economic activity and wealth in different parts of the world and within different regions of a country can have a marked impact upon the prices paid for many goods and services. Variations in house prices in different parts of the UK are an example of this.

▶ Licences may be granted to produce or market goods and services. In the former case the licence relates to know-how. Royalty payments can be one-off payments or as a percentage of subsequent sales.

 Find out the amount of tax that is paid on the following goods and services. Can you account for any differences that occur?

cigarettes	books
beer	betting
spirits	theatre tickets
petrol	

▶ Government imposed political, fiscal and economic policies can restrict demand for goods and services and affect the business activities of firms.

Note: Information on taxes is provided in the *Marketing Pocket Book*, NTC Publications Ltd. PO Box 69, Henley-on-Thames, Oxfordshire, RG9 1GB.

War and trade

A British manufacturer of lead-acid batteries found that there was a substantial demand for its products in India and Pakistan. It set up assembly plants in both countries and supplied them with component parts from the UK.

During the conflict between India and Pakistan in the mid 1960s, a very large consignment of parts on board a ship bound for the Pakistan plant was intercepted and confiscated by the Indian Authorities. It was many months before the consignment eventually reached its destination and the company receiving the products suffered financial setbacks as a result.

The same British company took a different approach to marketing when it started to trade in the Middle East at about the same time. It entered into a licensing agreement with a company based in the Lebanon. In return for a royalty payment it agreed to provide the Lebanese firm with the know-how and expertise to produce and market batteries in its own right.

Technology

▶ The appearance of the microchip revolutionized the nature of many products. It is not widely appreciated that in order to operate a computer of comparable capacity to the palm top Hewlett Packard, Psion or Atari models of today a room of considerable size would have been required in the 1960s.

Technological advances and improvements are occurring all the time. Today's products rapidly become obsolete. A desktop computer purchased in 1985 is obsolete in 1992. Firms which do not react to technological advances run the risk both of product obsolescence and of going out of business. On balance it would seem better to adopt new technological innovations than to ignore them. The relationship between technological advances in product design and marketing strategy is however a curious one and does not always seem to support this argument. Sometimes there is a sizeable demand for products using an old technology. In such a case it may be the technology itself that people find attractive.

▶ Changes in technology effect what firms can produce and how they produce them.

 Next time that you go shopping make a list of some consumer durables that you see in the shops and that you think must have had some technological improvements made to them in the last five years (if you are not sure keep it on the list).

Next pay a special visit to your local library and ask for the bound volumes of *Which?* which are usually to be found in the reference section of the library.

Look up reports over the last five years that deal with products on your list. Compare the technical specifications of the ones which get the highest ratings by the *Which?* raters with those given the lowest ratings.

Distribution mechanisms

Changes in distribution patterns are taking place all the time. This is much in evidence in retailing. In the UK the growth in car ownership, the trend to a high percentage of husbands and wives both

Technology moves with time

Though it is still possible to buy pocket watches, clockwork wristwatches replaced pocket watches as portable timepieces many years ago. The story of the Elgin watch company's disappearance as a result of not moving with the times is well known. Clockwork wristwatches subsequently received a technological nudge with the invention of the automatic-wind mechanism. Many watch makers began to incorporate this feature into their products, though at a premium price.

In the late 1960s automatic-wind mechanisms were becoming the rule rather than the exception. Some companies, however, were already marketing battery driven watches and the Japanese watch company Seiko, in particular, had begun to attack markets world-wide making use of its precision engineering and automated production facilities. A major shift in technology occurred in the mid 1970s when LCD watches began to appear for the first time. Seiko, having already developed an excellent reputation for automatic-wind watches, led the way at the higher end of the market with the new technology.

The strategic dilemma facing manufacturers at that time was one of how to react. High quality manufacturers with international reputations chose not to follow suit and adopt LCD displays though some of them did begin to change to quartz movements while keeping the traditional analog display. By the late 1980s the LCD display had become the standard for many cheaper watches. Up-market manufacturers had returned to differentiation on brand name and the aesthetic appearance of the analog display.

Some of the producers at the quality end of the market had adopted quartz movements but others such as Rolex had relied on their brand name and exclusive appeal to withstand the impact of technological innovation. They continued throughout the period to market self-winding clockwork watches.

working, together with increasing standards of living, have led to less time being available for shopping and greater mobility of the shopper. All of these factors, in turn, have led to the need for one-stop shopping facilities and thence to the development of supermarkets to provide this specialist facility. Many of the traditional retail outlets have suffered severely from the competition – fishmongers, butchers, pharmacists, etc.

Over the years some of the chain stores such as Boots and Marks and Spencer have increased the range of products they offer to customers. Marks and Spencer's movement into food retailing is an example of this. There are now also large specialist retailing establishments (superstores) emerging to cater for specific market segments, for example, Texas.

► The British Market Research Bureau has estimated that in 1991 seventy-four per cent of regular grocery shopping is carried out once a week or less. In addition sixty-five point six per cent is carried out from Thursday to Saturday inclusive. Sainsburys, Tesco and Asda between them provide for sixty-three per cent of the regular major grocery shopping. (Source: TGI, April 1990 – March, 1991)

▶ Changes in patterns of retailing have revolutionized shopping over the past years.

▶ On the 16 September 1987 more than 70 countries agreed on measures to reduce the threat to the Earth's ozone layer. Under the agreement drawn up in Montreal use of CFCs were frozen at existing levels and were to be reduced by half by 1999.

Reshaping the world

'I don't care what the salesman told your teacher. We are not going to grow a rain forest in your bedroom.'

▶ It is worthwhile to note that whereas in the UK it is customary to wrap goods bought at most retail outlets in some countries this is not the case - in the south of Germany, for example.

Halfords, traditionally retailers of cycle accessories and parts for the DIY motorist trade, now offer a car servicing/repair service to motorists at their new out of town stores.

Green marketing

Green principles are concerned with preserving the environment. There are a number of issues which have important implications for marketing. The issues relate to:

- damage to the Earth's ozone layer by chlorofluorocarbons (CFCs). These were at one time present in aerosol products and are still to be found in some forms of packaging, refrigeration and air conditioning equipment
- the greenhouse effect (also known as global warming) which is the result of certain gases (carbon dioxide, nitrogen oxides, methane and CFCs) being released into the atmosphere. The way to combat this problem is to use less hydrocarbon-based energy together with any action taken to conserve energy. Preserving the tropical rainforests and the creation of new forests also helps to come to grips with this problem
- acid rain causes considerable damage to trees, soils, rivers and lakes. Power stations, factories and car exhausts are producers of the pollutants. Solutions to this problem are similar to those associated with the greenhouse effect
- intensive farming methods, use of artificial fertilizers and pesticides, use of phosphates and bleaches in household detergents and the dumping of waste into rivers and the sea can all cause damage to the environment. Different working practices provide the solution to this problem
- the creation and disposal of waste in general produces another problem. In particular, attention needs to be given to packaging which is a major contributor to waste. Over-packaging needs to be avoided and reusable or recyclable materials encouraged
- the amount of unspoilt countryside in many parts of the world is diminishing due to continued urban expansion. Better use of existing urban retailing and manufacturing sites provides a partial answer to this problem
- the welfare of animals is suffering as a result of commercial and industrial developments which threaten to destroy their natural habitats. Animal abuse and cruelty are taking place for a wide variety of purposes is also a most undesirable feature of twentieth century living. Elimination of products associated with any of these acts is essential.

The issues raised above have long-term implications for consumer behaviour. It is possibile that consumers may begin to favour products which possess quality, reliability, durability and safety. In addition, the days of throwaway products may be limited.

The smog menace

Trafford Park in Manchester has been a huge, sprawling complex of industry for a long time. Many years ago it was beautiful countryside. It developed alongside the Manchester and Salford Docks which were themselves by-products of the building of the Manchester Ship canal.

For many years factories in Trafford Park churned out effluence and incinerated chemicals which added to pollution in the Manchester area. Thick, yellow-tinged smogs clung to the streets of the neighbouring towns in the winters bringing death to older people with respiratory problems, accidents to road travellers, delays for everyone and dirt and grime that got in people's clothes and hair before they even got to work in the morning.

The introduction of national legislation to combat problems caused by air pollution alone has had an enormous impact on the area.

Green labels

The government's latest plans for an official eco-label on green products were outlined in a Department of Environment (DOE) white paper in November 1991. It laid down the criteria for products to be covered by the first eco-labels in 1992. The kind of products likely to be covered by the eco-labelling scheme are those where there is:

● a significant impact on the environment
● a high degree of consumer confusion about the environmental claims.

Next time you are in the supermarket make a note of those products which now indicate that they are making use of materials which are in keeping with green policy. Also, make a note of those products which do not mention the green issue at all.

Take the list of items which do not mention green issues and see if you can find out whether any of these products contain materials which are environmentally unfriendly. Can you account for why these products have not been produced to meet green requirements?

In the case of some products you will note that some brands or items are green and other are not. Why do you think this should be the case? A useful source of information, here, is the *The Ethical Consumer*, back issues of which can be found in the your local library.

► Green issues are starting to dominate our way of life and this is reflected in the types and of products we want to use. It is forcing firms to change the nature of their products so that they meet with the needs of a green society.

RESPONDING TO CHANGE

Firms have adopted a number of ways of coming to grips with the ever-changing complexity of the marketing environment. Foremost among these are the use of effective marketing information systems and the use of on-going market research so that reaction time to change can be speeded up. These will be considered in more detail in Chapter 4 on information gathering systems in marketing.

► See Chapter 4.

Another approach involves what is called **fast track marketing**. Increasing rates of technological change and the shortening of the life of products mean that companies have to act very quickly when they are introducing new products to the market (the process of new product development is discussed in Chapter 12). Late entrants to a market with a new product may find that the product does not offer attractive financial prospects since the product's commercial life is much shorter than might have been typical say twenty years ago. The response is to look for ways of reducing the amount of time spent in developing and testing a product. The implication of this is that firms have to **manage in parallel** and not sequentially. This means that instead of one stage following on from another, wherever possible the two stages take place at the same time. Spending more money to speed up the process of innovation is another strategy and spending more effort on planning things out before something is actually put into action also appears to bear dividends.

► This is obviously most applicable to those industrial markets where product development times can be counted in years, for example, military and commercial aircraft.

► Marketing research and fast track marketing are ways of keeping up with the ever changing marketing environment.

MARKETING LAW AND ETHICS

It may not always be apparent at the time of purchase that goods are not of merchantable quality, so laws are enacted to protect consumers from unscrupulous manufacturers and dealers who produce shoddy, defective or dangerous goods. The same principle also applies to the purchase of services. Laws may also be enacted for a variety of other reasons to protect the consumer interests – for example when goods or services are bought on credit. Another purpose of legislation is to curb unfair trading practices where companies engage in trading practices which are likely to be counter to the interests of the customer. For example, firms could enter into agreements to fix prices for essential goods such as fuel thereby giving themselves excessively high profits.

There are a variety of important Acts of Parliament which have either a direct or indirect effect on marketing. Some examples of legislation are:

- Food and Drugs Act, 1955 (as amended) – covers matters relating to the labelling and advertising of foods
- Trade Descriptions Act, 1968 – makes it an offence to deliver or offer goods for sale which do not match with the descriptions given of them. It applies to services as well as products

Unsolicited goods

'No officer, I'm sure I didn't order it AND I know I don't have to pay for it. The problem is that I don't know who sent it or what to do with it.'

- Unsolicited Goods and Services Act, 1971 – makes it an offence for anyone to ask for payment for goods or services that they have not ordered
- Prices Act, 1974 – relates to products which are offered at 'sale' prices. Sale prices are defined as being prices below that which would normally be charged for the same items. The normal price should be shown and there has to be evidence that the product has been on sale for a period of at least twenty-eight days during the previous six months at the 'normal' price quoted.

 Indicate how you might seek redress in the following instances:

1 A dealer sells you a second-hand Land Rover and the engine seizes after 200 miles. The dealer says you must have misused it and refuses to put the matter right.

2 You order a chair from a retailer and pay cash. The wrong colour and type of chair is delivered. You refuse delivery and send the goods back to the dealer. After two months you have still not received the goods you ordered so you write and request your money to be returned. After two further letters the money has not been returned nor goods supplied.

3 A shop at the end of the street is emitting nasty smells and creating a local nuisance. The matter has been brought to the attention of the owner of the shop but he just shrugs his shoulders and says that it cannot be helped.

4 You bought a cardigan in a sale for £15. A friend tells you that it had been on offer for the previous six weeks at £14,

which was the regular price. You return to the shop and bring it to the owner's attention but she just says that you cannot prove the matter and refuses to do anything about it.

Hint: call in at your local Citizen's Advice Bureau to obtain pamphlets which can help you to tackle some of these issues. Alternatively consult any consumer law handbook such as *Business Law*, K. R. Abbott and N. Pendlebury, DP publications.

▶ The Consumer Credit Act was introduced partly as a result of problems which arose when people agreed to high value sales, often after pressure had been put on them by door-to-door salespeople. Often decisions were made by the customer without due deliberation in the matter as to whether the customer could really afford to make the repayments.

- Consumer Credit Act, 1974 – makes it obligatory for suppliers of goods on credit to provide a cooling off period for credit agreements signed away from trade premises. In addition, for goods that are bought on hire-purchase, once the hirer has paid at least one third of the agreed amount, repossession of the goods cannot be obtained at will. Moreover, in the case of goods bought with credit cards there are specific remedies in the case where goods do not match with what customers might reasonably expect. In addition, all promotions relating to credit business must state both the cash and credit prices together with the rate of interest to be charged
- Consumer Transactions Order, 1976 – makes it an offence to offer guarantees or conditions of sale which mislead the customers into believing that their statutory rights are adversely affected
- Unfair Contract Terms Act, 1977 – means that traders cannot limit or contract out of liability for death or personal injury arising from negligence or from breach of duty
- Competition Act, 1979 – is directed against anti-competitive practices in both public and private sectors. The Director General of the Office of Fair Trading can investigate such practices and refer them to the Monopolies and Mergers Commission
- Consumer Protection Act, 1987 – covers defects in products which give rise to damage. It assigns liability to the producer or importer of the product.

▶ Laws exist to protect consumers from unscrupulous business practices and the selling of shoddy goods. They also exist to prevent firms from engaging in unfair competition.

(ACT) Despite legislation, infringements to fair competition and consumer protection do occur. Over a period of time, observe business practice in your neighbourhood, scan the newspapers and other periodicals, listen to the news, and watch television to produce a list of such infringements. Enter these infringements into a file (paper or electronic) and subsequently tabulate them to discover which infringements appear to occur the most often.

Ethics and codes of practice

Ethics refer to the principles of morality. In the context of marketing it relates to activities which while not actually illegal raise moral questions. We must distinguish between practices which are illegal and those which are unethical. The distinction is necessary because of the way in which society responds to breaches of conduct. In the case of illegal practice the remedy is to seek redress through the law. In the case of unethical practice one can only seek redress through pressure groups or 'watchdogs' (see below).

There are many ethical issues which marketers should be aware of. In the first instance some people believe that marketing creates wants for goods and services that did not previously exist and perhaps which are not needed. It is felt this is not in the best interests of society since it can lead to all kinds of undesirable social consequences. In the case of products such as drugs legislation exists to outlaw trading except under medical supervision. However, there are a range of other products that are more difficult to deal with since the products themselves are not actually illegal. Cigarettes, alcohol, pornography and chat-lines are among the products which are the subject of contention.

Ethical issues also relate to how firms set about marketing their products. Advertising which makes misleading claims about products or services and advertising which operates at a subliminal level are cases in point. Price fixing while legally outlawed may still operate because its existence is difficult to substantiate. Distributors may fail to live up to agreements they have made with producers without the latter's knowledge.

► Subliminal – below the conscious threshold.

► As with all matters relating to law enforcement it has to be proved that an offence has taken place. Collusion in the fixing of prices can be difficult to prove beyond doubt.

Consumerism, pressure groups and watchdogs

Pressure groups exist to influence how decisions are made. **Consumerism** is the action of organized movements to protect the economic interests of consumers by forcing companies to behave in a more socially responsible manner. The Consumers' Association (the main UK consumer body) publishes a monthly journal, *Which?*. Information is provided in the journal about certain goods and services based upon the first hand experience of CA members or other independent bodies which test the products. A wide range of products and services are covered in this journal.

Watchdog organizations exist to deal with complaints about public sector organizations such as the Post Office, British Rail and the NHS. Complaints received from users of these services are publicized. There are also environmental watchdog organizations that look out for matters relating to environmental protection. They seek to oppose plans to build factories or houses in the open countryside and watch for environmental pollution caused by factories.

One of the results of consumerism is that it has caused firms to produce voluntary codes of practice relating to matters which may give rise to environmental pollution. At the same time the government has established the Office of Fair Trading. The basic aim of the Office of Fair Trading is to encourage competition that is both fair between firms and fair to the consumer.

Various other consumer protection agencies exist and are listed below:

► Consumerism refers to consumers acting to exert control over the quality of goods and services and the way in which they are bought and sold.

- Consumer Protection Advisory Committee deals with:
  - terms and conditions of sale
  - prices
  - advertising, labelling and promoting goods and services
  - selling methods.
- National Consumer Council deals with:
  - presenting the opinions of consumers to industry and government.
- County Council Trading Standards/Consumer Protection departments deal with:
  - complaints from members of the public.
- District Council Environmental Health departments
  - enforce offences against particular Acts. Matters of interest to these bodies include Sunday trading (at the time this book goes to press this is the subject of review), food and drink which is not fit for sale and any other matters relating to shop hygiene.
- Advertising Standards Authority
  - monitors the standard of advertising in the UK. Complaints can be made by members of the public direct to this body. A monthly report is issued which lists complaints received and the action taken by the Advertising Standards Authority.

A question of age
Re: Levi-Strauss & Agency Bartle Bogle Hegarty Ltd.

The Advertising Standards Authority received objections to an advertisement in *Elle* magazine with respect to clothing which was captioned 'Age doesn't improve everything'. The visual featured a black and white photograph of a glum middle-aged couple sitting on a park bench semi-naked. Objectors found the unflattering image of the couple to be offensive on the grounds that it was undignified and mocked the middle aged.

The advertiser said the advertisement was one of a series designed to convey the message that their product improved with age and stood the test of time. It was intended as a humorous play on the glumness of the characters' poses. The editor of *Elle* explained that the publishers had agreed to run the series of advertisements but that she had subsequently had reservations about publishing this particular advertisement and had received several complaints from readers. The Authority considered it unlikely that the image would cause grave or widespread offence in the context of the humorous approach, but the advertisers were advised to take into account readers' sensibilities with regard to the depiction of the elderly or middle aged if considering similar approaches in the future.

Adapted from : The Advertising Standards Authority, monthly report no.6, 1991, p. 17.

► Consumer watchdog organizations are on the look out for breaches of the law relating to bad business practices and unethical trading methods.

CHAPTER SUMMARY

1 Patterns and changes in patterns in social and cultural values have an impact on customers wants and needs in the marketplace. This in turn influences the nature of goods and services which firms offer in different regions or countries and to different cultural groups.

2 Political, fiscal and economic policies have an effect on the demand for products both in home and overseas markets. Governments may try to restrict demand for certain goods for economic, fiscal or political reasons or to protect infant industries. Restrictions can pose marketing problems which exporters have to find ways of surmounting.

▶ Fiscal – financial or treasury, for example, purchase taxes, import tariffs, etc.

3 Technological advances exert a considerable influence on the types of product that can be offered to customers. Firms which do not take note of the trend run the risk of going out of business.

4 Legislation exists to protect consumers and outlaw unfair competitive practices. These are regularly under review and amendment.

5 Changes have taken place in establishments distributing goods over the past thirty years which have had a marked impact on the marketing of consumer products. Notable developments have been the growth of supermarkets and specialist supermarkets aimed at improving convenience shopping.

6 Green issues are beginning to dominate the way firms think and do business. Environmental pollution is an important issue with implications stretching into the centuries to come. As a consequence firms are starting to take the kind of steps that are required to keep in line with green policy.

7 Ethical issues involved in the marketing of goods and services are important. Misdemeanours may fall short of actually being illegal but they may be socially unacceptable and not part and parcel of what is considered to be good business or marketing practice.

8 In addition to legislation there have been various bodies set up to monitor and report on firms not meeting with legislation enacted. Other bodies report on matters which while not illegal may be considered to be not in the best interests of the consumer or society. The global term relating to such organizations is watchdog and they form part of the ever increasing consumerism movement.

▶ Now that you have reached the end of the chapter, turn back to the objectives and make sure you have achieved each of them.

④ Information gathering systems in marketing

Chapter objectives

By the end of this chapter you should:

▌ know what kind of information marketing researchers are seeking

▌ be able to describe the sources of information which marketing researchers can consult

▌ know what kind of research methods market researchers can employ

▌ be able to describe in very broad terms how a survey might be conducted

▌ be able to describe how a sampling plan is drawn up and be conversant with different probability and non-probability sampling methods

▌ be able to put together a simple questionnaire for use in a survey

▌ be able to describe the main types of marketing information systems

▌ be familiar with the following terms as used by marketers : market research, marketing research, marketing information systems, field experiments, laboratory experiments, observation, surveys, sample, sampling plan, probability samples, non-probability samples, simple random sample, stratified random sample, cluster (area) sample, convenience sample, judgement sample, questionnaires, closed-ended questions, multiple choice questions, attitude scales, unstructured questions, word association, sentence completion, story completion, picture completion, quantitative data, qualitative data, research risk, research cost, planning systems, control systems, market research systems, monitoring systems, marketing intelligence.

Introduction

Information gathering and analysis in marketing play an important role in helping firms to make decisions. This chapter outlines some of the basic elements of market research and indicates developments in the rapidly expanding field of marketing information systems. **Market research** is an aspect of marketing research, a term which relates to all areas of marketing activity. The bulk of time and money is spent on market research activities and hence prime attention will be given to this topic in this chapter.

▶ According to the Market Research Society market research is the means used by those people who provide goods and services to keep themselves in touch with the needs and wants of those who buy and use the goods and services. We see market research extending to measure the effectiveness of marketing decisions.

REASONS FOR RESEARCH

A firm undertakes market research to find out about those people who buy a product or service and those people who do not. It involves ascertaining the nature of wants and needs and assessing the current and potential demand for consumer and industrial products and services. Information obtained can help to reduce the element of uncertainty and guesswork in making marketing decisions. For instance, information on income levels and customer perceptions of a fair price can be used to advantage in setting prices.

Market research takes the questions how, when, where, what, who and why and applies them to basic questions such as:

- who buys or does not buy the product/service?
- why do they buy or not buy the product/service?
- how do those who buy the product obtain it; get to know about it; pay for it; etc. ?
- how often do they buy?
- where do they obtain it?
- when do they obtain it?
- what do they buy ?
- in what quantities do they buy ?
- in what quantities are they likely to buy?

► Market research enables a firm to identify customer wants and needs.

Who undertakes market research?

Many firms undertake their own market research but there are also specialist consulting firms that undertake to collect and provide information for a fee. This is particularly useful for small firms that do not have their own market researchers. There are also specialist market research firms that concentrate on specific aspects of marketing – such as branding or packaging. Even where firms do have market research departments they can still benefit from the specialized service offered by such market research companies. In addition there are market research companies that collect trade or consumer data to sell to client companies on a fee subscription basis.

► The Association of Market Survey Organizations (AMSO) indicated that its members turnover almost doubled in the period 1985–90. Food/soft drinks manufacturers accounted for more than twice as much of the business as any other group of firms. The AMSO accounts for more than seventy-five per cent of the market for survey research.

Sources of information

There are many sources of information. We can consider sources under two headings – information that the firm already has itself in company records and information that it obtains from outside sources.

Company records

Firms have a wealth of marketing information in their internal company records. These include customer sales records, salespersons' reports, and correspondence with individual customers. In addition there are the company's own sales statistics and competitive information gleaned from a variety of sources. The important point here is that there must be some formal means of collecting this information and making it readily available to marketing executives. This is generally the role of the marketing information system. We will return to this later in the chapter.

Outside sources of information

There are many different outside sources of information. They include trade associations. These organizations produce reports, surveys and other statistics for companies which belong to the association. Independently published reports and surveys on specific markets are also produced by organizations such as Mintel and the Economist Intelligence Unit. Another source of useful information are government statistics (census data, family expenditure surveys, national income statistics, etc.). Company reports and accounts of competitors can give some ideas on what companies intend to do in the future and can be obtained from Companies House in London.

► Government statistics can be obtained on request from the Central Statistical Office (CSO).

Market Research companies

There are many market research companies located in different parts of the UK. Some are large companies which have branches in different towns and cities. The companies undertake to do research on behalf of clients or can provide reports on topics which they have researched on their own initiative.

Information based on consumer panel data (see below) is available from market research firms that specialize in collecting data on people's purchase habits. There is also retail audit data based on continuous sampling of retail stocks. Such audits can be bought from market research firms (for example, Audits of Great Britain).

Market research companies undertake **omnibus surveys**. Omnibus surveys cover a wide range of products and services and probe into people's attitudes and opinions concerning the products covered. The information obtained in these surveys is sold to client companies on request. Omnibus surveys will contain information which is not of interest to clients as well as information which is pertinent to their requirements. Specific surveys relating to a company's products and those of its competitors may also be commissioned and in this case the results are only made known to the clients sponsoring the research.

► Information can be obtained through company records, government sources and market research specialists.

Panel data

With **panel data** a sample of respondents is retained for a period of time and all members of the panel are asked to keep a diary record of their purchases over a period of time. This is the best method of recording purchases over time since people have difficulty in remembering what they have purchased and when they purchased it. A major problem with using this method is getting together a representative panel and keeping it going. People drop out or die and getting a replacement who matches the lapsed panel member can be difficult.

 Assume you are the marketing manager for a national brand of ice-cream. Suggest the best approach to finding answers to the following questions:

- who buys or does not buy the brand?
- why do they buy or not buy the brand?
- how often do they buy the brand?
- where do they obtain the brand?
- when do they obtain the brand?

What other questions might be asked and what would be the best way to find out the answers?

THE PROCESS OF RESEARCH

Whatever kind of research is conducted there are a number of stages in the research process which have to be gone through. The stages are:

- problem definition
- consulting company records and published data sources
- deciding whether field work is required and if so what is the best research method
- specifying the location and size/type of sample
- collecting the data
- analysing the data
- evaluating the results
- setting down recommendations for action.

Problem definition
The first stage in the research is problem definition. This is an initial statement of the research objectives. Objectives are usually to provide information on people's:

- opinions
- attitudes
- beliefs
- intentions
- knowledge
- behaviour
- social background.

▶ Audits of Great Britain have a panel of 8500 households which record purchases of packaged grocery, household goods, fresh food and similar items. The panel is representative of the whole of Britain. Data is collected via personal data terminals which read bar codes. Each terminal is linked via a modem to the telephone socket and data are polled overnight. In addition to personal data of the panel member, data is obtained on all purchases regarding: brand name; size; flavour/variety; actual price paid; weight of purchase; quantity bought; name and address of shop and type of shop.

Consulting company records and published data sources

The next stage in the process involves consulting published data sources such as company records and previous research or outside bodies and relevant periodicals. Some of these sources of data may be able to provide answers to aspects of the problem. Information can be obtained more cheaply from such sources than from research which involves undertaking a survey or some other form of **field research**. Not all the answers can be obtained in this way. It is quite likely that field research will have to be undertaken.

► Field research involves actually going out and finding things out by asking questions, doing experiments, etc.

Deciding whether field work is required and if so what is the best research method

Assuming that field research is necessary, the next step is to decide whether to commission an agency to undertake research or whether the firm itself should carry out the research. Much will depend on the size of the firm and its resources. Small firms usually do not have the resources to conduct their own research. Another factor to take into account is that market research agencies have skilled staff and expertise in conducting research and can probably conduct it more efficiently.

An appropriate research method also has to be decided. The main methods of conducting field market research are survey interviews, observation and experimentation. Here we will consider experimentation and observation and look at surveys in the following section.

Experimentation and observation

Experimentation and observation are used across the whole range of marketing research activities. Advertising research employs **experimentation** to determine the effectiveness of different advertisements. Researchers also use experiments in supermarkets and large stores to assess the impact of varying the space and shelf positioning given to different brands of goods.

► Space is the amount of shelf-space given to displaying a product in a store. Shelf positioning is where the foods are displayed in the store and can also refer to the height or level at which they are placed. Some store sites attract more attention and customer traffic than others, for example goods displayed at eye level have a greater chance of being seen seen than those displayed below knee level.

► Sometimes competitors may deliberately intensify marketing activities in an area where they know controlled experiments are taking place.

Field and laboratory experiments are used to evaluate the effect of changes in a product or service, its price, type of packaging, distribution method or method of promotion. **Field experiments** study the effect of changes in these variables on customer reactions. They are usually carried out on fast-moving consumer goods and take place in selected stores or supermarkets. A major problem is to ensure that the stores or supermarkets used are representative of the universe of shops or stores. Another problem is the distortion effect that can occur if competitors start to undertake heavy promotions in the area.

The **laboratory experiment** is a controlled method of determining the effect of changes in the marketing mix variables on customers' reactions. It takes place in a laboratory setting – that is in a hall or room specially acquired by researchers for this purpose.

Critics of laboratory testing argue that because the situation in which participants find themselves is contrived, they will not behave normally.

Observation can be an effective method of research. It may be used when trying to ascertain whether the siting of a new shop on a particular street is likely to be worthwhile. Simple head-counts of passers-by at different times over a prolonged period will give some idea of the amount of potential custom. Observation can take place either in a laboratory or in the field. Advertising research, for example, may be conducted in a laboratory. A variety of medical instruments can be attached to people to measure their reactions to different stimuli (usually advertisements). These include eye cameras which measure changes in pupil size which in turn indicate the level of interest in a given advertisement.

Other observational methods include traffic audits, television and radio audiometers, store audits, pantry audits and information on brand or stock levels at retail outlets, observing children's reactions to clothes or toys in shops.

▶ Observation can take place either in a laboratory or in the field. Advertising research, for example, may be conducted in a laboratory.

(ACT) Observation is a powerful technique when applied effectively and can often provide answers to otherwise unanswerable questions.

List as many questions as you can for which you feel observation provides the only way of finding the real answer. Indicate the kind of difficulties you would expect to encounter in making observations.

Surveys

Surveys are techniques for collecting information from a large number of people in order to ascertain facts, beliefs, opinions and attitudes.

The most appropriate way of carrying out a survey will depend on the type and amount of information required, and the cost, ease and accuracy of questionning. Surveys may use interviews, which can be conducted over the telephone. Alternatively, they may be face-to-face with individuals or groups. Not all surveys, however, depend on interviewing to obtain information. A postal survey may be used. However, since interviews play an important role in surveys, we next look at the different kinds of interview situation in more detail.

Personal interviews

Personal interviews give the interviewer the opportunity to clarify potential ambiguities and misunderstandings in the questions. This is a strong point in favour of conducting personal interviews since the ambiguity of questions can be a major problem in designing effective questionnaires. Personal interviews also make it easier to show visual material. Response rates tend to be good when using this method. Despite their advantages personal inter-

► Training of interviewers is most important. People will record their own interpretations of what other people say to them and, depending on how a question is put to a respondent, may prompt quite a different response. Eliminating personal bias in recording answers in personal interviews is very important. Through training in the use of a particular questionnaire, it is hoped to standardize the approach adopted and to minimize this kind of error.

► Surveys are a popular way of collecting data. They may be undertaken through personal or telephone interviews or conducted by post.

Personal interview bias

'So you undertake voluntary work for Eddie the Bookie, but you're officially registered as unemployed. I think I'll record you as working part-time.'

views are expensive and the interviewer can introduce personal bias into the recording of answers. Personal interviews can be useful during exploratory research – that is when we are not yet sure exactly what it is we want to find out. They enable decisions to be made about the kinds of questions that can be posed in a larger and subsequent survey.

Telephone interviews

Telephone interviews can only be directed at telephone subscribers. In 1991 it was estimated that 90 per cent of UK homes had a telephone. Therefore, despite some obvious limitations and biases, this method does allow a large number of interviews to be conducted in a short period of time, without the interviewer having to travel. The cost per interview is low and the sample can be spread out country-wide. On the other hand, it is likely that only a short questionnaire can be used by comparison with the personal interview method. Response rates also tend to be lower. Another point is that one can only really ask straightforward questions. Attitude measurement and rating is not amenable to this form of interview.

Postal surveys

Postal surveys can be the cheapest way of collecting data. A covering letter and a stamped addressed envelope should accompany the questionnaire to encourage completion. It is usual to send a follow up letter and a duplicate questionnaire after a period of time has elapsed without a response. The main problem with postal questionnaires is the non-response rate which is typically much higher than with other methods of inquiry. There may also be problems if the respondents misunderstand questions that cannot then be explained as in a personal interview.

Sampling Plan

Surveys are conducted with respect to populations. Populations may comprise people or firms. A **population** for survey purposes refers to all the persons or companies to which one would like to direct questions. Clearly, it would be advantageous to contact all members of a population and have them all answer the questions we want to put. If this could be done we could produce very accurate results indeed. However, it is seldom possible to contact or gain a response from all the members of a population. The exception is in industrial market research exercises where it may be possible to contact all firms in a particular population because the population is comparatively small.

For the most part, populations in the market research sense are very large and it is impractical or too expensive to contact all members of the population. In such instances we have to take a **sample** from the population. We must ensure that the sample we choose represents the population as a whole.

There are three decisions to be taken in drawing up a **sampling plan** :

1 Who is to be surveyed?

This defines the **target population** . Once this has been done the next step is to develop a **sampling frame** – that is a way of giving everyone in the target population a known chance of inclusion in the sample.

2 How many people/companies should be surveyed?

Large samples give better results than smaller ones. However, samples of less than one per cent of a population can provide good reliable information if the sampling procedure is sound.

3 How should the respondents be chosen?

Probability samples permit the calculation of confidence limits for sampling error, i.e. to calculate how confident we can be that our data is representative of the whole. However cost and time often make it impractical to collect data through probability samples, so researchers may use non-probability samples – particularly **quota samples** . Strictly speaking, sampling errors cannot be measured in such cases.

Probability sample
There are different kinds of probability sample:

Simple random sample – each member of the population has a known and equal chance of selection. For example, the names of each person or firm in a sample may be written on to slips of papers and the slips deposited in a box. The box is then shaken so that all the slips of paper become thoroughly mixed up. A blindfolded person drawing successive slips of paper from the box will be taking a random sample.

Stratified random sample – the population is divided into mutually exclusive groups and random samples are drawn from each group. For example the sample might be divided into five groups A, B, C1, C2, D and E reflecting the social background of the people involved (see pages 105–6 for a definition of social class). Slips of paper with person's name on them are then   put into a box marked A, B, C1, C2, D or E as is appropriate. Random samples are then drawn from each box. A stratified sample is chosen to make sure that all groups, including minority groups, are adequately represented.

Cluster sample – the population is divided into mutually exclusive groups (such as blocks of houses) and the researcher draws a simple random sample from these groups. Again, assuming that the population is people, this time we are not interested in a person's social class but in where he or she   lives, or some other

► C. A. Moser, *Survey Methods in Social Investigation*, London: Heineman, 1969, points out that quota sampling has been criticized by statisticians for the theoretical weakness of its method. On the other hand opinion reaserchers have defended it for its cheapness and administrative convenience.

characteristic. Assuming that it is where they live and that we want to interview household heads, then we first divide the locality under study up into individual areas of housing. We then take a random or stratified sample of the areas we have identified and interview every head of household within each area we are sampling.

The preceding example is a **single-stage** cluster sample since only a sample of the blocks or areas of housing is taken. A **two-stage cluster sample** might involve undertaking the same number of interviews but making sure that a large number of blocks are covered but that only a sample of households in each block is interviewed. For example, if an area comprises three high rise tower blocks of flats, one might randomly select one of the three blocks and interview all heads of households within that block.

Non-probability sample

Convenience sample – the researcher takes the most accessible population members from which to obtain information. This happens for example, when a firm producing a prototype new washing machine gets some of its employees to test the product out in their own homes.

Quota sample In **quota sampling** the sizes of the various sub-classes or strata in the population are first estimated from some outside source, for example census of population data. We have to specify which strata will be relevant to our study. Age may be something which we think is relevant and so we will want to take account of age when drawing up the sample. If for example we find that in the population twenty-five per cent of people are aged between twenty-five and thirty then we will try to make sure that twenty-five per cent of the people in the sample fit into this age band. We would make similar requirements for other age bands. In addition we might want to take account of other factors as well as age.

Quota sampling may be **interlocking** or **parallel**. In the case of interlocking quota sampling the researcher finds and interviews persons who simultaneously meet with each of several requirements. For example an interviewer may have a total of say one hundred interviews to obtain and the age, sex, education proportions in the population may be the key discriminating variables. This could lead, for example, to four interviews with respondents who are between eighteen and thirty years of age, female, with some college education; twelve interviews with respondents who are aged between thirty and forty-five years of age, male, with no formal post school education, etc.

In the case of 'parallel' quota sampling it is not necessary for each respondent to fit all the criteria simultaneously. Interviewers are simply instructed to obtain say one hundred interviews and that within that sample size there should be a certain number in each of the specified category groups.

▶ Chisnall points out that care should be taken in deciding on strata so that only those relevant to the problem being surveyed are included. He notes that their relevance may not be apparent before the survey is done and that in such cases judgement and experience are valuable. P. M. Chisnall, *Marketing Research*, 3rd Edition, London: McGraw-Hill, 1986, p. 75.

The 'interlocking' quota sampling method is more effective in minimizing error that can arise in sampling in an on-going survey.

**Quota sample interlocking versus parallel methods
– an illustration -**

Interlocking method (only one way to do it)

There are 400 interviews to be completed.

(1) 25% in Salford and 75% in Manchester.
(2) 60% are to be males and 40% females.
(3) 25% aged between 16 and 24 (a),
    50% between 25 and 50 (b) and
    25% over 50 years of age (c).

```
                               400
                    (Total Sample Size 100%)
                      /                   \
                   100                      300
             (Salford 25%)           (Manchester 75%)
              /        \                /          \
           60           40          180            120
       (males 60%)  (females 40%) (males 60%)  (females 40%)
       / |  \        / |  \        / |  \        / |  \
     15 30  15     10 20  10     45 90  45     30 60  30
     (a)(b) (c)    (a)(b) (c)    (a)(b) (c)    (a)(b) (c)
     25%50% 25%    25%50% 25%    25%50% 25%    25%50% 25%
```

Parallel method (many ways to do it)

For the same task using a parallel method of quota sampling the instructions might be:
There are 400 interviews to be completed.

(1) 100 (25%) in Salford and 300 in Manchester.
(2) 240 (60%) are to be males and 160 females.
(3) 100 (25%) aged between 16 and 24 (a),
    200 (50%) between 25 and 50 (b) and
    100 (25%) over 50 years of age (c).

There are a very large number of different ways in which this could be achieved. Here is one way which would satisfy the target.

```
                               400
                    (Total Sample Size 100%)
                      /                   \
                   100                      300
               (Salford)               (Manchester)
              /        \                /          \
           40           60          200            100
        (males)     (females)      (males)      (females)
       / |  \        / |  \        / |  \        / |  \
     20 10  10     20 20  20     40 130 30     20 40  40
     (a)(b) (c)    (a)(b) (c)    (a)(b) (c)    (a)(b) (c)
```

Note : exactly the same numbers are specified in terms of respondents required, including percentages in both cases. We can see, however, that the profile of the respondents is quite different.

Market research makes wide use of quota sampling since it is cost effective. The method works because it is possible to introduce representativeness by stratifying the quota sample by objective and known population characteristics such as age, sex, family status, socio-economic group, etc. Quota samples may be accurately constructed using classifications such as ACORN. This is because such classifications are based on objective distributions of statistical variation in demographic, housing and occupational factors.

▶ See Chapter 8 for a full discussion of the ACORN system of classification.

Judgement samples **Judgement sampling** relies on sound judgement or expertise. It depends on selecting elements that are believed to be typical or representative of the population in such a way that errors of judgement in the selection will cancel each other out. Judgement samples are sometimes used in market research. They tend to be used more often in industrial market research than in consumer market research. In industrial market research a firm may get sixty per cent of its business from ten large purchasers and the remaining forty per cent from 300 smaller firms. A judgement sample might therefore comprise five of the large purchasers (fifty per cent) and 150 of the remainder (fifty per cent). Judgement would be exercised to ensure that the firms chosen in the sample represented the sub-grouping.

▶ Research employs samples. Both non-probability and probability methods may be used. Quota sampling is the most popular method.

 A local newspaper has launched a Friday supplement which is directed towards the under twenty-five segment of its target market. It wishes to gauge reaction to the newspaper from readers. Indicate how you might draw up a sampling plan and the type of sampling method you would use. Assume the newspaper is prepared to spend up to £2000 for the information.

Collecting the data

Questionnaires
Questionnaires must be carefully developed, tested and debugged before administering them on a large scale. There are many potential sources of mistakes when compiling a questionnaire, some examples are:

● including irrelevant questions
● including unanswerable questions
● omitting important questions
● including ambiguous questions
● including leading or biased questions

▶ All questions should be pretested with a sample of respondents who are representative of the population, before giving the questionnaire final approval.

Questions can be **open-ended**, where the respondent must answer in his or her own way, or, **closed-ended** where all possible answers are pre-specified. Open-ended questions can reveal more information and are often useful during exploratory work when one wants to discover what people think. Data from closed-ended questions is easier to interpret and tabulate.

The sequencing of questions is important. The earlier questions should attempt to create interest in the respondent. The questions should also follow a logical order and questions relating to age, salary, etc., should be left to the last. Types of questions:

1 Closed-ended

(a) Dichotomous

A question offering two choices: usually yes and no.

> Did you buy your used car from a Ford distributor?
>> Yes [ ] No [ ]

► Closed-ended questions mean that all possible answers are supplied with the question.

(b) Multiple-choice

Offers three or more choices.

> Which of the following countries have you visited?

France [ ] Germany [ ] Holland [ ] Belgium [ ] Spain [ ] Portugal [ ] Sweden [ ] Denmark [ ] Norway [ ] Finland [ ]

(c) Likert Scale

A statement with which the respondent has to express their degree of agreement:

> 'Politicians try to speak the truth'

Strongly disagree Disagree Don't know Agree Strongly agree
1 [ ]   2 [ ]   3 [ ]   4 [ ]   5 [ ]

► **Likert scales** are named after their inventor and are intended to measure attitudes. There are other types of attitude scale including the **Semantic differential** which is also shown. These types of scale are the most popular for use with questionnaires.

(d) Semantic differential

A scale running between two bipolar adjectives. Respondents select the position between the two that represents their feelings.

British Rail

Fast	[ ]	[ ]	[ ]	[ ]	[ ]	[ ]	[ ]	Slow
Comfortable	[ ]	[ ]	[ ]	[ ]	[ ]	[ ]	[ ]	Cramped
Economical	[ ]	[ ]	[ ]	[ ]	[ ]	[ ]	[ ]	Expensive

(e) Rating scale

The TV series the *Darling Buds of May* was:

Excellent   Very good   Good   Fair   Poor
1 [ ]   2 [ ]   3 [ ]   4 [ ]   5 [ ]

(f) Stapel Scale

+5	+5
+4	+4
+3	+3
+2	+2
+1	+1
Helpful	Reliable
−1	−1
−2	−2
−3	−3
−4	−4
−5	−5

Select a plus number for words that you think describe the service (or product) accurately. The more accurate you think the description is the larger should be the plus number selected. Conversely select a minus number for words which do not describe the service (or product). The less accurate you believe the description to be the larger should be the minus number you select.

2 Open-ended

(a) Unstructured
Offers the respondent almost unlimited ways of answering the questions.

What do you think about American foreign policy?

(b) Word association
Respondents are asked to give the first word that comes to mind when presented with the word:

apple	....
penguin	....
shoe	....
circus	....
train	....

► This is quite a useful method to employ when trying to gauge reaction to words that might be used in an advertising message or for a brand or company name. Clearly, the right kind of associations with the target word are required.

(c) Sentence completion
Respondents are required to complete a sentence.

People who go to parties with a bottle of vodka in their hands are ....

(d) Story completion
Respondents are asked to complete an incomplete story
Jane caught the 5.31 pm from Paddington. It was crowded with commuters and sped off in a westerly direction. NOW COMPLETE THE STORY.

► **Projective techniques** such as sentence, story and picture completion are borrowed from the domain of abnormal psychology. They were devised in the belief that people have various blockages which prevent them verbalizing their true feelings. The assumption is that normal people, too, experience blockages and that the method is valuable in these circumstances, too.

(e) Picture completion
An ambiguous picture is presented to the respondent in which one character is making a statement. Respondents are asked to identify with one character and fill in the empty balloon.
(Picture showing two people on a train)

One is looking at his/her watch and saying:

I am sure my watch isn't right.

A postal questionnaire
Here is an example of a questionnaire. See if you can work out how the designers attempt to maximize the chances of it being completed or returned. Specifically, look at the ordering of the questions, the nature of the phrasing and the marketing reasons for including particular questions. Can you suggest any other ways of getting the information sought by the questionnaire?

Example of Postal Questionnaire enclosed with the *Journal of Creative Marketing* for its Reader Survey 1992.

We at the *Journal of Creative Marketing* would like your help to improve your journal. The questions below will help you to tell us what you think of the magazine and how you would like to see it developed. Please return the completed questionnaire to *JCM*, Freepost 12325, Manchester M91 2XX by 14th July. You do not require a stamp. Thank you.

In answering the questions below please put a tick in the appropriate box.

1 How often do you read *JCM* ? (Please tick box)
   Every month   Yes [ ] -1
   Once every two months   Yes [ ] -2
   Once every three months   Yes [ ] -3
   Less than once every three months   Yes [ ] -4

2 Do you have any difficulties obtaining a copy of *JCM* ?
      Yes [ ] -1   No [ ] -2

3 How many other people read your copy of *JCM*?
      None [ ] –1   1 [ ] –2   2 [ ] –3   3–5 [ ] –4
      6–8 [ ] –5   9–11 [ ] –6   12–15 [ ] –7   15+ [ ] –8

4 Some *JCM* items appear every month – please indicate how
   often you read them:

	Always	Often	Sometimes	Never
a Advertisements	[ ] –1	[ ] –2	[ ] –3	[ ] –4
b Editorial	[ ] –1	[ ] –2	[ ] –3	[ ] –4
c Notes on authors	[ ] –1	[ ] –2	[ ] –3	[ ] –4
d Book reviews	[ ] –1	[ ] –2	[ ] –3	[ ] –4

5 How interested were you in articles we published under the
   following categories in the past year?

	Very	Quite	Mildly	Not
a Branding	[ ] –1	[ ] –2	[ ] –3	[ ] –4
b New products	[ ] –1	[ ] –2	[ ] –3	[ ] –4
c Advertising	[ ] –1	[ ] –2	[ ] –3	[ ] –4
d Selling	[ ] –1	[ ] –2	[ ] –3	[ ] –4

6 How interested would you be in our publishing articles under
   the following categories?

	Very	Quite	Mildly	Not
a Exporting	[ ] –1	[ ] –2	[ ] –3	[ ] –4
b Merchandising	[ ] –1	[ ] –2	[ ] –3	[ ] –4
c Sales promotion	[ ] –1	[ ] –2	[ ] –3	[ ] –4
d Market research	[ ] –1	[ ] –2	[ ] –3	[ ] –4

7 Which article that we published in the last twelve months did
   you like most?..

Could you please supply some details about yourself?

8 Age
   Under 25   [ ] –1 25 under 35 [ ] –2   35 under 45 [ ] –3
   45 under 55 [ ] –4 55 under 65 [ ] –5   over 65   [ ] –6

9 Sex
   Female [ ] -1 Male [ ] -2

10 Are you in full-time education?
   Yes [ ] -1 No [ ] -2
   If yes go to question 15

11 Are you in full-time employment
   Yes [ ] -1 No [ ] - 2
   If no go to question 15.

12 Which category does your job title fall into and in which type
   of industry?

► The numbers shown after the boxes here are used to help with subsequent analysis of the questionnaire. The number beside the box which has been ticked will be the code which represents the answer given to that question. Ambiguity in answering the questions should not be possible.

Job title

Head of department/professor/reader	[ ] -1
Lecturer (various grades)	[ ] -2
Chief executive	[ ] -3
Director	[ ] -4
Manager	[ ] -5
Executive	[ ] -6
Representative	[ ] -7
Administrative	[ ] -8
Clerical	[ ] -9
Other	[ ] 10

Industry

Insurance/banking/finance	[ ]-11
Government/national/local	[ ]-12
Manufacturing	[ ]-13
Distribution	[ ]-14
Media	[ ]-15
Education	[ ]-16
Consultancy	[ ]-17
Other	[ ]-18

13 Size of Organization (number of employees)

Up to 50 [ ] –1   51–100 [ ] –2   101–200 [ ] –3
201–500 [ ] –4   501–1000 [ ] –5   Over 1000 [ ] –6

14 Please indicate your income bracket

Up to £10 000 [ ] –1   £10 001–£15 000 [ ] –2
£15 001–£20 000 [ ] –3   Over £20 000 [ ] –4

15 Which other marketing journals do you regularly read?

....
....
....
....

 Below is an example of a poor questionnaire which is attempting to establish how customers rate and perceive the products and services of a supermarket. The questionnaire has to be completed by someone who has only a few minutes to spare while waiting to pay at the till. Determine what the questionnaire should be trying to elicit. Cut down the number of questions asked. How could you improve the questionnaire?

Hand the completed questionnaire to the cashier as you leave.

1 What is your name?
2 How old are you?
3 Do you come here often?
4 What dont you like?
5 How much have you to spend?
6 Would you come on Friday nights after 6 pm if you thought we were open?

7 Have you a car?

8 What do you think about the quality of our service?

9 Where do you go for your holidays?

10 Can you park your car alright?

11 Are the trolleys the right size?

12 Do you bring your children with you?

13 Have you any complaints?

14 Do you like our green products?

15 Do you not think that we should not close on every other Sunday?

16 What is your sex?

17 How often do you come here?

18 Do you think we are a clean shop?

19 Do you think we should diversify?

20 What promotional offers would you like?

Although there are modern ways of collecting data such as computerized data entry terminals, old well-tried methods still prevail. Interviewers have to be trained in the methods of interviewing and usually identify potential members of a quota sample in shopping precincts or on a door-to-door basis.

Any questionnaire must be properly introduced to the respondent whatever method of data collection is employed. Interviewers must introduce themselves to the respondent indicating the purpose of the study and must establish their credentials. This is also true of postal questionnaires, but in the latter case either the introductory part of the questionnaire must do this or else an accompanying letter must explain the purpose and benefits of the study.

► Much of the data collected in survey research is done so with the aid of questionnaires. A good deal of care needs to be taken in their construction to ensure that data collected is useful and accurate.

Analysing the data

Data analysis is not always straightforward. Tabulation and cross-tabulation are the simplest ways to show findings. Frequencies and percentages, averages and measures of dispersion can be worked out for major variables. This may be all that is necessary to produce meaningful results. Of course, if the data is suitable then more sophisticated statistical analysis can be conducted if required. However, it is the interpretation of data and the turning of data into information that often presents the greatest difficulty.

Simple Tabulation of data

Number of cigarettes smoked per day	Per cent of men
0	67
1 less than 20	18
20 or over	15

From this we can see quite simply that there are significantly more men who do not smoke than those who do. Also we can see that there is very little difference between the percentage who smoke more than twenty cigarettes a day and those who smoke fewer than twenty. There are statistical tests to show the significance or lack of significance of the differences. In this case however, the data speaks for itself. The difference between all smokers and non-smokers is so large that we don't need statistical tests to help us interpret this aspect of the table. However, the difference between those smokers who smoke under twenty and those who smoke over twenty cigarettes a day is very small and it may well be that these figures are accidents of the way in which we drew our sample rather than accurate reflections of the smoking habits of the population as a whole. There are statistical tests which can be used to tell us the likelihood of the difference between fifteen per cent and eighteen per cent being due to chance, or as it is usually put, not being statistically significant.

Cross tabulation of data

Number of cigarettes smoked per day.	Per cent of men	Per cent of women
0	67	70
1 less than 20	18	20
20 or over	15	10

Source: *Marketing Pocket Book* , 1992

Here we are considering the percentage of men and women and their smoking habits. Where there is more than one variable under investigation we use cross-tabulation. There appear to be no significant differences between non-smokers and smokers according to sex. Moreover, there appears to be little difference in terms of gender as far as smokers of less than twenty cigarettes a day are concerned. In both of these cases the data 'speaks for itself'.

An interesting point however concerns the difference in the number of men and women who smoke more than twenty cigarettes a day. The difference does seem to be large and we could test to see if it is statistically significant given that the sample size is known.

▶ Books on quantitative methods and/or statistics provide information on how to test to see if the difference between two proportions is statistically significant.

How would you interpret the following data?

(ACT)

	Accidents/10,000 vehicles	Total casualties	Fatal/serious injuries
Best small car			
VW Polo	106	58	12
Rover metro	117	81	14
Worst small car			
Fiat Uno	143	90	13
Ford Fiesta	142	97	14
Best small/medium car			
Skoda Estelle	97	59	20
Mazda 323	103	57	19
VW Golf	106	62	12
Worst small/medium			

Ford Orion	167	99	13
Ford Escort	155	99	16
Vauxhall Astra	154	84	14
Best medium car			
Volvo 340	88	47	19
BMW 3	118	64	17
Worst medium car			
Ford Sierra	179	97	17
Ford Sapphire	170	96	16
Best large car			
Volvo 740	98	42	15
Worst large car			
Ford Granada	171	78	12

Cars registered since 1 January 1987

► Tabulation and cross-tabulation are employed to analyse survey data. Data interpretation is a skilled exercise.

'The report produced few surprises for the Automobile Association. While welcomimg the report, it said that driver error rather than cars was responsible for most road accidents. Bert Morris, the AA's highways and traffic manager said it might change the views of manufacturers who advertise the speed and performance of their cars.'
Source: Adapted from the *Guardian* , 26 April,1991

Quantitative and qualitative data

Quantitative data is simply numerical data. It refers to such things as volumes of goods bought, amounts of money spent on various goods and services, age and salary of respondents in a survey. It is anything which can be expressed in numerical terms.

Putting numbers to things makes it easier for us to make comparisons and judgements – it helps in the decision-making process. It helps in answering questions relating to the size of markets, their salient features, the distribution of features and in assessing the importance of different features to different types of consumer. What we have to recognize, however, is that quantitative data are not necessarily precise but can be subject to error. Statistical methods enable us to get some idea of the error in quantitative data when it is based on sampling a population.

► Quantitative data answers the question 'how much?' or 'how many?'. Qualitative data answers the question 'why?'.

Qualitative data is data which conveys motives, impressions or attitudes often in words or pictures. Qualitative studies emphasize not what consumers do but why they behave in such a way.

The majority of data which passes through a marketing information system is quantitative in nature (see later in the chapter). In market research we obtain both quantitative and qualitative data.

Risks of research

Since the marketing environment is changing rapidly, competition is usually exceptionally keen and failure to act at a precise moment in time can lead to a loss of strategic impetus and position. If a competitor gets in first with a new idea it may be too late to respond. Undertaking research can give advance warning to the competition of a firm's intended marketing strategy. Under these circumstances undertaking research which may give advance warning to competitors may be inadvisable.

Carrying out research can be time-consuming and expensive. Occasionally, it may even be undesirable. Nevertheless the general rule would be to undertake research unless there are good reasons not to do so.

Cost of research

The cost of collecting information must be weighed against the benefits to be derived from using the information. A knowledge of costs and benefits can help marketing researchers determine which projects should be carried out, which research designs to use and how big a sample size to taken.

Review: Market research

Firms undertake research to find out why some people buy their products and others do not. Research is also undertaken to help provide information for making marketing mix decisions (pricing, product, place and promotion).

Research is undertaken both in-house (by a firm's own employees) and by specialist marketing research companies. In the latter case research can be tailor-made to a client's requirements or bought off the peg if a suitable research report is available. There is a variety of other sources which provide research data that is useful to companies. These include trade associations and government departments.

A wide variety of research methods is used including surveys, experiments and observational methods. A key component of research is how the sample has been drawn from the population. Quota sampling and simple random sampling methods are widely used.

The bulk of marketing research carried out is actually market research which relies very much on survey methods. Questionnaire design and analysis, along with sampling, are key aspects of survey methods.

There are costs and risks involved in undertaking research. The implications of these have to be fully appreciated before entering into research.

MARKETING INFORMATION SYSTEMS

Marketing information systems developed from marketing research. The ways in which marketing information systems differ from marketing research are as follows:

- MIS (marketing information systems) produces largely quantitative data on sales, profits and costs whereas marketing research produces qualitative information about peoples attitudes, beliefs and opinions about products or services, etc.
- MIS is a continuous study of the market and provides a continuous stream of information. This contrasts with marketing research and market research studies which are carried out on an ad hoc basis.
- MIS employs both internal and external information sources and makes use of a far greater volume of information inputs than does marketing research.

Information is needed for decision making but it is often difficult to obtain information of the right kind. The kinds of complaints made include:

- there is too much information of the wrong kind
- there is not enough information of the right kind
- information is too dispersed to be useful
- information arrives too late to be useful
- information often arrives in a form that leaves no idea of its accuracy and therefore lacks credibility.

Source: Kotler, 1983

► Kotler P (1983) and G Lilien, *Marketing Decision Making: a model building approach* , New York: Harper and Row

Clearly there is a need to overcome these kinds of problems and complaints and it is for this reason that marketing information systems have evolved. The concept of marketing information systems has been around for many years. Early systems were paper based but with the emergence of computers with large storage capacities and later microcomputers with similar features, marketing information systems have become more 'electronic' in nature. Modern electronic marketing information systems are able to produce, to manipulate and to summarize data in such a way that its presentation to management overcomes the problems listed above.

MIS (marketing information systems) can be classified under four headings:

- planning systems – which provide information on sales, costs and competitive activity together with any kind of information which is needed to formulate plans
- control systems – these provide continuous monitoring of marketing activities and enable marketing executives to identify problems and opportunities in the marketplace. At the same time they permit a more detailed and comprehensive review of

performance against plans
- marketing research systems – such systems allow executives to assess the effects of marketing actions and encourage better learning from experience
- monitoring systems – these systems provide management with information concerning the external environment in which they are operating.

A marketing information system can be defined as one which scans and collects data from the environment, makes use of data from transactions and operations within the firm and then filters, organizes and selects data before presenting it as information to management.

Using a marketing information system

There are two basic components to a marketing information system. On the one hand there is a database or a number of databases containing a variety of data about the firm, its competitors, its markets and the environment. On the other hand there is the provision of a wide variety of analytical tools capable of exploring the data and turning it into meaningful information for management.

Competitive information and information on customers wants and needs can be gleaned from salespeoples' reports. Reports, of course, need to be filed into the information system in electronic form. This requires that either the sales staff do this themselves or alternatively someone else has to scan all sales reports and abstract information to put into the computerized system. The former method is decidedly more attractive but it calls for the design of electronic forms which can easily be completed by sales staff. Sales reports tend to be filled in at home at weekends or in hotel bedrooms during the working week. A portable laptop computer directly connected via a modem link with the firm's mainframe computer provides an attractive solution to the problem. Alternatively, floppy disk files handed in weekly to the computer support staff in the company could provide an adequate method.

Data on the environment and competitive activity can often be bought from consultants and marketing research agencies in an electronic form. Data should as far as possible be kept in a disaggregated form in the database. This allows anyone to manipulate and analyse the data to suit their own particular purposes. Summary statistical analyses of data may well be kept in a separate file within the database, if it is felt that it is information which people may want frequently. Having computer- based information means that information in the form of reports can be made available quickly to management.

User requirements of a marketing information system

Sales management requires information to help it allocate the

▶ 'The Martech Survey into Marketing Information Systems', Martech Information Systems, June 1989, found that in the companies it surveyed, computerization had grown very rapidly over the previous two years with penetration increasing from 15% to about 50% – that is 70% of the systems mentioned had been implemented in the previous two years.

sales force effectively and assess the performance of sales staff equitably. Sales staff, too, should be able to access the system easily and get support and information about such things as:

- the quantity of the product on hand
- prices and price discounts
- status information on invoices, time of delivery and back orders
- delivery dates
- complete product specifications.

The system should also aid the process of entering orders and reduce the sales person's paperwork.

As we shall discuss in Chapter 6, on planning for control purposes, sales performance analysis is required. The MIS system can facilitate this kind of analysis. Sales performance analysis amounts to a detailed study of the total sales revenue of a company over a specific period of time. An analysis is made of total sales volume by product line, by salesperson, by territory and by customer group. These sales are then compared with company goals and industry sales.

The MIS system can help to produce forecasts. Marketing budgets, sales strategies and sales quotas are influenced by these estimates. The forecasts also help the planning and control of manufacturing, distribution management and advertising and promotion activities. Information on sales profitability is also made available. This shows the relative profitability of customers, territories, product lines, etc.

Marketing research helps to define marketing problems. It also helps executives find new customers and to adapt products to meet changing customer requirements. User friendly software and large relational databases help advise users on which segments to target. Marketing research can tell customers how to price a product, which distribution channels to use and how to get more out of advertising and other promotional expenditure.

Outputs of the marketing information system can take the form of reports. Example reports might be:

- a new product report, comprising of an estimation of sales potential and customer buying habits and motives
- a pricing strategy report to help management reach pricing objectives
- a product mix report to advise management on how to manage the product mix to best advantage, for example, by changing the number of lines or the depth within a line or simply pruning or simplifying lines
- a product life cycle report to help marketers manage the product through its various stages in the life cycle and possibly anticipate marketing requirements at a subsequent stage
- an advertising effectiveness report to help assess who is the target audience, what to communicate, when to communicate and what media to use

- a customer analysis report to spotlight customer trends, complaints and requests and a complete breakdown of profitability by customer
- an order processing control report to allocate stock, to fill customer orders, process backorders, answer order status enquiries, produce shipping reports by invoice and produce freight and labour costs.

CHAPTER SUMMARY

Marketing information systems exist to help marketing managers get to grips with the volumes of data with which they are constantly bombarded. Four types of system have evolved these are:

1 Planning systems – providing information on sales, costs and competitive activity together with any kind of information which is needed to formulate plans.

2 Control systems – which continuously monitor marketing activities to identify problems and opportunities. At the same time they permit a more detailed and comprehensive review of performance against plans.

3 Marketing research systems – allowing executives to test effects of marketing actions.

4 Monitoring Systems – providing an opportunity to assess the external environment in which managers are operating.
The marketing information system provides management with a variety of reports to aid its decision making.

► Now that you have reached the end of the chapter, turn back to the objectives and make sure you have achieved each of them.

⑤ Competition

Chapter objectives

By the end the end of this chapter you should:

■ know how competitors make use of product positioning to obtain a competitive advantage in relationship to their rivals

■ be able to describe the bases on which a competitive advantage may be built

■ know how leaders, challengers, followers and nichers define their marketing strategies

■ be able to describe the various factors which influence competition in an industry or market

■ know how firms analyse the competitive positions of rivals

■ know the various sources of information available to firms that enable them to gauge competitors' strategies, strengths and weaknesses

■ be familiar with the following terms used by marketers: differential advantage, product positioning, added value, experience curve, cost advantage, value advantage, differentiation strategy, market leader, market challenger, market follower, market nicher, product innovation, product flanking, multibrand strategy, brand extension, barriers to entry, product substitution, cross-elasticity of demand, business battlemaps.

Introduction

Being successful in the marketplace depends not only on an ability to identify customer wants and needs but also upon an ability to be able to satisfy those wants and needs better than competitors are able to do. This implies that firms need to look ways of achieving a differential advantage for their products or services in the eyes of the customer.

PRODUCT POSITIONING

Firms have to develop **product positioning strategies** within every segment in which they operate. Product positioning is the way the company puts forward its product image so that customers can make comparisons with competitors' products. A firm may, for example, seek a 'high quality position' or 'a leading edge technology position' and try to create these images in the minds of customers.

The product of differential advantage

John – 'I think car A is best – it has so many safety features.'
Henry – 'Car B's best – it's more economical.'
Jill – 'You're both wrong. I think C is the best – it has an excellent dealer network throughout the country and I'll be able to get it repaired very easily.'
Can they all be right?

The task of positioning involves three steps:

- identifying the potential competitive advantages
- selecting the most appropriate one
- signalling to the market the firm's positioning idea

Bases of Competitive Advantage

A **competitive advantage** can be derived either from having a cost advantage or having a value advantage or even a combination of the two. Having a **cost advantage** means that firms can produce and distribute their products at a lower cost than their competitors. A value advantage, on the other hand, means that the firm is able to offer a product which is perceived to provide differentiated benefits to customers – it has greater added value.

Cost advantages arise where a producer derives economies of scale by having a large sales volume. Fixed costs can then be spread over a greater output. In addition there are the added benefits of what is called the **experience curve**. The experience curve is similar to the learning curve we experience as people. As we perform a task or job again and again we develop our skills. In time we become more efficient at doing the task or job. The experience curve extends this concept to show that efficiency increases and value added costs decline as the volume of production increases. This means that where a firm has the predominant market share it

► Economies of scale reflect the efficiencies that come with size. Fixed costs such as administration, facilities, equipment, staff work and R&D can be spread over more units.

should be able to reap the benefits of experience and hence enjoy cost advantages. These same benefits do not, however, apply where a firm has deliberately sought to increase its market share by buying it through price reductions, increased marketing effort and product development at the expense of long-term profitability.

The implication of cost advantages for marketing strategy is that they can be used to lower the product's price or to earn higher margins at the same price. A preferable alternative, however, may be to reinvest in the product rather than run the risk of initiating price wars.

A **value advantage** or **differentiation strategy**, as it is sometimes called, is an attempt to distinguish a product or service in some way from its competitors through the benefit it offers to customers. It requires an approach based on market segmentation, i.e. different groups of customers attach different degrees of importance to different benefits.

Given that firms will generally adopt a strategy based on a combination of value advantage and cost advantage it is possible to make some general comments about how firms stand in this respect. Firms which are able to derive little cost advantage and little value advantage are those which tend to operate in commodity market situations. In a mature market where it is difficult to increase market share, the only real prospect for development is in terms of moving towards a **market niche strategy**. Niche strategies are available to firms that are unable to gain any cost advantage but are able to find ways of achieving product differentiation (these are discussed later in the chapter).

In the absence of a value advantage, a firm can only achieve a high cost advantage early in the life cycle of a product. A cost advantage strategy can be used to achieve price leadership and a firm adopting this strategy can make it impossible for higher cost competitors to survive. Price may also be maintained enabling above average profits to be earned. Some of the retained profits can then be reinvested in the product or service. The strongest position is one where a firm enjoys the benefits of both a cost advantage and a value advantage. Streamlined, automated production facilities coupled with active and effective product differentiation strategies have enabled many Japanese consumer goods manufacturers to achieve very strong competitive positions which are very difficult to dislodge.

 Pay a visit to your local library's reference section and obtain a copy of a *Which?* report. Take any of the reports and look at the criteria used to evaluate competing product offerings. For each product you consider, list the ways in which the producers are trying to gain a competitive advantage for themselves in the marketplace.

Fragrance with rubbish

Tracy – 'Bin liners – they're just a commodity!'
Sharon – 'But these are fragranced bin liners. Our kitchen smells like a rose garden.'

► Honda motorcycles have maintained their initial success in the US over the years by consistent actions to sustain a competitive advantage based on distribution and brand image in addition to low cost realized through high volume production. (Wensley R. 'Marketing strategy'. In M. J. Baker (ed.) *The Marketing Book*. 1987. Butterworth-Heineman, p. 39.)

► The differential advantage in washing powders is less clear to customers. Hence the strong development of marketing in the companies involved and their very high promotional spending to try and create a perceived advantage for particular brands.

► A competitive advantage can arise from having a cost advantage or a value advantage or both. The strongest position is where both are enjoyed.

Finding ways of establishing a competitive advantage is a major task for marketing management. For many firms the opportunities may be few. Companies can often find minor advantages to be exploited but these are soon copied by competitors and the advantage then becomes only a temporary one. The implication of this is that firms need to be constantly finding new advantages. Companies have to advertise their competitive advantage and must not assume that it will be automatically apparent to the market.

(ACT) The Flying Kite

Teresa and Liz run the The Flying Kite public house, off Rose Street in the centre of Edinburgh. Edinburgh has many bars which cater for a very cosmopolitan trade. The Rose Street area contains restaurants as well as bars and is in very close proximity to the main Princes Street shops. Trade has not been as good recently as in the past at the The Flying Kite because there are fewer shoppers with money to spend.

Sandy McTavish a marketing lecturer who frequents the establishment on Saturday lunchtimes has told Teresa and Liz that they should look for ways of achieving a differential advantage to keep their trade buoyant when there is not much money around.

Can you suggest various ways in which Teresa and Liz might aim to try and establish a differential advantage for their business?

UNDERSTANDING THE MARKETING STRATEGIES OF COMPETITORS

If a firm is to analyse competition properly it has to understand what strategy the competitors are following. Simply looking at the markets/segments in which competition is operating and examining market shares and financial performance of products/services will provide the firm with a picture of what other firms are doing. It will not however help to predict how things will develop in the future. To do this firms have to understand the strategies that competitors are pursuing.

Strategy typologies

Various suggestions have been put forward to account for the strategies adopted by firms. A commonly adopted framework is to consider firms according to the role they play in an industry. The suggestion is that a firm can act as:

● market leader
● market challenger

- market follower
- market nicher.

These roles are discussed below.

Leader

Not surprisingly the **market leader** has the largest market share. It usually leads other firms regarding price changes, new product introductions, distribution coverage and promotional intensity. Dominant firms want to stay in the leading position and this requires them to:

a Find ways of expanding total market demand
b Protect market share
c Even increase market share.

The key point to remember here is that the market leader is conscious of economies of scale of operation and is happiest when making inroads into large and substantial markets. Small specialist markets (niches) are not the prime interest of market leaders.

► Market leader
Market challenger
Market follower
Market nicher

► For example, the Ford motor company produces a range of cars for high volume markets, e.g., the Fiesta for the small car market. Ferrari, on the other hand specialize in producing high performance sports saloons, etc. for a very small market segment that is prepared to pay a very high price for such a car.

Strategies of Leaders

1 Product innovation – with accompanying heavy R&D expenditure.
2 Product flanking – introducing brands in several sizes/varieties to satisfy varying consumer preferences, thereby closing up gaps in the market
3 Multibrand strategy – producing several brands in the same category each one with a different positioning
4 Brand extension – extending the brand name to a wider range of products.

Challenger

Just behind the market leader are the **market challengers**. Challengers can attack the leader and other competitors in order to try and gain market share. They do not usually attack the leader directly but gain market share by attacking markets in which the smaller and less efficient firms operate. Such markets, of course, have to be of a substantial size and must not be too small or specialized to deter the larger firms.

One strategy that challengers can adopt is to produce a variety of types, styles and sizes of products including both cheaper and more expensive models. This was a strategy adopted by the Japanese company, Seiko, when it attacked the watch market. Seiko accompanied this strategy with another which involved distributing its watches through every possible channel. The wide

► The railway pioneer George Stephenson overtook the established canal transportation system. Xerox captured the copying market from 3M. In both of these cases the process was aided by a change in technology.

Strategies of challengers

1 Price-discount – comparable products with a temporary price discount
2 Cheaper goods – an average or low quality good at a much cheaper price
3 High quality products with a premium price
4 Reducing manufacturing and bought in cost – leading to a lower price

---

variety of models it had available (over 2000) meant that it could supply different types of channel with different models and thereby avoid the adverse effects of channel conflict.

Follower

A third role that firms can adopt is that termed **market follower**. Firms which undertake a good deal of innovation often have to recoup massive investment costs. Market followers are able to copy what the leading firms produce and save themselves the burden of massive investment costs. This means that they can operate very profitably at the going price in a market. Such firms will obviously have to forego the market share which comes from being first into the field.

► Compaq followed IBM and produced a perfectly compatible microcomputer. It became one of the fastest growing companies of all time.

Strategies for followers

1 Emphasis on efficiency of operation
2 Keep costs under tight control.

Providing they can stay cost efficient and obtain a reasonable share of the market they can survive. Less efficient ones however are open to attack from the market challengers.

Market niching

Most industries include smaller firms that specialize in producing products or in offering services to specific sectors of the market, i.e. in specific segments. In so doing they avoid the competitive thrusts of the larger firms for whom specialization does not offer attractive economies of scale (where segments are too small to generate the kind of return on investment that the larger firms require). This is a strategy called **market niching**.

Market niching is not only of interest to small firms but also to the small divisions of larger companies. The latter seek some degree of specialization. In cases where the latter occurs the position of small firms is not quite so secure. From a firm's point of view an ideal market niche is:

- of sufficient size to be profitable to a firm serving it
- capable of growth
- of negligible interest to major competitors
- a good fit with the firm's skills and resources.

Specialization is the corner-stone of market niching.

Stratagies of market niching

1 Serving only one type of end-use customer
2 Specializing at some stage in the production–distribution chain
3 Specialization in the size of customer served
4 Serving only certain geographical areas
5 Producing only certain products or product lines
6 Specialization in terms of a specific product feature
7 Producing only customized products
8 Operating only in one quality/price segment of the market.

It has been shown (Profit Impact of Market Strategy, PIMS, study) that there is a strong relationship between market share and return on investment (however remember the caveat about buying market share mentioned earlier in the chapter). The definition of market share here presents problems – a specialist car manufacturer, for example, may only hold a small share of the total car market but a very significant share of a particular market segment. We have to think therefore in terms of the served market (the market segment) rather than the total market.

▶ There is strong evidence to show that a strong brand in a niche market earns a a higher percentage return than a strong brand in a big market. In the case of large markets, competitive threats and retailer pressure can hold back profits even for the top brand. (Clifford D. K. and Cavanagh R. E. 1985. *The Winning Performance: How America's high growth midsize companies succeed*. Sidgwick and Jackson)

 Fast food restaurants are a booming business. Names like Macdonald, Kentucky, Wimpy and BurgerKing have become household names. Using the four categories market leader, market challenger, market follower and market nicher how would you classify the various fast food outlets that you see round about you?

▶ Firms may adopt a number of different strategic roles. They may be market leader, challengers, followers or nichers. Each has opportunities and problems.

Niching based on skills

After more than twenty years' experience working as joiners Sam and Bill were both made redundant on the same day. They decided that they would take advantage of the government's enterprise allowance scheme and set up in business together, not as joiners but as manufacturers of imitation antique dining suites.

For many years they had been producing one off items as a hobby which they both enjoyed doing. At first they had produced furniture for their own homes. Next they made up items for relatives. Soon friends and associates had been asking if they could produce items to meet with quite clear specifications. Of course, because they both had permanent jobs, it was difficult to meet the requests which were made of them.

Before making the decision to go into business together they had been contacted by a dealer in the furniture trade who indicated that he felt he could sell certain types of furniture without any difficulty but other types would sell more slowly. He provided them with lists of the kinds of items that he felt would be fast moving and recommended that they gave prime attention to them. Furthermore, he placed a firm order with them for a half dozen reproduction antique dining tables with accompanying sets of chairs to a pattern he had seen in Sam's dining room.

Bill rented space in a nearby mill and the two men began work with a full order book for several weeks. More orders followed from the same dealer and eventually, by word of mouth, other enquiries were received from further afield.

Within two years the partnership had been turned into a company and they actually employed staff to make the furniture and run the office. Sam stayed in control of the production side and kept his eye on the accounts. Bill took up the marketing side of the business and spent most of his time trying to find new dealers and different ways of marketing the products.

FACTORS INFLUENCING COMPETITION

Industries have special peculiarities of their own. These peculiarities change over time. They are often referred to as the **dynamics** of the industry. It is important to note that no matter how hard a company tries, if it fails to fit in to the dynamics of the industry ultimate success may not be achieved.

Porter (1985) sees competition in an industry being governed by five different sets of forces:

▶ Porter M. E. 1985. *Competitive Advantage*. New York: Free Press

1   Rivalry among firms increases if numerous and/or similar sized competitors compete in the marketplace. This is exacerbated where industry growth is slow, costs are high and there is a lack of product differentiation. Moreover, in times of economic recession competition intensifies. High exit barriers from a market or industry contribute to increased competition. Firms may find it difficult to get out of a business because of the relationship of the business with other businesses in which the firm is engaged. There may also be high investments in assets of the firm which are used for the specific business and for which no advantageous alternative use can be found.

▶ Price cutting or even price wars can occur. A good example is the market for microcomputers where price reductions occur very regularly.

Increased competition also exists when there is a high degree of diversity of the competitors and high strategic stakes. The relative cost structures of the various firms in the market have a considerable bearing on the nature of competition. A promising market also attracts a high degree of competition as new entrants to a market vie to make themselves felt.

▶ As was the case in the UK home computer market in the early 1980s.

2   Customers can exert influence on what producers are able to do. For example, a small number of buyers or a situation where one buyer predominates limits the producer's opportunities for action.

3   Suppliers, too, can exert similar pressures by controlling supplies. Moreover a powerful supplier is in a position to influence the profitability of a whole industry by raising prices or reducing the quality of the goods supplied.

4   The threat of new entrants can increase competitive activity in a market. Outsiders will be tempted to enter a market or an industry if they feel that the opportunity is sufficiently attractive in terms of profitability and sales. Markets which have grown to a substantial size become potentially attractive to large powerful firms provided that the level of competitive activity will enable them to achieve the kind of profits and sales they expect. This provides an incentive for the firms already operating in the market to make the prospects appear less attractive to would-be entrants by increasing the level of competitive activity.

5   The threat of substitute products or services.

Suppliers in monopoly positions or operating as members of a cartel certainly can exert considerable influence on an industry in the short run. If there are alternative products or services available then their power will be curtailed in the long run. In the 1970s OPEC forced users of their oil to pay much higher prices because there were no alternative sources available. This made North Sea oil drilling appear an attractive economic proposition and within a few years oil production in the North Sea was under way. At the same time a greater incentive was given to the importing countries to look for ways of conserving oil fuels and to look for alternative fuel sources.

▶ The nature and size of firms in a market, barriers to entry and exit, suppliers, customers, substitute products and threat new entrants influence the amount of rivalry in a market.

Nature of competition analysis

Understanding competition is central to making marketing plans and strategy. A firm has to be constantly comparing its products, prices, channels of distribution and promotional methods with those of its competitors to ensure that it is not at a disadvantage. In doing this it can also identify areas where it can gain a competitive advantage.

Key information requirements about competitors include:

- who are they?
- what are their strategies?
- what are their objectives?
- what are their strengths and weaknesses?
- how do they react to competitors' initiatives?

Who are the competitors?

This may seem a simple question for most firms to answer. For example, one might suppose that Kelloggs' main competitors are manufacturers of breakfast cereals. This is, of course correct. However, one also has to consider *product substitution*. This involves looking more broadly at the types of business in which the firm operates. If this is done one can identify many producers of products that people consume at breakfast time. Many of these products could be used instead of Kelloggs cereals, i.e. they can be substituted.

 See if you can identify substitute products or services for the following:

journeys by bus	insurance
college or university courses	building society deposit
carpets	accounts
cigarettes	building society mortgage
discos	loans
restaurants	football pools coupons
dry cleaning	

Cross-elasticity of demand means that essentially the same need can be satisfied by more than one product. Product substitution takes place between products that have a high cross-elasticity of demand. For example, if the price of coffee rises in relationship to soft drinks then it is possible that some people may switch from drinking coffee to drinking soft drinks. Similarly, if soft drinks become difficult to obtain then consumers may again switch back to coffee. Thus a coffee manufacturer might initially think of other coffee manufacturers as its prime competitors. However, because

► See Chapter 13 on pricing and note the implications of the cross-elasticity of demand. Another point is that as some products become socially less desirable, e.g., for health reasons, other products may come to take their place. Current projections indicate a fall in the demand for beer by some twenty per cent by 2010 and a rise in soft drinks consumption of nearly eighty per cent.

Who are the competitors?

A fishmonger once boasted that he had no rivals. 'I'm the only fishmonger in town', he said. 'No-one else will set up in business as a fishmonger here because the market is too small to support another fishmonger. I'm a specialist retailer and I operate in a market niche meeting local demand. I know all about marketing strategy.'

Two years later his premises were empty and he'd moved away from the town. A large supermarket had opened in the centre of the town and featured a fish counter among its many offerings.

Convenience shopping, very competitive pricing and good choice had been the marketing communications theme promoted by the store.

of the product substitution effect manufacturers of soft drinks such as Pepsi-Cola and Coca-Cola are potential competitors for coffee manufacturers.

Assessing competitors strengths and weaknesses

A firm needs to have a continuous supply of information about competition. The main need is for competition information regarding:

- sales
- market share
- profit margin
- return on investment
- cash flow
- new investment
- capacity utilization

A firms also needs to keep track of its competitors' financial performances. Such information enables a firm to gain a complete impression of its competitors which may in turn be useful in predicting the short-term strategies of competitors. Knowing the specific objectives competitors are likely to pursue may be difficult to identify but can often be inferred from present or past activities. Moreover, a firm with some idea of the objectives and strengths and weaknesses of its competitors may be able to predict how they will respond to its own changes in strategy.

A Business Battlemap

In the illustration below there are two firms, A and B. Each firm is competing with the other in several market segments with three products X, Y, Z. There are no other firms competing in these segments at the present time. The current size of each market segment, or 'penetrated market', in £ m. is indicated by the crosshatching of the cell as shown in the key. Next to each firm is given the current market share of the firm. This is a simple battlemap and many variations on the illustrated approach, incorporating additional data, are possible.

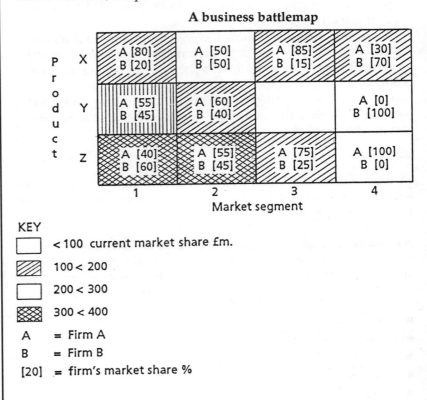

A business battlemap

KEY

☐ < 100 current market share £m.

▨ 100 < 200

☐ 200 < 300

▩ 300 < 400

A = Firm A

B = Firm B

[20] = firm's market share %

 Put yourself in the position of company A in the battlemap shown above. You know that company B is preparing to increase its sales. You guess that company B is going to do so by moving into a new market segment. Which one do you suspect company B will target? What information would company B need in order to make its choice?

Sources of information about competitors

Marketers should find out what competitors say about themselves and and what others say about them. Sources of information fall into four categories:

- public
- trade and professional
- government
- investors.

▶ Firms need to know what drives or motivates their competitors; what their competitors are currently doing; and what competitors have the capacity to do in the future.

Public sources

Advertising, promotional materials and press releases are the prime sources of information on what competitors have to say for themselves. Articles in journals and newspaper reports provide a good source of information on what others have to say about them. In both of these cases, however, one does have to be wary of the information gleaned since it may be biased or even distorted.

Trade and professional sources

Courses, seminars, technical papers and manuals prepared by competitors often provide detailed insights into their activities. Actually making sense of it all, however, can be very time consuming. It can take a considerable amount of time to distil and analyse it all. Distributors, the trade press and even customers are good sources of information when it comes to what other have to say about competitors.

Government

In the UK firms have to lodge their annual reports at Company House in London and the contents of these reports provide constructive insights into the operations of competitors. In the case of what others say about them, lawsuits, government ministries and national plans are useful sources of information.

Investors

Annual meetings, annual reports and prospectuses are primary sources of what competitors have to say about themselves. Credit reports and industry studies provide an outsider's viewpoint.

► Key information needed about competitors includes who are they, what are their strategies, what are their strengths and weaknesses, and how do they react to competitors' moves? Information can on competitors is to be found in what firms say about them.

 Imagine you are the marketing manager of a firm which manufactures car batteries and you are trying to find out as much information about competitors as you possibly can. Try and get hold of information from the sources mentioned in the text above which relate to competitors' activities.

CHAPTER SUMMARY

1 Firms make use of added value to manipulate a product's position and to put themselves at a competitive advantage with respect to their rivals. The bases on which a competitive advantage may be forged fall into two categories: those based upon achieving a cost advantage and those based upon obtaining a value advantage.

2 In the marketplace there are firms which can be thought of as market leaders, market challengers, market followers and market nichers. Each one adopts a different marketing strategy to the other. Being able to classify firms in this way is helpful in

predicting what moves competitors are likely to make in the near and more distant future.

3 Porter sees competition in an industry as being governed by different sets of forces: threat of new entrants, bargaining power of suppliers, bargaining power of customers and threat of substitute products or services.

4 Understanding competition is central to making marketing plans and strategy. A firm has to be constantly comparing its products, prices, channels of distribution and promotional methods with those of its competitors to ensure that it is not at a disadvantage. In doing this it can also identify areas where it can gain a competitive advantage.

5 A firm needs to have a continuous supply of information about competition. The main need is for information regarding sales, market share, profit margin, return on investment, cash flow, new investment, capacity utilization and financial performances. Naturally there would be benefits from knowing the specific objectives competitors are likely to pursue. These may be difficult to identify but may be inferred from present or past activities.

6 You should look for what competitors say about themselves and and what other say about them. Sources of information fall into four categories: public, trade and professional, government and investors. Knowledge of the various sources of information available to firms that enable them to gauge competitors strategies, strengths and weakness is of key importance.

► Now that you have reached the end of the chapter, turn back to the objectives and make sure you have achieved each of them.

6

Marketing planning and control

Chapter objectives

By the end of this chapter you should:

∎ be able to describe the stages in the marketing planning process

∎ know how the corporate plan systematically seeks to establish an organization's current position and aspired position, and how it should organize resources to help reach that position

∎ know the kinds of financial goals that an organization sets for itself and how these are related to marketing planning

∎ know what is involved in assessing marketing strengths, weaknesses, opportunities and threats and in evaluating the impact of these on the organization

∎ know how gap analysis is undertaken and be able to describe the various strategies that can be used to reduce the gap

∎ be able to describe how to set objectives and strategy using SWOT analysis

∎ know how marketing effort is evaluated through the use of sales analyses, market share analyses, sales to expense ratios, financial analysis and monitoring of the attitudes

∎ know how profitability and efficiency control is effected

∎ be able to describe strategic control

∎ know how marketing and its related functions operate as control centres

∎ be able to describe what is involved in customer profitability analysis

∎ know how management implements planning and control through the management of people and appreciate the alternative management styles that can be used

∎ be familiar with the following terms as used by marketers: planning, objectives, strategies, corporate objectives, goal setting, auditing, gap analysis, marketing effort, corporate plan, marketing audit, market penetration, market development, product development, diversification, horizontal integration, vertical integration, SWOT analysis, brainstorming, marketing plan, control, resource allocation, marketing budgets, profitability control, efficiency control, strategic control, budgetary control, control centres, budget variances, profit centre, cost centre, customer profitability analysis, management style.

Very small firms may keep their plans in their heads

▶ Planning involves outlining the way ahead, deciding what objectives have to be achieved and how this is to be carried out.

Introduction

Planning is an activity which is found in all walks of life. We plan our weekend shopping, maybe even going to the extent of drawing up a detailed shopping list. We plan our holidays for the coming year, setting aside a time when it is convenient for all members of the family and for our work as well. Planning is an activity which we do naturally but sometimes when we are asked or forced to draw up plans we may say that we have not got the time to do so. That is because planning does take time and effort to do properly and we may feel that we would prefer to spend that time doing something else.

PLANNING FOR BUSINESS

Planning is an important activity in all kinds of enterprises. Very small enterprises may not adopt the formal procedures which are outlined in this chapter but nevertheless they should still adopt the principles involved, albeit in an informal manner.

In business, planning involves outlining the way ahead; indicating what objectives have to be achieved and how they are to be achieved. Plans are often multi-tiered with one plan being interrelated with and dependent on another. In business the key plan is the **corporate plan** and this pulls together all the other plans. Marketing planning has to be seen within the context of the overall corporate plan for the organization. This specifies where the company is heading, what its overall objectives will be, and how these translate (where appropriate) into profit and sales targets. From this plan, marketing objectives and strategies are also formulated. The marketing plan is thus inseparable from the corporate plan. This chapter starts by looking at the nature of the corporate plan and then looks more specifically at the marketing plan.

Stages in the marketing planning process
1 Corporate objectives
2 Goal setting
3 Auditing
4 Gap analysis
5 Setting marketing objectives and strategy based on assumptions
6 Writing down the marketing plan
7 Implementing the marketing plan
8 Evaluating the marketing effort

The corporate plan

The corporate plan is the plan for the company as a whole. It defines the business in which the company operates, indicates financial objectives that have to be achieved, specifies how sales revenues are to be generated through various marketing programmes and estimates the various costs involved in meeting these objectives.

> **The corporate plan answers the questions:**
>
> Where are we now?
> Where do we want to go?
> How do we organize resources to get there?

► Defining the nature of the business in which the firm operates is a crucial point. If Cunard had not seen its business as being that of transportation it less likely that it would have moved into containerization from its position as a passenger liner business.

► The corporate plan is the blueprint for all the activities of the organization.

Goal setting

The goals set have to be realistic and therefore a company must know where it stands in relationship to the competition and the various markets it serves. It also has to be realistic in specifying where it wants to get to. For example, it may be unrealistic for a small electronics firm to expect to grow to the size of GEC within five years. Having said that one has to recognize that in the Far East there are now some giant corporations competing successfully in international markets, which did not exist twenty-five years ago.

The first stage involves setting long-term goals in terms of sales turnover, profit before tax and return on capital invested. In the case of non-profit making organizations target revenues should be specified. Planning horizons vary from five to twenty-five years ahead.

► Honda was a relatively small Japanese producer of motor cycles in 1951. Seven years later it had captured over sixty per cent of US motor cycle market.

► Goals should be realistic, measurable and attainable.

Auditing

The next step involves undertaking a **management audit**. An audit is taken of each of the four functional areas of management: marketing, production, finance and personnel. Here we will look at the marketing audit.

A marketing audit is an assessment of all factors, both within the firm and in the external environment, which affect the firm's marketing performance. This includes all the elements of previous plans, together with an account of the results achieved.

The internal marketing audit

The **internal audit** is a detailed analysis by product/service of the market share and profitability of the various lines. In addition, strategies relating to pricing, promotion, distribution and the products are reviewed and studied at length, together with the use made of marketing research data. Simultaneously, a careful study is made of marketing budgets and how they were drawn up and related to agreed objectives that have been set.

► An internal audit will help identify strengths and weaknesses. An external one will help identify opportunities and threats.

The external marketing audit

The **external audit** takes stock of the organization's external environment. Normally it starts with a review of information pertaining to the general economy and continues by assessing the prospects for the markets served by the company. The external audit attempts to estimate what the desired action should be, bearing in mind economic and market indicators. All the possible aspects need to be considered. There are many factors which should be taken into account, including economic, fiscal, social, business, legal and technological developments. From the point of view of the market such things as segments, channels, products, end uses, needs, tastes, attitudes, stocks and profits have to be considered. In addition, attention has to be paid to the activities of competitors and potential competitors.

Gap analysis

A further development of this stage involves trying to predict what is going to happen in each sector of the business in the immediate and longer-term future. The firm has to prepare forecasts that take into account factors which are external to the firm such as market trends, economic trends, competitive trends, socio-cultural trends and technological trends. The implications of these trends are then compared with the likely performance of the company based on internal factors such as product strengths, material costs, technical ability, productivity prospects and financial capacity. The next step is to project earnings from existing business over the time-scale of the forecasts and to make comparisons with the required objectives. For example, a manufacturer of microcomputer disk drives would recognize that laser technology and the market demand for larger size drives are likely to have an impact on future product requirements. The next step is to examine its current position. It will see that if it carries on producing the current size of disk drive, based on existing technology, it will start losing sales sometime in the foreseeable future as competitors introduce larger capacity disk drives using laser technology. It has to predict when the changes are likely to occur and what impacts these will have on its own sales and profitability.

Usually, because of factors arising from such things as the product life cycle a profit **gap** will be perceived. That is a gap between what the firm wants to achieve in terms of profit and what it is likely to achieve given the existing portfolio of activities.

The way in which the gap is measured is of paramount importance when determining the best way to reduce it. For example, if the gap is simply expressed in terms of profit (gross, net, pre-tax or after-tax) then clearly any action which generates extra profit could be considered as a means of reducing the gap. What a firm has to do is to relate the expected profit to the amount of resources employed to achieve that profit. The measure it needs to consider is the probable return on investment generated by a product-market opportunity or strategy.

▶ Cross impact analysis is a useful technique that can be used to assess the impact of environmental changes on a firm's prospects. Good illustrations are to be found in Aaker D. A. 1988. *Strategic Market Management*. Wiley, 2nd edition, Chapter 7

▶ Forecasting methods are discussed in Chapter 9.

▶ The concept of the product life cycle is discussed in Chapter 10.

▶ A gap usually exists between where a firm wants to go and where it is likely to end up if it continues with its current mix of products or services and strategy.

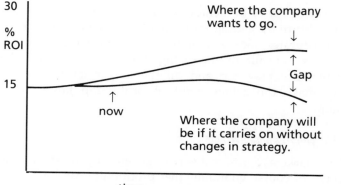

Diagram showing the gap between expected and required profits.

Return on investment for individual products is linked to the overall rate of return on capital employed by the business. Performance of the firm in the latter respect is reflected in the general confidence of other firms and financial institutions in dealing with the firm in the marketplace and in the firm's ability to attract and retain shareholders' investments.

Assuming that the firm wishes to maintain its existing rate of return on invested capital then it should only accept new projects which indicate a return of investment potential which is at least equal to the current rate of return on capital employed. Of course, even then, as its more profitable offerings start to decline, it still may not actually maintain the existing rate of return on invested capital.

Strategies for reducing the gap.

There are several ways of making up the difference indicated by the gap analysis. Some of these ways can be seen in Ansoff's product/market expansion grid shown in below.

Ansoff's product/market expansion grid

Market penetration strategy	Product development strategy
Market development strategy	Diversification strategy

► *See* Ansoff I. 1965. *Corporate Strategy*. Harmondsworth: Penguin Books Ltd.

Strategies include the following:
1 *Increased penetration of existing markets*

This involves increasing sales of existing products while maintaining the current margins of profitability on sales. In an expanding

► Increasing market share is a heavy drain on marketing expenditure and can affect short run profitability. If economics of scale or the impact of the experience curve are to be felt as a result of increased supply to the market, then this may more than offset the impact of any additional marketing expenditure on profitability.

market this may be achieved with modest outlays of marketing expenditure by getting more first time users to buy the product. In a saturated market it may only be possible to achieve extra sales as a result of increasing market share. Even short-term profitability may dip and, in the longer term, market decline may make the achievement of profit gap targets difficult to attain.

2 *Developing new markets*

New markets represent a way of generating additional sales. They do not of course guarantee that profitibility can be maintained in the long term or the short term. Economies of scale in producing for the market or in supplying the market will contribute to profitability. In addition, there may well be barriers to entry into the market which mean that neither short-run nor long-term contributions to overall profitability are attractive.

3 *Developing new products*

New products should promise rates of return on investment which are at least equal to the current rate of return on capital employed. Sometimes this may not be possible and firms may have to accept the prospect of lower profitability, just to stay in business.

4 *Reducing costs*

Reduction in the costs of running the organization is yet another way of reducing the gap. This involves using materials or labour more efficiently or reducing distribution, management costs and other overheads. There is often a lot of scope for this kind of approach to cost saving.

► New developments in technology lead the way for more efficient production processes. But in the latter context one has to bear in mind that competitors also can take advantage of such improvements.

5 *Adjusting prices*

Adjusting prices and discounts to push the firm to a new higher gross profit platform without any loss of sales revenue can enable a firm to close an identified profit gap. Such a strategy could imply repositioning the products or services or modifying them in one way or another.

6 *Diversification and vertical integration*

Should the firm be unable to close the profit gap through any of the means listed above, and assuming that the long-term objectives of the company are realistic, other action may be required. This may involve **diversification** or **vertical integration** and an **acquisition programme**. It can lead to long-term increased return on capital employed. Diversification involves moving simultaneously into new products and new markets. It is a high-risk strategy but with careful selection of the right kind of businesses, considerable improvements in profitability can be experienced. Vertical integration comprises moving backwards or forwards in the chain of production/distribution and is usually achieved by merging with or acquiring ownership of a supplier (backward integration) or a customer (forward integration).

Diversification and vertical integration

Diversification or horizontal integration can take place into related or unrelated products. A firm in textiles might diversify into carpets. This might be seen as diversifying into related products. The same firm diversifying into computer systems would be moving into unrelated products.

Moving into areas where a firm does not have any prior experience can be risky. For this reason firms may prefer to move into related markets rather than into unrelated ones. A further point is that there may be some **synergy** to be gained from moving into related markets. The synergy may be in marketing or even in production.

Vertical integration represents another way in which a firm can expand. The integration can be forward as when a producer takes over a distributor or backward as when a manufacturer takes over a supplier. Integrative strategies enable firms to gain greater control over the chain of production and distribution. For example, a manufacturer may have difficulty in gaining vital components from a supplier. It may be because the supplier is also selling the same component to other firms and cannot produce enough to satisfy everyone. Under such circumstances the manufacturer may be tempted to try to buy out the supplier (i.e., become the owner of the supplier's business) to ensure that it can always have supplies of the key component.

Diversification through internal development can take a long time to implement. A preferred strategy is to acquire existing businesses and develop these businesses. Research seems to indicate that short-run overall return on capital employed dips following merger or acquisition. However, in the longer run, provided a good choice has been made, profitability appears to improve.

▶ Synergy is the 2+2=5 effect. It is where the combined effect of the parts is greater than the effect of the individual parts.

ACT John is a keen golfer and spends most of his spare time on the local golf course. Soon he will be able to take early retirement and will have the benefits of a pension and a lump sum payment. His best chum, Eddie, has just taken early retirement and together they have been discussing setting up a golf equipment shop close by the golf links. A suitable shop is available to let from the borough council and they feel they have sufficient capital to establish the business.

▶ Cost and price adjustments together with increased market penetration, new markets, new products and diversification are gap-reducing strategies.

List the kinds of matters that John and Eddie ought to consider and indicate the kind of planning exercise they ought to go through prior to making this important decision.

Setting objectives and strategy

SWOT analysis is derived from the initial letters of strengths, weaknesses, opportunities and threats. The procedure followed is shown below:

Strengths, weaknesses, opportunities and threats are listed for the marketing aspects of the strategic business unit as a whole and strategies developed for each cell in the grid. Not all strengths weaknesses, opportunities and threats need to be used to formulate a strategy and more than one strategy, of course, can be developed for each cell:

Product : Metal Containers

► See Weihrich H, The TOWS Matrix: 'A Tool for Strategic Analysis', *Long Range Planning*, Vol 15 no 2, pp 54-56 where the construction of the Matrix is discussed and examples are outlined.

	Strengths 1 Brand name 2 Distribution 3 Know how 4 Low costs	**Weaknesses** 1 Marketing 2 Quality 3 Exports
Opportunities 1 Demand for lightweight robust metal containers 2 Export markets 3 Inflammable liquid containers 4 New developments in metal alloys	Develop lightweight cans for inflammable liquids using new alloys (S1, 01, 03, 04)	Improve quality and marketing. Look for export opportuniteis (W1, W2, W3, 02)
Threats 1 Higher prices for metal materials 2 Imports 3 Competition in existing markets	Diversify into non-metal container markets (S1, S2, T1, T2, T3)	Raise quality standards (W1, T3)

One of the most powerful uses of **SWOT** analysis is in conjunction with **brainstorming**. In such an instance one uses brainstorming techniques to generate strategies based upon identified strengths, weaknesses, opportunities and threats. Brainstorming often takes the form of a group activity. A warm-up session is advocated where participants have not had previous experience of the technique. The group members are invited to call out ideas relating to the problem as they occur. There is a group leader who records on a flip-chart all the ideas generated during a session. The aim is to generate as many ideas as possible – the wilder the ideas the better. Ideas are never evaluated during the generation process. By

► Brainstorming helps to overcome the restrictive nature of evaluation that takes place in most business meetings. Social pressures inhibit individuals from stating their ideas. This can be remedied through the medium of structured meetings at which ideas are freely expressed prior to evaluation.

being able to see other people's ideas recorded other individuals are able to find new combinations or 'hitch-hike or freewheel' on those ideas to produce new insights.

SWOT analysis produces a list of possible strategies some of which will enable the firm to fill the profit gap. Plans have to be prepared which indicate how the company intends to implement the strategies and estimated costings and revenues are worked out for implementing the identified options. When this information is available decisions can be made about priorities for implementation, bearing in mind the availability of resources.

(ACT) Fabio Menotti runs a small café on the main street (a pedestrianized way) in the centre of Weingarten, a small town with a student population, in the south of Germany. An Italian by birth, he came to Germany ten years ago and through hard work and personal endeavour eventually came into possession of his own café. He has expertise in producing the most delicious and highly original ice-creams and the café is also famed for its iced coffee.

Fabio is ambitious and wants to do well. He can speak three languages (Italian, German and Spanish) and is keen to expand his business. He has only limited cash available but his business is successful and he has a good credit rating at the bank and has other financial backers. There are several other cafés in the town but none has such a good position as he does and none has expertise for ices. During the summer he sets up tables on the pavement outside the café and is extremely busy with customers until late in the evening.

Opportunities for setting up additional cafés exist in Ravensburg, a tourist centre some three miles to the south, and in the Bodensee centres of Friedrichshafen, Meersburg, Konstanz and Lindau, which are thronged with locals and tourists in the summer.

An old friend has offered him a half share in her private hotel in Cork, in the Irish Republic. Situated close to the University College of Cork it offers good prospects in an area of Ireland that is undergoing substantial commercial development. Recently, while on holiday in Spain, Fabio saw an advertisement offering a café for sale in the Plaza Mayor, Salamanca. Such a move would require him to sell his existing business but he was extremely interested in the opportunity which had a prime location in the town which boasts the oldest university in Spain.

What do you think Fabio should do?

Hint: use a SWOT analysis.

► SWOT analysis together with brainstorming present a way of generating strategies

The marketing plan

The next stage involves devising plans and programmes to meet objectives. The exact nature of the plan will vary from organization to organization. The overall marketing plan is built from separate sub-plans. Sub-plans consist of:

► For a full undertanding of product decisions see Chapters 11 and 12.

● **A product mix plan**. This shows product deletions, product modifications, product additions, when they are to occur, and the volume, turnover and profit objectives, broken down by product groups and even product items. Each product group should have its own objectives in terms of market share, etc.
● **A sales plan**. This plan indicates objectives for levels of service to be provided to existing customers and objectives for obtaining new accounts. Figures include regional targets. There should also be sub-plans relating to key accounts.
● **An advertising plan**. The exact nature of this will vary according to the importance an organization puts on advertising. It indicates the timing, nature, weight and media to be used. It should contain information relating to communications objectives, such as increasing the level of awareness of a brand or achieving penetration of new users for each main brand.
● **The sales promotion plan**. This is put together in the same way as the advertising plan. However, in this case sales promotion activities are considered rather than advertising ones.

Other sub-plans could include physical distribution, market research, research and development, pricing and even regional plans.

Marketing Planning a one year plan

The following illustrates specific marketing objectives for a one year plan in an industrial product company:

Sales

10 per cent increase in unit sales
15 per cent increase in sterling sales
No change in unit sales of products A and B
15 per cent increase in unit sales of product C
20 per cent increase in unit sales of product D

To complete market tests and launch new product E with an expected 0.5 m. sales in the current financial year.

Share of the market

To increase overall company share of the market by 3 per cent

Distribution

To add 5 per cent class A distributors
To add 10 per cent class B distributors

No change in the number of class C and D distributors.

Sales coverage and stock

Class of distributor	Annual sales calls	% lines in stock
A	12	100
B	6	80
C	3	50
D	2	40

Advertising

Aimed at users

5 per cent increase in the general public's awareness of the company's name and product lines

2 per cent increase in customer preference for the firm's product lines

5 per cent increase in co- operative advertising space

Marketing expenses

3 per cent increase in sales expense

5 per cent increase in advertising expense

No change in sales promotion expense

5 per cent decrease in head office expense

1 per cent decrease in distribution expense

Apart from advertising and certain expense items, goals should be broken down by region, district and salesperson's territory. Establishing goals for each territory should be undertaken jointly by the sales person and his or her manager. Sales goals are then broken down by weeks, taking seasonal variations into account. These then become budgeted figures against which subsequent performance is measured.

The next stage of the procedure involves strategy selection and tactics. **Strategy selection** amounts to determining what is the best way to reach specific objectives. **Tactics** relate to the specific action that must be taken, by whom, when, and within what constraints. Together they specify how the plan is to be implemented.

Control procedures have to be built into the plan. Control entails identifying those measures in the organization which must be monitored in order to assess how well a plan is succeeding. For example, if the objective is to achieve £200,000 sales of a product each month, some means has to be identified by which it is possible to ascertain that this objective is in fact being achieved. A similar situation exists with respect to profitability on products and to marketing costs. A system of control must establish the necessary standards, measure the activities and results, compare the measurements to the standards, and report variances between the measurements and the standards. In this way the plan can be kept on course and decisions made as to how to modify the original plan if there is a need to do so.

Some marketing decisions are taken under very uncertain conditions. It is necessary therefore to undertake contingency planning to specify what action will be taken if key objectives cannot be accomplished. (At the same time attention must also be given to the contingency plan so that it is much less than what can in fact be achieved.)

Following implementation, plans must be reviewed so that corrective action, if need be, can be taken.

► The marketing plan includes various sub-plans for the product mix, sales, advertising and sales promotion. Control procedures also have to be built in.

(ACT) Three years ago Mark set up as an estate agent in Ormskirk, a small west Lancashire town within commuting distance of nearby Liverpool. Despite the problems caused by recession and competition in the town from established agents, Mark has managed to stay in business.

He now feels that it is necessary to take stock and start planning ahead. In particular he is thinking of putting down on paper a marketing plan for the coming year.

How might Mark outline his marketing plan? What other aspects of planning does he have to consider?

ALLOCATION OF RESOURCES

Time, space, people and money make up an organization's resources. In a well-planned organization budgets are made available to enable tasks agreed by management to be implemented. Since resources are usually in short supply, what is available is

Resource allocation meeting

How much one gets depends on the power and influence one can muster

allocated to those plans or programmes which are generally thought to be the most important to the survival or growth of the organization.

In some organizations departments compete for the resources. How much is allocated to departments tends to be a reflection of how much power or influence the manager of the department can exercise. In such a case plans may not succeed.

Marketing budgets and budget allocation

Since the marketing department in any organization is a key element it should receive a budget appropriate for its needs. If the marketing department does not receive an appropriate budget then clearly it will not be able to perform its task properly. Since marketing is central to the success of an organization, all departments will suffer in the long run.

► Planning and budgeting processes described in this chapter assume decision processes are handled in an objective and fair manner. Often, however, the persuasive abilities of departmental managers has an effect on how resources are shared out. Ability may be based on such things as who has the most clout with the person allocating resources.

EVALUATING THE MARKETING EFFORT

Planning by itself is of little value. It has to be accompanied by systems of evaluation and control. Plans are implemented and subsequent performance is monitored. Marketing effort is evaluated through various control mechanisms.

The major plan is the annual plan. The purpose of control in this case is to examine whether planned results are being achieved. Sales analyses, market share analyses, sales to expense ratios, financial analysis and monitoring of the attitudes of users all form part of the control process. There are three other types of control to be found in an organization:

1 **Profitability control** – this examines where the company is making and losing money. Profitability by product, territory, customer group, trade channel and order size are scrutinized.

2 **Efficiency control** – which evaluates and tries to improve the spending efficiency and impact of marketing expenditures. It is applied to the sales force, advertising, sales promotion and distribution.

3 **Strategic control** – this examines whether the company is pursuing its best opportunities with respect to markets, products and channels.

► Plans may fail to come to fruition simply because they are not properly implemented. Another possibility is that they may never be adjusted in the light of experience and evaluated after they have been put into action.

The process of control and evaluation

The process of control and evaluation simply involves comparing actual performance with objectives and goals that have previously been set. This involves establishing **budgets** which relate the responsibilities of departments and employees to the requirements of plans and policies. This is accompanied by a continuous comparison of actual results with the targets set in the budget so that the latter may be achieved, or adjustments made to the objectives upon which they were founded.

► A budget is a quantitive and financial plan of activities that have to be pursued during the financial year to achieve the year's objectives.

Control which is exercised in this way is usually referred to as **budgetary control**. The basic notion behind it is that of **responsibility accounting** whereby areas of employee responsibility such as sales or distribution become control centres within an organization.

There are two kinds of **control centre**:

- **cost centres** which are responsible for costs
- **profit centres** which are responsible for costs and revenues (profits).

Marketing is usually a profit centre while departments which specialize in advertising or distribution are cost centres.

Analysing variances

Control involves measuring the variations of costs, revenues, etc. from the budget and analysing why variations have occurred. Action then has to be taken. Clearly in a company which is offering many products or services the task of analysing variances and suggesting appropriate courses of action is a major one.

Customer profitability analysis

A multitude of discounts may be offered to intermediaries and retailers in an attempt to obtain the volume of business stipulated in the budget. It is, however, quite difficult for a company to estimate the effect this will have on costs and margins. **Customer profitability analysis** provides a means of coming to grips with this problem.

The method involves individually analysing the revenues and costs attributable to any one customer or distributor. It enables the firm to establish which accounts make the greatest contributions to profit and which ones the least. It also enables the firm to establish why this is so. Such an approach enables us to look closely at large customer accounts where margins may be low and turnover high. We can establish whether the margins are adequate in terms of their ability to generate contributions to profits and overheads. We can also establish the amount of leeway that may exist to offer better terms at the next round of renegotiation of contracts.

Alternative management styles.

Marketing planning is an important management function and plans have to be put into action. This can only be achieved through people and thus people management is an important element in the task of marketing management.

Getting people to do things is not quite as straightforward as just telling them what has to be done. Managers have to know how to deal with situations and individuals to get the best out them. Much has been written about management and about leadership

▶ Evaluation involves comparing what has been achieved with what was planned to be accomplished. Cost and profit centres may be established. Variances between planned and achieved profits and costs are explored. Customer profitability analysis helps to establish where most of the profitable business lies.

Analysing variances – the sales mix

Freeway foodstuffs market two brands of cat food – Miaow and Paws – to retailers. Sales performance and targets set for the year to date are as follows:

	(a) Units cases		(b) Average price		(a x b) Sales revenue	
			(£)		(£m)	
	Actual	Budget	Actual	Budget	Actual	Budget
Miaow	112,345	105,219	51.80	50.00	5.82	5.26
Paws	146,787	177,318	48.80	45.30	7.16	8.03
Total	259,132	288,537	100.6	95.30	12.98	13.29

We can see that unit sales of Miaow are well up on budget and that the price per case obtained is also above what had been set in the budget. The effect of these factors on sales revenue is extremely positive indicating a considerable surplus over the budgeted amount. Some thought needs to be given to raising the price of Miaow. A small increase might keep actual unit sales on target while at the same time increasing sales revenue.

Unit sales of Paws on the other hand are well below what had been budgeted. The sales price asked is above the budgeted price but it still leaves a large deficit between the actual sales revenue and what had been budgeted. Brand switching from Paws to Miaow may account for some of the lost sales units and the actual selling price of Paws is above budget making it too close perhaps to Miaow. Possibly tighter control over the selling price of Paws and a slightly less ambitious unit sales target could lead to a greater likelihood that the budget would be achieved.

The combined effect of the actions suggested would lead to a better performance in terms of achieving unit sales while at the same time increasing total sales revenues.

in particular. The only real conclusion is that there is no one best method to get a job done.

Most of the time management involves dealing with contingencies and people are no exception to this. A manager has to adapt his or her style to deal with individuals. It is true that some managers may be classed as job-oriented or people-oriented but this does not really explain the task of management. The key is to find out how subordinates are motivated to do things and then to try to find ways of making it possible for them to achieve their own level of satisfaction.

What is true, is that under certain conditions autocratic styles of management may appear to work for a particular group of individuals. But should the make-up of the group change substantially

► R. R. Blake and J. S. Mouton wrote a book entitled *The Managerial Grid* in which they differentiated between management styles according to whether they were employee-oriented or job-oriented. The best style was considered to be one which scored highly on both dimensions. Managers scoring high on the concern for job dimension but having low concern for people were seen as 'promotable'.

and different personalities join the group then the same style may not work at all.

The manager's task is a very difficult one since he or she will be unable to please everyone. Clashes in personalities between the manager and the staff are almost inevitable. A manager who adopts a democratic style of management may be seen as too easy going by some members of the group while by others the style may be viewed as just right for the situation.

Different managers may have a preferred style of interacting with people in general. This preferred style may appear to be a pervasive characteristic of the way they behave. Several writers on organizations have come up with ideas or suggestions which relate to effective and ineffective management styles. Reddin's classification of basic managerial styles is a case in point. He differentiates between less effective and more effective managers. A summary of his types is given below:

Less effective managerial styles

- the 'missionary' who is enthusiastic about new ideas, tries to sell them to others and then tires of the job and moves on to other things
- the 'deserter' who has become totally disillusioned with the organization and does the minimum required
- the 'autocrat' who shows most concern for getting the job done and relies on power. He or she tends to keep information to himself or herself and communicates downwards. Fear and threats are constantly used to cajole people into doing things
- the 'compromiser' who prefers things to run smoothly and tries to avoid conflict.

More efficient managerial styles

- the 'developer' who likes to teach, train and help others to put ideas into practice
- the 'bureaucrat' who sticks to the rules, remains impartial and stays remote from the action
- the 'benevolent autocrat' who delegates a little but keeps close policy control. Rewards rather than punishments are the order of the day in motivating people. Managers exercising this style of management see loyalty to the organization as an important quality in staff
- the 'executive' who exercises authority when the occasion demands it but who also consults and involves people in decision making.

In practice we may find managers showing a mixture of the various styles suggested by Reddin.

▶ Reddin W. J. 1987. *How to Make your Management Style more Attractive*, Maidenhead: McGraw-Hill.

The missionary

'Well, now you're all so enthusiastic about it all, I''ll be off.'

The benevolent autocrat

'It's a bonus for those of you who tell me you're not looking for another job.'

Exercise your creative talents and see if you can draw a cartoon, write a header and a caption for each one of the managerial types discussed above.

The key point to bear in mind is that managers themselves are accountable to others for their work and for their responsibilities. They certainly delegate their work to others but they are still accountable for how well the work is performed. No manager can afford to overlook this point. An employee who fails to perform satisfactorily in accordance with the work that has been delegated to him or her can expect little sympathy in the long term from a good manager.

 The difficult salesman
Everyone knows that Pete is the best salesman in the business. Someone once said that he could sell a kangaroo to an eskimo. Pete's basic problem though is that he sells what he feels like selling and doesn't take a great deal of notice of what the firm want him to sell. 'I sell more than any other two salesmen put together', he boasts.

The old-hands in the company want him sacked because he creates more problems than he solves. There are always customers on the telephone screaming for orders they have placed with Pete but for which the firm is out of stock. Dan, Pete's boss, however, feels that it would be a great pity to sack Pete. 'There has to be a better solution than that', he says.

What do you think?

Management of change.

Planning will always involve introducing change of one kind or another into an organization. This being the case, it is important to remember that when introducing change the following points should be taken into account:

* people should be given ample warning and indications of the kind of change that is likely to occur
* an explanation should be offered as to why the change has taken place
* people should be involved at all stages in the discussions relating to the change
* people should understand what the benefits and rewards are that result from the change
* training should be provided in relationship to changes in practice.

The launching of new products or services and or changes in marketing methods are examples of where changes take place.

► Management is about getting jobs done with the help of groups of people. Different managers may have different styles or approaches and some are intrinsically better than others. Experiencing change is a stressful experience and needs to be sensitively managed.

Members of one's own organization and distributors should be involved.

CHAPTER SUMMARY

1 Marketing planning may be seen as part of the corporate planning process in which a firm reviews its current situation, decides where it would like to get to and specifies how it is going to do so. The marketing planning element refers to how the firm is going to use its marketing resources to achieve specific objectives which contribute to the overall corporate objectives.

2 The planning process involves setting corporate objectives, setting goals, auditing marketing resources, undertaking gap analysis, setting marketing objectives and strategy based on assumptions, writing down the marketing plan, implementing the marketing plan and evaluating the marketing effort.

3 An organization sets itself overall financial goals that have to be attained and these are then translated into goals for marketing planning.

4 In order to develop marketing strategies which will enable an organization to achieve stated goals and objectives it has to analyse marketing strengths, weaknesses, opportunities and threats and evaluate their impact on the organization.

5 Gap analysis is undertaken to identify the nature of the likely financial requirements, assuming that the organization carries on with its present strategy and does not undertake any changes. An organization can pursue various strategies to reduce the gap, for example:

a Increase sales of existing products
b Look for new markets
c Look for new products
d Diversify
e Reduce the costs of running the organization
f Adjust prices and discounts

6 Choice of marketing objectives and strategy can be aided by skilful application of SWOT analysis to identify the strengths and weaknesses of the organization and the opportunities and threats that exist in the environment. Through a careful matching process and creative thinking, strategies will emerge.

7 Plans in themselves are not sufficient to ensure that an organization achieves its desired objectives. Marketing budgets have to be established to provide a specific target to achieve and resources to allocate. Control has to be effected to ensure that the organization keeps to the specified plan.

8 Marketing effort is evaluated through the use of sales analyses, market share analyses, sales to expense ratios, financial analysis and monitoring of customer attitudes.

9 Planning and control is implemented through the management of people and it is important to appreciate the alternative management styles that can be used.

► Now that you have reached the end of the chapter, turn back to the objectives and make sure you have achieved each of them.

7

Understanding the customer

Chapter objectives

By the end of this chapter you should:

▌ know how marketers define market segments by such attributes as social class, age reference groups and life style

▌ be able to describe the way in which messages pass from marketers to consumers involving selective attention, selective distortion, selective remembering and cognitive consonance and dissonance – and the implications of this for marketing practice

▌ be able to describe consumer behaviour in terms of the influences people have on each other's purchasing decisions

▌ be able to distinguish between habitual purchasing and one-off purchasing

▌ have considered the difficulties of getting consumers to switch brands and the techniques which can be used to encourage brand switching

▌ be able to describe complex buying decisions in terms of a given model and be able to identify the model's implications for marketing practice

▌ know that although industrial goods are bought by organizational buyers, more people actually influence business buying decisions than consumer buying decisions

▌ be able to describe the differences and similarities between industrial and consumer buying

▌ be able to describe the various roles in the industrial buying process, i.e. users, influencers, deciders, approvers, buyers and gatekeepers

▌ be familiar with the following terms as used by marketers: market segment, culture/sub-culture, social class, reference groups, roles and status symbols, life cycle, life style, motivation, selective attention, selective distortion, selective retention, cognitive dissonance, drive, stimulus, cue, response, reinforcement, attitudes, habitual purchases, one-off purchases, gatekeepers.

Introduction

Marketing involves satisfying customer wants and needs and in so doing making a profit or achieving other organizational or individual objectives. It is important to understand how the customer makes decisions with regard to purchasing or using a product or service. Armed with such knowledge an organization is in a better position to market itself and its products or services. First we will look at consumer behaviour and then we will look at industrial or business buyer behaviour.

CONSUMER MARKETS

The **consumer market** in effect comprises all individuals or households buying or acquiring goods or services for personal consumption. In the EEC alone there are over 300,000,000 persons. However consumer characteristics, buying power and wants and needs vary considerably from one region to another. For example some 30% of the population of Ireland is under 15 years of age whereas in West Berlin the figure is a mere 14% of the population. Only 8% of the Canaries population is over 65 years of age, whereas in West Berlin the figure is 20% of the population. In Denmark, the dependency rate is 0.8% whereas in the Sur region of Spain the figure is 2.1%. In Northern Ireland the birth rate per 1000 of the population is around 17 while in the Nord-Ovest region of Italy it is a mere 7%. The above figures reflect extremes and regions are spread out across the range between the extreme values.

► Dependency rate – the number of dependents in a family.

► In the UK populations seem to be relatively stable over time.

Mobility Patterns

How far is where you currently live from where you grew up?

Still live in the same home as I grew up in	11%
3–5 –> miles away	36%
6–25 –> miles away	22%
26–50 –> miles away	7%
51–100 –> miles away	7%
101–250 –> miles away	10%
over 250 –> miles away	6%

Planning for social change survey, Henley Centre 1990.

All over the world consumers vary considerably from one region of a country to another in terms of age, income, educational level, mobility patterns and taste. Fortunately, it is possible to distinguish groups of consumers who have much in common with respect to wants and needs. These groups form **market segments** and firms develop products and services to serve the needs of these market segments. Whitbread, for example, segments its beer market on a regional/local basis. A few years ago the firm offered a total of twenty distinctive local ales. These ranged from small brands with a distinct local appeal such as Bentley's Yorkshire Bitter, to major regional brands such as Welsh Bitter and Whitbread Best Scotch.

► A market segment is a group within the whole; identifies the target for a particular product.

What firms need to know about the consumer

> The 7 Os of the marketplace
>
> | | |
> |---|---|
> | Who constitutes the market? | Occupants |
> | What does the market buy? | Objects |
> | Why does the market buy? | Objectives |
> | Who participates in the buying? | Organizations |
> | How does the market buy? | Operations |
> | When does the market buy? | Occasions |
> | Where does the market buy? | Outlets |
>
> *Source:* Kotler *(1988)*

▶ Kotler P. 1988. *Marketing Management: Analysis, Planning and Control.* New Jersey: Prentice-Hall

Market research studies provide insights into the kind of questions shown in the box above. However, it is also important to understand the major factors influencing consumer behaviour.

> The major factors influencing consumer behaviour
>
> | Marketing | Environmental | Buyer characteristics |
> |---|---|---|
> | Product | Economic | Social Background |
> | Price | Technological | Personal situation |
> | Promotion | Political | Psychological |
> | Distribution | Cultural | |

▶ Marketing factors are dealt with in Chapter 2.

▶ Environmental factors are dealt with in Chapter 3.

Elsewhere in the book we consider the impact of the marketing and environmental forces, here we will look in some detail at buyer characteristics.

Social background

Culture consists of values, perceptions, preferences and behaviours. Many Western societies put value on achievement, success and materialism. This is good for the sale of goods and services which enable consumers to demonstrate their success and achievement through the kinds of products which they purchase.

Other societies have a somewhat different set of values. While materialism has not been absent in these other cultures, it has not been as prominent as it is in Europe and the USA. Moreover, much of the paraphernalia of Western societies is not generally revered in such countries. Nevertheless, we live in a changing world and there are signs of some Western artefacts being adopted in countries which have hitherto been slow to show an interest in Western ideas, values and goods.

▶ Promising material success may sell some products but there is also a market for what is apparently anti-materialist. One of the most rapidly developing business sectors in the 1980s and early 90s has been the occult 'mind, and spirit' sector with its crystals, UFOs, alternative medicines and meditation. These are profit-oriented businesses despite the image of anti-materialism.

Subculture reflects nationality groups, religious groups, racial groups and geographic areas. One can observe its effects in the way consumers form preferences or tastes. A geographic example was given at the beginning of this chapter when we discussed Whitbread's approach to market segmentation based on the tastes of a particular region.

Many of the larger European cities are extremely cosmopolitan in terms of their populations. People from many nationalities and racial backgrounds make up the populations in these cities. There has been a tendency for people with similar ethnic backgrounds to live in close proximity to one another within a geographic area of a city. The communities have developed their own business activities and in many instances this has led to the development of local retailing establishments which cater for the particular needs of the community. Such developments recognize that the needs and wants of such communities are in some ways different to those of the larger national community and have been set up to serve those specific differences.

► The specialist needs of ethnic minorities have usually been ignored as market opportunities by established British companies. This leaves a market niche for ethnic minority groups to satisfy.

Social class indicates societal stratification. Members of a social class share similar values and attitudes. These are different to those of members of other social classes. The identification of the social class to which a person belongs can be rather an involved business but broadly speaking it is based upon the recognition of such points as job, pay, personal wealth, education and value orientation.

Research appears to indicate that social classes have distinct product and brand preferences in areas such as clothing, leisure activities, home furnishings and motor cars. There are also signs that social classes have media preferences. Lower classes show a preference for television while upper classes favour magazines and journals. Moreover, within the media division itself, such as TV, we find upper classes favour news and drama while lower classes prefer soap operas and quiz shows.

► Although social class is a way in which the market is segmented, many people in Britain do not like to be identified as belonging to a certain social class. For example many women's magazines are read mainly by 'working-class' women. But it is editorial policy to avoid any mention of social class.

In the UK much use has been made of a social grading system which classifies the head of the household and allocates people to one of six social grades (see inset on page 106). The method was devised many years ago and is still in use. However, over the passage of time there has been considerable social change which has resulted in more social diversity. This method no longer explains consumer behaviour in many situations. Two newer systems are:

- **SAGACITY**, which is used extensively by Research Service Ltd which also takes account of differences in aspiration levels and other behavioural patterns as well as income and stage of the life cycle. There are four main stages of the life cycle which are subdivided by income and occupation groups.
- **ACORN**, which has been developed by the CACI Marketing Analysis Group. The method reflects the fact that people living in particular types of district tend to show broadly similar patterns of behaviour. It is thought by many people that the system

► The ABCDE classification devised by Market Research Services Ltd has been the system most frequently used to classify people into social classes for marketing purposes. Its failure to capture the complexity of class differences has led to new systems such as SAGACITY and ACORN.

The Market Research Services Classification of social class

Grade	% 0f Population	Status	Head of household's occupation
A	3	Upper middle class	Higher managerial, administrative professional
B	13	Middle class	Intermediate manegerial adminstrative or professional
C1	23	Lower middle class	Supervisory or clerical junior managerial, administrative or professional
C2	32	Skilled working class	Skilled manual workers
D	19	Working class	Semi and unskilled manual workers
E19	10	Those at lowest levels of subsistence	State pensioners or widows casual or lowest grade workers

Source: JICNARS National Readership Survey 1981

may ultimately replace the social grading system shown in the inset.

Take a copy of a popular tabloid newspaper (such as the *Sun*) and a copy of one of the quality broadsheets (such as the *Times*). The first will be read mainly by people falling into the C1, C2, DE categories, and the second mainly by As and Bs. Compare the advertisements in the two newspapers. How do they vary in terms of:
a) the purchasing power of the market served by these different papers?
b) the images and aspirations conveyed by the advertisements?

Reference groups are made up groups of people who directly or indirectly influence a person's attitudes or behaviours. Teenagers, for example may be influenced by a pop-star cult. Marketers attempt to identify the reference groups of their target customers and make use of ideologies associated with such groups in their marketing communications.

Make a list of the kind of categories you think you belong to, for example 'Southerners', '30- somethings', 'students' – these are reference groups to which you belong. Which of these reference groups do you think are targeted by advertisers? Find some examples.

Make a list of the categories of people to which you don't belong, for example 'graduates', 'beautiful women', 'dynamic businessmen'. These are also reference groups. Find examples of ways in which marketing encourages you to believe that if you buy a certain product you can join a particular reference group.

Family is perhaps the strongest reference group which influences consumer behaviour. It is not reasonable for marketers to attempt to identify the influence that individual families have on individual people's behaviour. As a consequence marketers concentrate on the roles and relative influence of the various members of a family in the purchase of a large variety of products and services.

Parents no longer make decisions about what their children will wear. When it comes to buying shoes, children decide which products will be purchased. Children are becoming more and more fashion conscious, and at an early age. This trend is slower to emerge than in France and Germany where parents have always spent as much time and effort on their children's apparel.

Clarks Courier, Clarks Ltd, May 1985

Traditionally, the wife or female partner in a family has tended to purchase the weekly shopping and buy small value items, but this situation gradually changed throughout the 1980s. In the case of expensive items there is generally joint decision-making. The marketers main task is to identify which member of the family has the greatest influence in choosing various products. An example is given below:

▶ *See R. M. Cozenza, 'Family decision making: decision dominance structure analysis – an extension; Journal of the Academy of Marketing Science*, vol 13, p. 99, 1985.

Husband dominates	Neither dominate	Wife dominates
life insurance	holidays	washing machines
cars	carpeting	housing

Take your own family as an example. How are decisions to purchase the following made?

toothpaste	holidays
curtains	male underwear
children's shoes	wine

What implications do your answers have for how a marketer should target your family for these different products?

Roles and status symbols

People identify with different groups. Moreover, within each group they adopt a role which reflects their status within that group. One of the most important statuses relates to their job and how it is viewed by their various reference groups. People often buy products that relate to their role and status. The company chairman usually drives an expensive car and wears expensive suits. Status symbols vary for different social classes and it is the job of the marketer to recognize what the status symbols are for different groups of people.

Personal situation

Age and life cycle

People pass through various recognizable stages during their lives. Of course, people may have different life cycles according to whether or not they decide to establish a family unit. The inset gives an illustration of the life cycle concept, assuming that people decide to build a family unit. It will be observed that people exhibit different buying patterns according to the stage in the life cycle they are passing through.

Life style goes beyond a person's social class. It is an expression of an individual's personality. Some women may have a life style which people might describe as being oldfashioned or traditionalist. Other women may be described as socialites, and yet others as family-centred. Marketers have to look for relationships between their products and the life-style groups which they can identify.

 Heritage homes owns a large number of self-catering holiday cottages and flats. All are conversions of period cottages, barns or houses. The accommodation is in three area groups: Pembrokeshire, Northumberland and the Cumbrian Lake District. The company wishes to add value to its rental business by selling holiday packages – Heritage Holidays – consisting of self-catering, bed and breakfast,

▶ *See* F. W. Derrick and A. E. Linfield, 'The family life cycle: an alternative approach, *Journal of Consumer Research*, September 1980, pp. 214–217.

historical and/or wildlife tours with lunch and evening meals provided. You can invent any further details for yourself.

Look back at the previous pages and try to identify the market segment most appropriate to Heritage Holidays in terms of class, sub-culture, reference groups, roles and status symbols, age, life cycle and life style. Think of the activity as one of producing an Identikit picture of the typical customer.

Stages in the family life cycle and associated behavioural buying patterns.

Stage in the family life cycle	Buying interests
1 Young and single – away from home	Fashion clothes, sport and leisure products, cars, music centres and records, holidays
2 Young married couples – no children	Cars, consumer durables, holidays, furniture
3 Married – small children	Washers, driers, baby items, economy food
4 Married – children mainly under 13	Children's toys, educational products, domestic appliances, many foods
5 Married – children mainly teenagers	Consumer durables, better furniture, hobby interests
6 Married – children left home – still employed	Travel, recreation, self education, investments, luxuries
7 Older – retired	Cheaper holidays, value for money goods
8 Solitary survivor	Economy living

▶ Age, life-cycle stage, occupation, economic circumstances, personality and lifestyle all exert an influence on buyer behaviour.

Psychological factors

Motivations, perceptions, learning, beliefs and attitudes all have an influential part to play in a person's buying choices.

Motivation

Marketing people can benefit from understanding what motivates people to buy a product. Armed with such knowledge it may be possible to steal a competitive advantage in the design and/or

▶ A need becomes a motive when it is aroused to a sufficient level of intensity. A motive (or drive) produces action in a person.

marketing of a product. This can be done by persuading consumers that a product is better able to satisfy their wants and needs because it has certain features.

There are various theories of motivation two of the most important, as far as marketing is concerned , were put forward by Freud and Maslow. **Freud** suggested that people may be influenced at an unconscious level. It may not be possible therefore to get people to talk rationally about why they make certain purchases. A person may indicate that the acquisition of a dishwasher will make housework easier. It could also be, however, that the purchase is being made in order to impress friends. Both of these motivations could be behind the purchase but the latter might never be discovered in the course of asking the person to explain his or her motivation. Freud makes us aware of these obscure motivations. As a result different methods of research have been developed to get at these hidden kinds of motives.

Freudian insights
Marketing to unconscious desires
A key Freudian idea is that people repress their sexual desires and find sexual gratification in all kinds of 'safe' ways that are not obviously sexual. Some marketing people have tried to exploit this by marketing products which satisfy unconscious sexual desires. The most notorious example is the 'squeezy' bottle for washing-up liquid which was designed to simulate a penis. Much market research time was invested in testing alternative bottles for the optimum point between rigidity and softness.

► A. H. Maslow, 'A theory of human motivation; *Psychological Review*, July 1943, pp 370–96.

Maslow's main contribution was to suggest that human needs are arranged in a hierarchy of importance. The most important needs he identified were the basic ones to do with physiological needs whilst the least important ones he identified were to do with self-actualization. Maslow argued that people would not seek to satisfy the less important needs until the more important ones were satisfied. This theory helps us to clarify how various products may fit in with peoples' plans. A person may consider buying a home before purchasing a motor car. A householder who has a car, a refrigerator, cooker, freezer, telephone, washing machine and spin-drier may next be interested in purchasing a dishwasher.

Perception
People do not observe the same phenomenon in exactly the same way. People differ in their perceptual process of:

● selective attention
● selective distortion
● selective retention

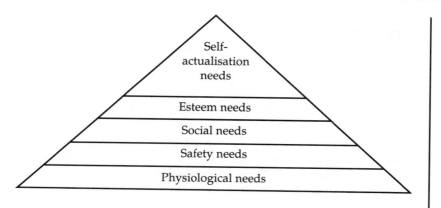

Self development & realization

Self-esteem, recognition, status.

Affection, love.

Security, protection

Hunger, thirst, sex

Source: Maslow's Hierarchy of Needs. A. H. Maslow, 1943.

Selective attention. People pay particular attention to only a fraction of what is going on around them in the course of their lives. Journeying to work in the morning it is quite possible that we are exposed to hundreds of advertising messages. We would probably screen out all of them except possibly the odd one or two which are some way related to our current thoughts and it is quite possible that we would be unable to recall any of them! The real challenge for the advertiser is to present messages in such a way that people will pay attention to them.

Selective distortion. People assimilate incoming information so that it fits in with their preconceptions. It is possible, for example, that in showing horrific accidents resulting from drink-driving people will not take notice of it because they feel that they cannot relate to such a situation. For instance, they might assume that horrific accidents only really happen to people who are habitually very drunk.

Selective retention. Much of what people learn is forgotten but there is a tendency to remember information that reinforces particular attitudes and beliefs. Where a strong belief or attitude exists, information received which reinforces the belief or attitude is likely to be retained.

Implications of selective attention, selective distortion and selective retention for marketers

The above phemomena are taken into consideration by marketers in the course of preparing and presenting marketing communications. They account for the amount of drama and repetition that takes place when marketers send their messages to their target audiences.

▶ **Cognitive dissonance** refers to the feeling of unease we experience when things don't fit into our expectations. Monty Python derives humour from exploiting cognitive dissonance.

Cognitive dissonance

Trying something new can be a stressful time. We may feel unsure about whether we should be trying it all. After all, we have managed alright without it before.

Progressive spectacle lenses are a case in point. Progressive lenses obviate the necessity to wear two different pairs of spectacles, one for reading (close up vision) and one for normal wear (distance viewing). As we get older there is a tendency for our eyesight to deteriorate so that often in middle and old age we are faced with the need for these two types of lens.

A recent product innovation has been the progressive lens. This is an alternative to the bifocal lens where the top half of the lens is for distance viewing and the bottom half is for close-to viewing. The progressive lens does away with the abrupt break in the type of lens specification associated with the bifocal. There is a much more gradual transition between the two types of lens.

Wearers of progressive lenses may experience considerable unease when they first wear the new lens. Initially, it is more difficult to see where steps are when descending staircases and one is apt to trip over easily if care is not taken. The lens also causes the eyes some strain if one works under neon lighting conditions. Furthermore there is some blurring of the image if one moves one's head rapidly from side to side. The eyes also have to become accustomed to looking through particular parts of the lens to ensure a clear image at various distances. After a while the eyes automatically adjust to making the kind of compensatory movements which are required by progressive lenses.

In some cases wearers of progressive lenses experience so much unease that they give up wearing the lenses and revert to two pairs of spectacles.

Take any weekday evening Monday to Thursday and watch television as you would normally watch it. Don't treat this as a memory test. Next morning jot down all the adverts you saw. Then watch for the same time period on the following day – the adverts will be much the same. How many did you remember? Is there any pattern in your remembering and forgetting?

Learning

Learning arises from experience and most human behaviour is acquired in this way. This applies to the purchase of goods and services and so learning is perhaps the most important factor underpinning consumer behaviour. Drives, stimuli, cues and responses and reinforcement are the key elements of learning. A **drive** is a force inside people that pushes them towards certain actions. Drives become motives when they are directed specifically towards a **stimulus** which will reduce the drive. **Cues** are minor stimuli which establish when, where and how a person will respond.

Firms build up demand for a product or service by linking it with strong drives, using cues to motivate people and giving positive reinforcement to people who respond. In effect this is really the whole basis of the marketing concept. Marketers seek to identify unsatisfied customer wants and needs (where there is a strong drive which is not fulfilled). The firm provides the product or service (stimulus) together with appropriate promotional messages (cues). The consumer responds by purchasing the product and the marketer follows this up with after sales service or promotional messages to reinforce the fact that the consumer has made a good choice.

Beliefs and attitudes

People develop beliefs and **attitudes** which in turn influence their purchasing behaviour. Brand images are based on the beliefs and attitudes of people and as a result of these images people make purchase decisions. An attitude is a predisposition to act in certain way towards an objective under given circumstances. Having a particular attitude towards something influences the way in which people may behave.

A principal objective of marketing communications is to inform customers that a product meets with their attitudes. Marketing communications are also concerned with correcting mistaken beliefs about a product or service. Recent advertising campaigns relating to the selling off of public utilities to the private sector in the UK emphasize this point.

► The marketing concept. Marketers seek to identify unsatisfied drives (wants and needs) by linking a product with them. The product is the stimulus and the promotional messages are the cues which encourage the consumers to respond by purchasing the product to satisfy their drives.

► Attitudes are predispositions to behave in particular ways towards particular objects in particular circumstances.

► The social background of consumers and psychological make-up are important influences on their behaviour. Marketers need to have ways of classifying consumers and need to understand the psychology of their behaviour

MODELS OF CONSUMER BEHAVIOUR

Several people may have a part to play in making a purchase. We may not be conscious of this until we come to look at what is involved in the actual decision. For example the boss at work, anxious to plan coverage for the office during the summer, may prompt me into deciding that it is time I did something about settling on this year's holiday destination. Someone in the office suggests Malaga as the destination, someone else suggests Malta, and yet another colleague suggests Madrid. Finally I decide on Malta and because of lack of time to arrange the holiday myself I get one of my parents to make the arrangements for me.

A number of persons were involved in the decision making

> **Roles in the purchase decision making process**
> ● Initiator – person suggesting the product/service in the first place
> ● Influencer – person who exerts some influence on the final decision
> ● Decider – person who takes the decision
> ● Buyer – person who makes the purchase
> ● User – person who uses the product or service.

process concerning the holiday in Malta. Each one of the persons, including me, has played a role in the decision making process. The boss was the initiator, a colleague in the office an influencer, I was the decider, one of my parents was the actual buyer and I was the user.

A firm needs to be aware of the different roles since they have implications for the product design and the various marketing communications that have to be made.

Habitual versus one-off purchases

We need to distinguish between complex decision-making situations and those in which little thought is given to the purchase being made. Where a product is relatively expensive and possibly technologically complex, prospective purchasers often go through a complex search and evaluation process prior to making a purchase. Where the product is relatively cheap and simple to understand the process often involves little or no search and evaluation and is based very much upon experience learned from using the product before. In both cases, however, attitudes and beliefs have an important part to play.

Habitual purchases

People purchase many food items at the supermarket out of **habit**. Such products tend to be low-priced frequently purchased items. There is no extensive search for information nor is there extensive evaluation prior to making a purchase. Consumers purchase a particular brand because it is familiar and the familiarity is emphasized by different types of advertising. The main task of marketers of competing brands is to persuade the consumer to try a different brand. If trial of a different brand can be brought about there is the possibility that the behaviour of repeatedly buying the same brand will be transferred to the new brand. Price and value for money are principal factors which consumers consider when buying goods of this nature. Price and sales promotion are the key marketing tools in this situation.

► Assael H., in *Consumer Behaviour and Marketing*, page 87, Kent Publishing 1987, gives a more elaborate classification of purchasing decisions.

(ACT) If you regularly go shopping for groceries try and observe yourself next time. How often do you 'make a decision' to purchase rather than go through a familiar routine? Do you have your own standard route of going through the super-market?

Based upon your own self observation and the likelihood that other people have similar experiences what implications do you think this will have for store arrangement and display?

The first step is getting people to switch from the brand they habitually purchase

Free samples of the product or special introductory prices are a feature of inducing trial in the case of low priced fast moving consumer goods. At the supermarket we may be invited to eat a piece of a new brand of meat pie or be handed free samples of a new brand of instant coffee as we enter a store. Notices at the point of sale pointing to price reductions on new brands also stand out and 'hit us in the eye'. Under such circum-stances it may be quite difficult to avoid trying a new brand. Whether or not we switch to using the new brand regularly, however, will depend on how satisfied we are with the new brand.

Complex buying decisions

Many people have studied consumer behaviour and a five stage model of the buying process has been distilled from these researches (see, for example, Engel *et al.*, 1986).

► Engel, Blackwell and Minard give an extensive treatment of the research on consumer decision making. See also Chapters 12 and 15.

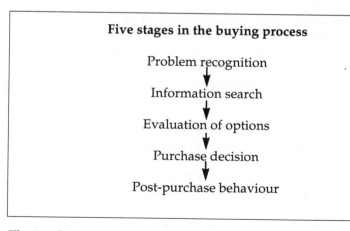

Five stages in the buying process

Problem recognition
↓
Information search
↓
Evaluation of options
↓
Purchase decision
↓
Post-purchase behaviour

► Engel J. F., Blackwell R. D. and Miniard B. W. 1986. *Consumer Behaviour* (5th Edition), Holt Rinehart Winston

The implication is that consumers actually pass through all stages in buying a product or service. In actual fact, of course, as we have seen in the case of habitual purchases, this is not necessarily the case. However, it is a useful framework from within which to view the purchase of many of the more expensive type of durable products and or services.

Problem recognition

The notion here is that the prospective purchaser experiences a need or drive to buy a certain product – for example a new washing machine. The need can be triggered by a variety of stimuli, for instance the unsatisfactory performance of the current washing machine or the fact that a neighbour has bought a new one. The marketer needs to identify the factors which give rise to the recognition of the problem and use these to advantage in marketing communications about the particular product, service or brand.

Information search

Once the problem has been recognized, prospective purchasers search for information about the product in question. A person who has recognized a felt need for a new home computer, for example, may scan many computer magazines for information on what is available and at what price. This scanning helps to identify locations where the products or service may be purchased and the intending buyer may well visit these locations to obtain more information and possibly to view the product working. The amount of search undertaken probably varies with the individual concerned, the amount of time available, and the availability of suitable products and services. The marketer is primarily interested in the sources of information that the prospective purchaser will consult and the kind of information which is likely to sway the consumer into buying one particular brand rather than another.

Evaluation of options

Current ideas about how consumers make decisions are based on the premise that consumers make them on a conscious or rational basis. We may have to bear in mind, however, that this may not necessarily always be the case. However, assuming a rational model of consumer choice, we can understand the process as follows:

- products are conceptualized as a bundle of attributes – desk top computer: memory (disk and ram), speed, IBM compatibility, portability, etc
- relevant attributes vary from one product or service to another – size and speed are important with cameras whereas variety and packaging are emphasized in the case of chocolates
- some product attributes are more important to consumers than others – tread life and safety may be more important than price when considering car tyres

Problem recognition
↓
Information search
↓
Evaluation of options
↓
Purchase decisions
↓
Post purchase behaviour

Problem recognition
↓
Information search
↓
Evaluation of options
↓
Purchase decisions
↓
Post-purchase behaviour

- the degree of importance of different product attributes to different consumer groups can form the basis of market segmentation – hardwearing relatively expensive shoes
- consumers develop beliefs about products with respect to their various attributes – this forms a brand image, for example Volvo cars are considered safe
- consumers have utility functions with respect to each one of the attributes. Product/service satisfaction varies according to the fit between the product's performance on the attribute and the consumer's expectations – a small car's petrol consumption is satisfactory provided that it is more than ten kilometres per litre
- attitudes towards brands are formed through the process of evaluation – Seiko watches are better value for money than competing brands because they offer the same product features and have equally elegant designs.

Firms need to understand what criteria consumers use to evaluate their products and services. If it is discovered that a product or service does not meet with consumer's expectations then the marketer can try one or more of a number of options:

- change the product so that it fits with consumer expectations
- change people's beliefs about the product or service
- change people's beliefs about competing brands and demonstrate that they are no better than the company's brand
- change people's perceptions of the importance of different brand attributes – if the product is considered weak on one attribute then the marketer could play down the importance of this attribute and stress the importance of others.
- move the consumer perception of what comprises an ideal product more in the direction of the existing brand's profile of attributes.

► For example, the advertising campaign 'It's a lot less bother than a hover'

Purchase decision

Intending purchasers are influenced by the attitudes of others. Other factors may also arise which prevent the purchase intention being put into practice. Unfortunately the marketer of the product can do little to counter these kind of problems.

Post-purchase behaviour

Post-purchase cognitive dissonance is commonly experienced by consumers after purchasing a relatively expensive product or service. There is a tendency to ask oneself whether one has done the right thing in making the purchase or whether one would have been better off to have purchased a different brand, product or service altogether. Consumers need to be reassured. If the marketer has exaggerated the benefits of the product then the consumer will

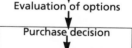

► Problem recognition
↓
Information search
↓
Evaluation of options
↓
Purchase decision
↓
Post-purchase behaviour

▶ Formal models of consumer behaviour help firms to establish a framework within which to both understand behaviour and formulate communication strategies.

▶ J. P. Marrian, provides an extensive account of the marketing characteristics of industrial goods and buyers in: 'Marketing characteristics of industrial goods and buyers' in A. Wilson (editor) 1966 *The Marketing of Industrial Products*, London: Hutchinson.

▶ See Chapter 13 for a discussion of price elasticity.

▶ Webster and Wind provide a detailed account of the various influences on industrial buyers. F. E. Webster and Y. Wind, *Organizational Buyer Behaviour*, Englewood Cliffs, N.J.: Pentice

more than likely experience dissatisfaction. This in turn can lead to poor word of mouth communication about the product.

Marketing people can do much to allay dissonance. Some of the methods include:

- directing specific advertising at people who have already bought the product, featuring contented, happy customers.
- writing booklets which are dissonance reducing to accompany the product or service
- arranging speedy redress of customer grievances.

ORGANIZATIONAL BUYER BEHAVIOUR

Industrial buyers are those buying goods and services for some tangibly productive and commercially significant purpose. There are various differences between the customers in industrial or business markets and consumer markets. In particular there are:

- fewer buyers
- larger buyers
- geographically concentrated customer groups

The demand for industrial goods arises from the demand for consumer goods. In addition the total demand for many industrial goods is relatively price inelastic – that is, it is not affected by price changes very much.

Industrial goods are bought by organizational buyers. In reality, however, more people actually influence business buying decisions than consumer buying decisions. Indeed there may be a buying committee consisting of technical experts and senior management personnel. These are often found in the purchase of relatively expensive industrial goods. Even if this is not the case, the same people may be involved or consulted in the course of making buying decisions.

The industrial buyer needs to know as much about marketing as salespeople s/he encounters. There are industrial buyers who simply place orders. They act on behalf of production management and require little or no skill. More often, however, the role of the buyer is more important and s/he needs to know all about the products and services. Buyers are also proactive rather than reactive and are constantly on the look-out for information which can enable them to make more judicious purchases decisions.

Major influences on industrial buyers

Industrial buyers respond to both rational economic and personal appeals when participating in buying decisions. There are various influences on industrial buyers and these may be classified as follows:

- environmental – economic recessions and resurgences, technological developments, legal constraints, competitive activities, etc.
- organizational – reflecting objectives, procedures, structures and systems
- interpersonal – arising from status differences between people associated with the purchasing decision
- individual – associated with the age, income, education, job position, personality and attitude to risk of the buyer.

Similarities with consumer behaviour

There are some similarities with the theory we have discussed earlier in this chapter relating to consumer behaviour. As is the case in consumer decisions making there are a variety of people who actually exert an influence on the decision:

- users – who will use the product or service
- influencers – often technical persons whose expertise is requested prior to making decisions
- deciders – those who actually have authority to take decisions
- approvers – those who hold the purse strings
- buyers – who select the supplier and arrange the terms of purchase
- gatekeepers – who can screen out information before it ever gets into the decision makers' in-trays.

Marketers of industrial and business goods have to be aware of the various influences on decision making. Moreover, they have to try to identify the key influential people and to persuade them that the product will meet a felt need.

Arnold runs a large window cleaning business employing around fifty people. His clients are not house owners but own shops, offices and business premises. Getting a contract is never quite straightforward. Using the framework of:
users
influencers
deciders
approvers
buyers
gatekeepers.

Consider the relevance of the above to the approach he might take in obtaining business in the following instances:

large retailer with branches all over the country
small local retailer
skyscraper office block – tenanted by many firms
airport
skyscraper – one firm occupier
local government offices
college, school or university
cathedral.

► P. J. Robinson, C. W. Faris and Y. Wind, *Industrial Buying and Creative Marketing*, Boston: Allyn and Bacon, 1967.

In the same way that there are models of the consumer decision-making process there also models of the industrial buying behaviour process. Robinson (1967), identified eight buying phases in the industrial buying process:

- problem recognition
- general need description
- product specification
- supplier search
- proposal solicitation
- supplier selection
- order-routine specification
- performance review.

► Organizational buyer behaviour is a complex process. While the job of buyer may exist in a firm there may be many people concerned in the purchase decisions. Marketers have to identify the various roles played and then influence the various actors in the decision-making process.

The model fits well where a product or service is being bought for the first time, but appears to be less applicable in other situations.

CHAPTER SUMMARY

1 The consumer market is extremely complex. It can be divided into segments in an almost infinite number of ways by classifying people according to social class, age, sex, ethnicity, marital status, life style, reference groups and so on, but the objective for the marketer is to find the best way of identifying the market segment for a particular product.

2 The motivations of consumers are equally complex and different kinds of psychology offer different theories of motivation. The marketer is interested in identifying kinds of motive which prompt someone to buy a particular product rather than in the general psychological theory of motivation.

3 The messages that marketers send to consumers are rarely received directly. People only attend selectively , interpret messages in the light of their previous experience and existing ideas and have very selective memories.

4 It is important for the marketer to understand that purchasing decisions are made by people in a social context. Many purchasing decisions are made as part of everyday routines which are difficult to change. Others are made subject to a wide variety of influences from other people. Understanding the context in which consumer decisions are made is a key to successful marketing.

5 Industrial buying decisions are also complex. There are many similarities and there are also differences. The decision making unit of a buying organization consists of people who play different roles in the process. The roles are those of : user, influencer, buyer, decider, approver and gatekeeper. The industrial marketer has to identify these people and their roles when trying to market goods or services to an organization. The buying process comprises eight stages which are similar to those encountered in consumer goods marketing.

► Now that you have reached the end of the chapter, turn back to the objectives and make sure you have achieved each of them.

8 *Market segmentation*

Chapter objectives

By the end of this chapter you should:

▌ know the procedure by which firms set about identifying market segments

▌ be able to describe the various bases for segmenting consumer markets – in particular family life cycle segmentation; life style segmentation

▌ be able to describe the various underlying principles used for segmenting industrial markets – in particular the use of the Standard Industrial Classification system

▌ know how firms set about picking target markets and how they approach them

▌ know how consumer goods marketers can target markets with the aid of the ACORN system of social classification

▌ be able to describe how segment synergies can be achieved through selecting specific combinations of market segments

▌ be familiar with the following terms used by marketers: market segmentation, niching, positioning, segmentation variables, life-style segmentation, family life cycle segmentation, Standard Industrial Classification (SIC), market targeting, ACORN system, segment synergies.

Introduction

A **market segment** is a part or section of the market. It possesses one or more unique characteristics which set it apart and distinguish it from other segments. Market segmentation involves dividing the market into a number of distinct segments according to some specific criteria which reflect different purchasing wants and needs. The purpose of segmentation is to make it possible for firms to produce products or services that fit more closely with people's requirements.

This chapter discusses various approaches to market segmentation and looks at some of the marketing strategy implications of moving into different segments. Markets consist of buyers of products and services and they differ from one another in one or more respects. These differences show themselves in buyer wants, resources, areas in which they live, buying attitudes and buying practices. We can use any one or more of these differences as a basis for segmenting a market. It has to be appreciated, however, that the existence of a group of people with common characteristics does not in itself constitute a market segment. It is only when they have common characteristics as buyers that they form a market segment.

Teenage market segment

Teenagers exist as part of the population but only to the extent that they behave differently to other age groups can one say that there is a teenage market. They are a distinct social group as well as an age group and have their own pattern of buying behaviour and particular brand preference. They exert a strong influence on family buying decisions. Addressing themselves to the special requirements of this segment, marketers have produced such things as compound beauty preparations specifically for adolescent complexions and they also advertise directly to teenagers using copy and commercials phrased in the teenagers' own language.

NATURE OF SEGMENTATION

If we consider the consumer goods markets then it is quite possible to conceive that every individual consumer has slightly different wants and needs as far as a product is concerned. Every consumer could in fact constitute a market segment. It is clearly not possible for any producer of consumer goods to cater for individual wants and needs. It is however possible to identify general classes of buyers who differ only slightly in their product requirements. The task is to identify those broad classes of similar requirements and to identify the common characteristics of people who share them. Products or services can then be offered which meet the wants of the identified segments. Marketing communications relating to the products or services can then be directed through suitable media to appeal to people possessing the identified characteristics.

► British Caledonian knew it could not compete across the board against the major airlines, nor could it hope to win on hardware. It identified special features of the business traveller segment and pieced together a package which would make the airline distinctive and appealing to that type of passenger.

 Take a varied group of people (say ten) and for each of the following products/services identify characteristics which appear to differentiate between them in terms of their purchase behaviour:

- holidays
- shoes
- breakfast food

- soft drink purchases
- pens

Segmentation and strategy

Modern marketing strategy employs three principles:

1 Segment the market
2 Target the users
3 Position the products

Market segmentation involves identifying characteristics which distinguish between customers according to their buying preferences. Profiles of market segments which reflect different combinations of these characteristics are then developed.

Market targeting involves assessing the financial attractiveness of every segment and then selecting target segments. Selection takes account of the relative financial attractiveness of the segments and the organization's ability to exploit them.

The term **positioning** applies to placing products in a part of the market where they will fare well in comparison with competing products. Markets consist of people with different wants and needs and it is unlikely that any organization can offer a single brand which will meet the requirements of the entire market. Marketing strategy should aim to match a product with that segment of the market where it is most likely to succeed. Product positioning involves identifying possible positions for products or services within each target segment and then producing, adapting and marketing products and services towards the target markets. The topic of positioning products is discussed in detail in the chapter on product decisions.

Bearing in mind that different consumer groups have different sets of preferences, it is possible to produce a product or service to meet the specific needs of an identified market segment. This can result in a demonstrable competitive advantage for an organization's product or service in relation to those offered by its competitors. Of course market segments must be:

► See Chapter 11 for product positioning

- clearly identifiable, so that marketing communications can be easily directed at the segment
- big enough to generate the volume of sales and profits that the firm requires.

If preferences within a market are roughly the same, competing products tend to be similar. Where there are distinct clusters of preferences, that is clearly identifiable market segments, then firms tend to do one of two things. Either they produce different brands to meet the requirements of each cluster (providing the number of

Appealing to different cluster with a single brand or appealing to each cluster with a different brand

'Shall we play "Abide with me" every time or shall we try something different outside each pub?'

potential purchasers is large enough) or they produce a brand to appeal to several clusters.

Wherever there are differences in consumer preferences, products, services or brands may be positioned in such a way as to appeal to most of the buyers. This can sometimes lead to dissatisfied customers. An observant competitor may position its offering to the market in such a way as to appeal to those dissatisfied customers.

► Market segmentation recognizes that there are groups of buyers who have similar buying requirements and that the preferences of individual groups may be sufficiently different from one another to warrant a separate product or service offering.

Can the market be segmented for all products?

Homogeneous products are ones which are roughly the same in terms of their physical appearance and functions. This makes it difficult for a marketer to create a distinction between his/her product and that which the competition is offering. Marketers, therefore, have to differentiate, if at all possible, in terms of benefits which are not immediately apparent. Salt is a commodity and is considered to be a homogeneous product. However market segmentation exists even for this product. All consumers require salt but they do not all need exactly the same product. The informed producer recognizes that some geographic regions require iodised salt because of the absence of iodine or other elements in the environment. Salt is also packaged to meet different consumer needs.

PROCEDURE FOR IDENTIFYING MARKET SEGMENTS

There are three stages:

1 Survey stage

Here researchers conduct informal interviews with groups of consumers to find out about their motives, attitudes and behaviour. Based on this preliminary research, researchers then collect further data by means of a formal questionnaire served on a sample of consumers. The information sought includes:

- the importance and ratings people give to certain attributes of the product
- the extent to which people are aware of the existence of different brands of the product
- if brand awareness exists, how people rate different brands
- how, when and where and by whom the product is used
- attitudes towards the product category
- demographic, psychographic and mediagraphic profiles of the consumers.

2 Analysis stage

There is a range of statistical methods which can be used to analyse the data in order to categorize the segments based on the identified characteristics.

3 Profiling stage

Each segment is profiled with respect to its distinguishing attitudes, behaviour demographics, psychographics and media consumption habits. Segment characteristics and make-up vary over time so the procedures have to be periodically carried out again.

▶ The techniques are cluster analysis and factor analysis. The manual for SPSSPC provides illustrative material.

Bases for segmenting consumer markets

In consumer markets the segmentation variables fall into two broad groupings. The first group comprises the geographic and demographic characteristics of the consumer and the second group comprises psychographic and behavioural characteristics. These are illustrated in the inset on page 127.

It is important also to note that companies usually employ more than one basis for segmenting a market. Many companies use geographic segmentation. Firms can easily identify their market segments on this basis and select the ones that they prefer.

In the case of **demographic segmentation** it has to be remembered that age and life cycle ideas can be difficult to make use of effectively. This is because, for example, there are forty year-olds

Market segmentation variables in consumer markets

Group 1

Geographic

Area of a country – South East England, Bavaria, Ardennes, Normandy, etc.

The population size of the area – under 10,000, 10,000–20,000, etc.

The predominant make-up of the area – urban, rural.

The climate – hot and dry, hot and wet, mild, cold, etc.

Demographic

Age – under 15, 15-24, etc.

Sex – male, female

Family size 1-2, 3-4, etc.

Income – under £4000, £4,000–9,000, etc.

Occupation – skilled work people, executives, retired people, etc.

Education – highest grade school, 6th form college, FE college, college of HE, polytechnic, university, etc.

Religion – Muslim, Hindu, Christian, etc.

Race – Afro-Caribbean, Asian, European, etc.

Nationality – French, German, Italian, etc.

Group 2

Psychographic

Social Class – A, B, C1, C2, D, E.

Life-style – outdoors, party-goer.

Personality – ambitious, retiring.

Behavioural

Occasions – regular, special

Benefits – quality, service, economy

User status – Non-user, ex-user, potential user, first timer, regular

Usage rate – light, medium, heavy

Loyalty status – none, medium, strong

Readiness stage – unaware, aware, informed

Attitude toward product – hostile, negative, indifferent, positive, enthusiastic

► Segmentation by sex is commonly used with products such as clothes, cosmetics, magazines, cars, and even cigarettes. Income segmentation is also used with such product categories as clothes, cosmetics and cars. Nationality segmentation can be important for firms that export their goods, or for companies in multi-racial countries, since different nationalities have different habits, religions, traditions and cultures.

with children at sixth form college or even at university, there are forty year-olds with children still at the nursery stage and there are forty year-olds who may even be grandparents!

Income may be a good predictor of what people can afford but people vary widely in their needs and wants. A bank clerk earning £12,000 a year may not have a car but may wear a Rolex watch. A university lecturer earning £24,000 a year might run a five year-old car worth less than £2,000 and yet own an up-to-date £4,000 micro-computer.

Targeting the needs of a particular segment

In November 1991 the French dairy producer Bongrain launched an innovative new fromage frais on the UK market. The new chilled deserts come in oyster-like packs. Once opened the fromage frais slides easily into the mouth. It was aimed specifically at children.

► Joseph T. Plummer, 'Applications of life style research to the creation of advertising campaigns', in *Life Style and Psychographics*. William Wells (ed.) Chicago: AMA 1974, p. 160.

Psychographic segmentation involves dividing buyers into different groups based on their social class, life style and/or personality characteristics. Life style and personality represent the two most modern approaches to market segmentation and are methods that are growing in popularity. Manufacturers try to endow a product with characteristics that correspond to a group of consumers' self-perceptions.

► Hertz was generally seen as providing all things for all people in the car-hire business. It discovered the disadvantages of such a commodity approach and moved to rifle-shot segmentation with its specially tailored business class and American vacation visitor packages. The features of each packet were developed as a result of deep research into the life style and special needs of the two customer segments.

Life-style segmentation

Joseph T. Plummer (1974) suggested that there are four different dimensions to life style and under each heading he suggested a number of attributes which relate to them. A selection is shown below.

Activities	Interests	Opinions	Demographics
sports	family	themselves	age
hobbies	home	social issues	education
work	job	politics	income
holidays	community	business	occupation
community	recreation	economics	family size
shopping	fashion	education	dwelling
entertainment	food	products	geographic

When carrying out segmentation using this method, the analysis requires that consumers are clustered according to common activities, interests and opinions. The market has to be measured along the relevant activities interests and opinions to uncover a homogeneous and sufficiently large life-style segment that will respond to a specific marketing programme.

Marketing strategies employing behavioural segmentation methods include marketing a product specifically to a segment that is celebrating an occasion. Examples might be going on holiday, having a wedding, celebrating a birthday or events to do with Christmas or Easter. The kissogram service and its associated offerings are a case in point.

Using the benefits people expect from a product is another way of segmenting the market. The wristwatch industry illustrates this point. Under-water diving watches, sports watches with stop-watch facilities, fashion watches with ornate dials to be worn for party going, etc. are examples of this.

We have also to acknowledge that people who are heavy users of certain products, for example, beer, often have other similar habits in common. This may include the type of television programme they watch or the newspaper they choose to read. Armed with this knowledge the seller can devise specific marketing strategies aimed at such market segments.

► The market for toothpaste can be segmented on the basis of benefits. There are those who are interested in decay prevention, those who are concerned about appearance (bright teeth) and those who are concerned about stopping bad breath.

Segmentation according to stage in the family life cycle

The idea of market segmentation by stage in the family life cycle was pioneered and developed by the Survey Research Centre of the University of Michigan. Customers have different needs at each stage in the life cycle. Newly married couples, for example, are especially large buyers of furniture and household goods. Families with young children are very good customers for labour saving devices. Families with teenage daughters spend sizeable amounts of money on girls' and women's clothing.

► Details of the stages in the family life cycle are to be found in Chapter 7.

 Suggest bases for segmenting the market for the following consumer products/services:

canned peas	breakfast cereals
bicycles	gents watches
theatre seats	handbags
women's shoes	umbrellas
men's shoes	writing paper
airline seats	tumble driers
holidays	pepper
dry cleaning	toilet rolls
life assurance	newspapers
novels	breakfast cereals

► There are numerous bases for segmenting consumer goods' markets, for example, usage rate. The most appropriate bases are influenced by the nature of the product.

SEGMENTATION IN INDUSTRIAL MARKETS

Like consumer markets, industrial markets can be segmented on demographic grounds. Demography in this case refers to such factors as:

● the industries that would be able to use the product or service
● the size of company likely to use the product.

The geographical location of the users can also be used as a basis for segmenting the market.

Segmentation by industry using the Standard Industrial Classification

► SIC classifications can be found in the KOMPASS directory of firms.

One of the most useful ways of segmenting industrial markets is to make use of the **Standard Industrial Classification** system (SIC). All places of business are classified into one of ten divisions covering the entire range of economic activity. These are:

1   Agriculture, forestry and fisheries
2   Mining
3   Construction
4   Manufacturing
5   Transportation, communication, electricity, gas and sanitary services
6   Wholesale and retail trade
7   Finance, insurance and real estate
8   Services
9   Government
10   All others

Each of the major divisions is broken down into several major groups such as printing and publishing or chemicals and allied products, with each major group having a two digit SIC number assigned to it. Still further classification is achieved through three and four digit numbers. Thus, by using the SIC system the industrial market can be divided into relatively small, medium, or large market segments.

An example of SIC	
SIC code	description
25	Furniture and fixtures
251	Manufacturers of household furniture
2514	Manufacturers of metal household furniture

We can also distinguish between whether a product is to be (1) supplied as a part or sub-assembly to other manufacturers to be incorporated into a finished product, for example, brake linings for new cars, or (2), supplied for maintenance or repair purposes, for example, brake linings for the DIY motorist.

Segmentation by size of company

Large users of a product buy in a different manner to small users of the same product.

Large buyers often:

- buy direct from the manufacturer
- buy from several different suppliers and have definite policies regarding their purchase patterns from these suppliers, i.e. they specify that they always have to deal with at least three suppliers for example
- make use of competitive bidding in order to obtain low prices from suppliers. That means that firms which can act as suppliers are invited to 'tender' – make a bid – for a contract. In the bid they say exactly what they can supply and how much it will cost. The lowest bid is usually the successful one but quality of the product also is taken into account
- have the technical expertise to measure and to evaluate differences in product performance. That is they can readily assess the quality of goods supplied and cannot easily be 'short-changed'.
- evaluate the supplier in terms of its ability to exercise quality control on the products it supplies, delivery punctuality, and level of technical service.

Small buyers often:

- buy from distributors rather than direct from producers
- may even buy from retail type establishments, for example, DIY stores
- will pay higher prices
- rely on supplier/producer for technical support and product education.

The difference between large and small firms in terms of their buying habits enables them to be considered as different market segments.

Geographic segmentation

There are often differences in how regional markets buy and how they should be approached.

Other ways of segmenting the market

These include:

- operating variables – reflecting the customer technologies employed and the firm's usage rate
- purchasing approaches – reflecting the different methods and criteria of purchasing employed by the firm, for example centralized versus decentralized purchasing
- situational factors – reflecting speed of service required, size of orders, and specific versus specialized service provided

- personal characteristics – reflecting such things as loyalty to a supplier, attitude towards risk, and whether the segment companies share the same values as the supplier company
- channel segmentation – reflecting the sales and distribution channels through which the end-user is reached
- market life cycle segmentation – reflecting different stages in the technology life cycle of a product or service.

 Suggest bases (for example, by industry) of segmenting the market for the following industrial products/services:

lathes	computers
nuts and bolts	staff recruitment services
aluminium ingots	office furniture
drive belts	overalls
mechanical diggers	industrial paint
fork lift trucks	lorries

► As with consumer goods, there are various bases upon which markets can be segmented. The Standard Industrial Classification system is a popular method.

TARGETING A MARKET

Market segmentation allows a firm to analyse the market and choose those segments in which it thinks it will be able to operate profitably. In analysing competition one has to identify in which segments the firms market their products and services and the strategies they employ to keep these products buoyant.

A company has to answer two important targeting questions:

- which are the best market segments for the firm?
- how many segments to cover?

Strategy and market segments

Expanding market segments would seem to be the most appealing option open to firms. Firms must take account of their resources and objectives when selecting segments in which to place products or services. The fit between the market needs and the company's capabilities is important.

A firm may decide that it will position its product or service within a single market segment. Few resources, or a lack of a competitor in the market segment, may make this strategy attractive to the firm.

By doing this firms have been able to develop a strong market position through gaining an in-depth knowledge of the segment's needs over a long period of time – the effects of the 'experience curve'. Such firms also enjoy operating economies obtained through specialization. The strategy is risky because if the market

► Rolex and Rolls Royce have products in the high price market segment.

suddenly turns down or a strong competitor forces an entry, sales and then profits can be drastically reduced.

A less risky strategy involves looking for a match between a firm's capabilities and the demands of several different segments. In so doing the firm spreads the risk so that if one segment starts to become unprofitable there are still others that can bring in cash for the firm.

A firm may concentrate on producing one product or service which it supplies to several different customer groups. In pursuing this strategy a firm is able to build a good reputation in the area of the specific product. Such a strategy also has its risks since it is concentrating on a single product or service. Another strategy is to concentrate on serving the needs of a particular group of customers. This can involve providing many different products or services. Again the strategy is risky since a downturn in the fortunes of the particular group of customers could end in disaster for the firm.

In many instances large firms are able to give full market coverage and serve all customer groups with all products that they need and want. There are two variants of the strategy. The first is referred to as **undifferentiated marketing** which means that firms disregard the possibility that there are segment differences and pursue the whole of the market with one offering. The offering and the marketing programme must appeal to the broadest number of buyers and therefore it relies on mass distribution and mass advertising. The other strategy is called **differentiated marketing** and is where a firm operates in most segments of the market but puts together tailor-made approaches for each significantly different segment.

Targeting and the ACORN system

ACORN is an acronym for A Classification of Residential Neighbourhoods which divides units of 150 addresses throughout Great Britain into 38 different types of residential neighbourhood. Addresses are divided on the basis of demographic, housing and socio-economic characteristics. It provides a basis for consumer targeting and makes it possible for targeters to use individual customer lists and market research survey data to identify the types of neighbourhood with the heaviest consumption of a particular product or service. This makes it easy to have accurate targeting of retail and product distribution, product promotion and advertising on specific geographical demographic customer segments.

Many UK companies have large customer databases and from the postcode of any address, the producers of ACORN, CACI, can categorize a customer according to his or her ACORN classification. A company can then take a sample of its own customers and discover which of its ACORN categories are its most valuable in terms of sales. From its records it can then determine what the

► The experience curve is discussed in Chapter 5.

► Small firms may choose to operate in one or a small number of specialist segments. Large firms may choose to operate in all of the large volume/value segments.

▶ The ACORN classification system can aid targeting in consumer markets.

people in different categories buy, how much they spend per head, etc. On the basis of this information messages and direct mailshots can be selectively targeted on those categories which are the companies best customers.

Selected ACORN types and groups

Group
C   Older housing of intermediate status
Type
C 8   Mixed owner occupied and council estates
C 9   Small town centres and flats above shops
C 10   Villages with non-farm employment
C 11   Older private housing, skilled workers

Group
J   Affluent Suburban Housing
Type
J 33   Inter-war semis, white collar workers
J 34   Spacious inter-war semis, big gardens
J 35   Villages with wealthy older communities
J 36   Detached houses, exclusive suburbs

Source: from CACI Market Analysis, 1989.

Segment synergies

If a firm decides to serve more than one segment it should give close attention to synergies between segments with respect to cost, performance and technology. Two or more segments might provide just the opportunity for exploitation because they share common distribution channels, manufacturing facilities, etc. The joint effect of marketing to all segments creates synergy. That is, the overall effect of marketing to two or more segments is to produce greater sales and profits than if each segment had been exploited one at a time in complete isolation from the others.

Take one fast moving consumer product, for example, ice-cream. List the various ways in which it is possible to segment the market for it. Choose one basis for segmenting the market. Identify what you consider to be identifiable and sizeable market segments. Identify where synergies might exist from marketing the product to combinations of specific segments.

Segment analysis

Segment analysis should be carried out before entering any new segments. Estimates of sales potential need to be obtained together with expected market share. Consideration has also to be given to the promotional mix that the firm has to employ in order to stimulate sales.

► Methods of measuring market size and forecasting demand in market segments are dealt with in Chapter 9.

 Jim McAlpine retired as a racing driver in 1991. A winner of many a Grand Prix, and world champion on several occasions, Jim had become a multi-millionaire. His main hobby was flying and on retirement in 1991 he founded the McAlpine Airway Company.

He began operating a shuttle service from Edinburgh to Oslo in the knowledge that there were many Norwegian students in Edinburgh who would welcome a relatively cheap and regular service. After two months of profitable operation one of the larger airway companies started to run a similar service and undercut McAlpine on price to such an extent that he felt he might have to withdraw from the market altogether.

Do you think that McAlpine adopted the right or the wrong market segmentation strategy? What should he do now?

Segment invasion strategy

Having selected segments to enter, the final strategic decision concerns the method of 'invading' the segments. The question is should a firm try to invade all segments at once or should it 'pick them off' one at a time? Much depends on the resources that the firm has at its disposal. Taking the military analogy, an army is more likely to concentrate its efforts on one strategic objective at a time, thereby ensuring that resources are not too thinly spread. Assuming that a firm intends to move into all segments which it has selected and which together possess synergy it is more prudent to enter one segment at a time and to conceal the overall plan.

► It is more productive to market goods to selective market segments where synergy can be achieved. In addition moving into one segment at a time is more effective than entering them all at the same time.

► Now that you have reached the end of the chapter, turn back to the objectives and make sure you have achieved each of them.

CHAPTER SUMMARY

1 Modern marketing strategy involves segmenting the market, targeting the users, positioning the products or services. The process involves undertaking a survey of the market to determine identifiable and discriminating customer characteristics, analysing the data collected by statistical procedures and identifying and profiling individual market segments according to distinguishing customer characteristics.

2 There are various bases along which markets can be segmented. In the case of consumer goods, family life cycle segmentation and life style segmentation are becoming increasingly popular options. In the case of industrial goods, the Standard Industrial Classification (SIC) system is commonly used.

3 Firms have to systematically set about identifying and measuring market segments and then decide which are the best market segments to cover and how many segments to cover. In consumer goods markets the ACORN classification system is a useful aid to targeting.

4 Segment synergies can be achieved through selecting specific combinations of segments. The approach to moving into different market segments should be a gradual one.

9 Market measurement and forecasting

Chapter objectives

By the end of this chapter you should:

▌ know how marketers decide what aspects of products and markets they want to measure and forecast

▌ be aware of the key sources of information which can be consulted in order to aid the process of market measurement

▌ be able to describe both objective and subjective approaches to forecasting

▌ be familiar with the following terms as used by marketers: potential market, available market, served market, penetrated market, total market demand, regional market demand, environmental forecast, industry forecast, company sales forecast, black box approach, cycle, trend, seasonal effect, erratic variation, time series forecasting, exponential smoothing, statistical demand analysis, curve fitting.

Introduction

Marketing plans can only be prepared and delivered well if the size of current and future markets is carefully measured and estimated. Such information is a useful starting point from which to determine which markets to enter and how to budget resources among markets.

DEFINING MARKET DEMAND

Defining what to measure and estimate is not quite as straightforward as it might seem. Demand can be measured at several different levels:

- **product levels** – product item sales, product form sales, product line sales, company sales, industry sales, national sales
- **space levels** – sales to individual customers, sales by territory – area, or country – world sales
- **time levels** – short-range, medium-range, long-range sales.

Choosing exactly which level or levels to measure and forecast is an important first step. The situation is further complicated by another factor. There are **penetrated markets**, **potential markets**,

available markets and **served markets**. To get some idea of the implication of this let us begin by assuming that a market comprises all those people who actually buy a product or service or who have the interest, money and opportunity to buy it.

A market comprises all those who have the interest, money and opportunity to buy

'So what if we don't have any money. Let's ask him to buy us a drink.'

The penetrated market

There are a number of different ways to establish the current number of users of the product or service and the sales volume they generate. This is the **penetrated market**. There may be figures readily available which indicate this or it may be necessary to establish it by a sample survey. Alternatively we can use the **chain ratio method** illustrated in the inset on page 139.

The potential market

The penetrated market leaves out those people who have an interest in buying the product or service, but who currently do not do so, for one reason or another. These latter people are important since in looking at future demand they provide a measure of the **potential** demand in the market.

We could ascertain the number of these people and their likely demand by conducting a survey and asking people who do not already use the product or service whether they would have a strong interest in using it. This would provide an idea of the size of the **potential market**. However, customers must be able to afford the product or service, so in the survey we must establish

> ### A way of estimating the penetrated market
> Market penetration can be estimated by a method known as the chain ratio method. An example will illustrate what is involved:
>
> Demand for crisps = Population
> x per capita discretionary income (pcdi)
> x average per cent of pcdi spent on food
> x average per cent of spending on food spent on snacks
> x estimated per cent of spending on snacks spent on crisps
>
> We can see that the method involves multiplying a base number by several adjusting percentages. Some of the figures, such as per capita discretionary income (pcdi), can be obtained from puplished government sources. Other data has to be estimated either from published information sources or from data bought from market research firms.

whether people can afford to purchase it. This will redefine the market size.

The available market
Opportunity to use product or service also cuts down on the size of the market. If it is not possible to use a product then this will obviously restrict the market size. Taking this into account will define the **available market**. For example, in certain areas of the north of Scotland television reception is so poor that it is not possible to operate battery operated portable TV sets. This clearly excludes the demand for such a product in those areas.

The served or target market
A company has only limited resources at its disposal and so selects certain market segments where it feel that it has the capacity to compete effectively and where the market size is sufficiently attractive. This becomes the **served** or the **target market.**

 What information would be required to estimate the penetrated market for chocolate covered gingerbread men?

Demand in regional markets

Because of limited resources, a firm may only be able to serve a number of geographic market segments. It needs to have information on the penetrated market, the potential market and the available market in individual areas.

Is there an available market for cars?

'No Mr Jones, I'm afraid I can't consider becoming a distributor for your cars.'

► The first step is to define the market one wants to measure and then measure the market demand.

Defining the market
Penetrated market – those using the product already
Potential market – those who might be interested in using the product and can afford to do so but who are not already doing so
Available market – those among the potential market who have the opportunity to use the product

The **total market** may be defined as:
the penetrated market + the available market
BUT the firm has only limited resources so it becomes redefined as:
Served or **target market** – those to whom the firm has the resources to make the product available

---

Consumer goods

A manufacturer of cakes, for example, might assume that the penetrated market is directly related to the size of the population. For example, if the population of Scotland is eight per cent of the population of the United Kingdom, the manufacturer might reasonably assume that there would be a market for eight per cent of the cakes sold in the UK in Scotland. A single factor, however, is seldom a complete guide to sales potential: per capita income and number of distribution outlets are also influential factors. The manufacturer could develop an index of purchasing power based upon the three factors (or even more, if it would produce more accurate estimates).

Industrial goods

Industrial goods producers may be able to approach the problem by identifying all the buyers of the product in an area and estimating what they buy. A good way to make an estimation involves using the SIC (Standard Industrial Classification system) to identify those firms which are likely to be users of the product. If the firm is not clear whether other firms are likely to be users of its product then it can find this out through a postal survey.

One way to assess the potential market is to relate sales of the firm's products to those of its customers. For example, a producer of tubular frames may find that it sells six tons of tubular framing p.a. to manufacturers of metal framed furniture (SIC2514) for every £100,000 p.a. sales turnover of its present customer base. Assume that in a known region there are five such firms operating, none of whom are current customers of the producer of tubular frames. Imagine that the combined sales of the furniture manufacturers amounts to £10 million p.a. then the market potential can be estimated as:

► See Chapter 8 on segmentation

► See Chapter 8 page 130.

Deriving the size of the penetrated market by an index method

A cake manufacturer

We make use of the equation
$$Bc = W_1I + W_2O + 0.3P$$
Where

Bc	=	regional buying power for cakes
W_1	=	a weighting factor
I	=	% of national disposable income in the region
O	=	% of national retail sales in the region
P	=	% of the country's population in the region

Note: sum of the weights adds up to 1

Using the index method, the estimate of the percentage of cakes sold in Scotland might be as follows:

$$0.4(7.3) + 0.3(6.5) + 0.3(8.0) = 7.27\%$$

Where 0.4, 0.3 and 0.3 are the chosen weights and 7.3, 6.5 and 8 are the estimated values for I, O and P. Values for I, O and P can be obtained from a variety of HMSO publications based on census data. The weights themselves are somewhat arbitrary – we may choose to give equal weighting to the variables. In addition other weights can be used if is thought they are more appropriate. Other factors too, such as the strength of competition, may cause a revision in the estimate.

$$\frac{10,000,000}{100,000} \times 6 = 600 \text{ tons p.a.}$$

The exercise has to be repeated for other SIC groups and regions.

Aluminium ingots
A firm produces aluminium ingots. Ingots are supplied to other firms which turn them into other intermediate products which can be used for further processing.

Use the SIC to identify possible industry users of aluminium ingots. Next, look up the potential users within the industry in a directory such as *Kompass* which you will find in the reference section of any good commercial library. Note that there are *Kompass* directories for different countries, so keep to the UK directory.

Make a list of potential users and their respective sales turnovers for one particular region or area of the country.

What other information would you need to estimate market demand for aluminium ingots?

▶ Since most organizations operate on a regional basis one has to predict the regional demand for goods and services.

Actual industry sales and market share

► Market share estimates may be available from trade association data. Otherwise it may only be possible to obtain such estimates from surveys.

Getting an estimate of actual sales and market share means that a firm has to find out who its competitors are and how much they are selling. Industry trade associations are a good source of information and enable firms to assess their relative standing in relationship to the industry. Every member of the association provides details of its own sales figures to the association which then in turn provides aggregated statistics for the members. This works well where most sales are made by members of the association.

There are other ways of acquiring this information. Market research companies collect data on brand sales of consumer goods through retail audits. They then make this information available to companies for a fee.

PREDICTING FUTURE DEMAND

In making forecasts we assume that what has happened in the past will continue to happen in the future. Thus if consumption patterns by age of consumers are known to be stable across time we assume that the stability will remain in the future. If there is a trend in such consumption patterns, for example a five per cent increase on average each year, then we take account of this trend in making projections, bearing in mind that the trend may eventually decrease or increase or ultimately flatten out. The difficulty is in forecasting when flattening out will happen. We will explore some of these points later in this chapter.

There are government publications in the UK together with a large number privately funded sources of information which enable us to gain a numerical estimate, and hence the growth history of many products sold to the UK market. Similar figures may be available for other countries but a good deal of research has to be undertaken to glean this information.

When there is no data available

Sometimes, there is no data available, for example when estimating the initial and long-term market sizes for new products, or where data is scant on existing products or services. In such a case we have to estimate the size of the initial market, its long-term potential and the growth pattern that the market is likely to exhibit as it moves towards its ultimate size. For example, assume we are trying to estimate the potential market demand for a robot which will help us around the house and in the garden, with many of the chores which we find irksome. We might firstly, identify what level of household incomes are likely to be interested in such a product (presumably higher household incomes, if the product is likely to be expensive). Then secondly, assume a given percentage of interest in buying the product based on past experience with other labour saving devices.

Some UK sources of information on market size and growth history of products and services

- *Market Intelligence* (Monthly), Mintel Publications
- *Retail Intelligence* (Monthly), Mintel Publications
- *Home, Office, Leisure Market Assessment* (fortnightly) BLA Management Services Group
- Keynote Publications Ltd, London
- *Retail Business* (Monthly), Economist Intelligence Unit, London
- Euromonitor Publications Ltd, London
- Business Services Ltd, Dorking
- *Nielsen Market Information Manual*, A C Nielsen, Oxford
- *Nielsen Researcher* (Quarterly), A C Nielsen, Oxford
- *The Food and Drink Forecast* (Quarterly), The Food and Drink Industries Forecasting Group
- *Family Expenditure Survey*, HMSO
- *The General Household Survey*, HMSO
- *Business Monitor*, Department of Industry and Business Statistics Office
- Attwood Statistics, Berkhampstead
- Audits of Great Britain Ltd
- British Market Research Bureau Ltd, London
- Trade associations.

▶ Past history of industry sales is important when it comes to forecasting. We can go to a variety of published information sources to try to obtain relevant data.

Number of dwellings in the country	23,000,000
% in which income > £30,000 p.a.	10%
Potential number of households	2,300,000
Potential sales (60% penetration)	1,380,000 robots

This is a light-hearted example but the same kind of approach will apply whatever the situation. For example, a firm introducing a new kind of machine tool might first identify the different kinds of buyer for its product in a region or country. The market might consist of manufacturing/engineering firms performing the particular kind of operation that the machine tool is designed to do. A sample survey of identified potential users would elicit the following information:

- whether or not the firms saw any applications for the new machine tools
- in what quantities they could use such a machine over various time horizons
- given that they could use such a machine whether or not companies would be interested to buy such a product – in what quantities and when.

All products have been new products at one time or other. Take five of the following products and suggest how the firms that launched the very first products of their kind might have estimated the potential market and the available market for the product:

dishwashers	home computers
colour televisions	sewing machines
video recorders	video cameras
loft insulation	sailing boats
cavity wall insulation	caravans
double glazed windows	electric hairdryers

► When no sales data is readily available firms have to estimate market size, trends and future demands. This may involve looking at sales histories of similar products and undertaking surveys to ascertain the nature of future demand.

FORECASTING METHODS

Good forecasting is a key component of business success. A company's production schedules, planned manning levels and financial budgeting are all related to the **sales forecast** that is made. An over-optimistic forecast can lead to excess stocks being accumulated, over-production and too-high manning levels, as well as over-borrowing or inefficient deployment of financial resources. An over-pessimistic forecast can lead to large **opportunity costs** and frustration amongst potential buyers if delivery is late or not forthcoming.

Firms adopt a variety of approaches to obtain a sales forecast but the basic approach is to:

► Opportunity costs arise when any investment decision is made. They represent the income that could have been obtained from investing the same amount of resources in the best alternative project.

1 Make an **environmental** forecast regarding: inflation, unemployment, interest rates, consumer spending and saving, business investment, etc.
2 Make a forecast of sales and profits to be earned by the industry using the data in (1) together with other information which links industry figures to environmental trends.
3 Make a **company sales forecast** using the data in (2) and assuming a given market share.

► Sometimes market share is not known because insufficient data on market size is available. In such cases sales forecasts will be based on how patterns in the company sales have varied relative to changes in environmental conditions.

Basically, there are two ways of forecasting sales for established products. On the one hand there are the methods which rely on asking questions of people and on the other hand there are those which involve the analysis of historical data.

Asking people questions
This applies to forecasting changes in environmental factors, industry sales and company sales.

Surveys of buyers' intentions
There are a number of research organizations which conduct periodic surveys of buying intentions.

The following provides an illustration of the kinds of questions that might be asked by a researcher looking at the market for

---

A builder's forecast of sales for houses

A builder knows from past experience that unemployment trends have an impact on his ability to sell houses. For every one per cent rise in the rate of unemployment he knows that industry sales will fall by five per cent. The firm's share of the national housing market has been consistently twenty-five to twenty-seven per cent over the past decade.

Industry sales in the current year amounted to 132,000 new homes. The latest government figures estimate that unemployment will rise by two per cent in the next twelve months.

The builder estimates that this means a 2 x 5 per cent = 10 per cent drop in industry sales next year to 132,000–13,200 = 118,800. He reckons that he will hold his market share at twenty-five per cent thus giving him 118,800 x 25 per cent = 29,700 houses to build.

---

major consumer durables (cookers, refrigeratrors, washing machines, etc.):

Do you intend to buy a refrigerator in the next six months?

Please tick one of the following categories:

No chance   [ ]
Slight possibility   [ ]
Fair possibility   [ ]
Good possibility   [ ]
High probability   [ ]
Certain   [ ]

The research organization then attaches a probability of purchase to each of the categories:

No chance   = 0
Slight possibility = 0.2
Fair possibility   = 0.4
Good possibility   = 0.6
High probability   = 0.8
Certain   = 1.0

Based on the results of regular sample surveys such firms are then able to make predictions of the likely demand for various items.

The same method can be carried out by a firm itself provided that it has the resources to conduct a survey. It is a good method for producers of industrial plant, machinery and supplies. Some modification to the questions asked is needed to take account of the quantity likely to be purchased. Probability estimates are usually based upon experience. The numbers shown in the example in the inset on page 146 might be considered to be reasonable estimates.

► Of course, such a method is only valuable as long as customers do have clear intentions and are willing to disclose those intentions.

► Surveys of buyers intentions are useful indicators of short-term demand for products and services.

► For more information on this method see: P Kotler, *Marketing Management: Analysis, Planning and Control.* 6 Ed. Prentice Hall. 1988 pp 270-3.

Random sample survey of 5000 people regarding intention to purchase a refrigerator:

		(a) Number of people	(b) Probability	(c) Expected Purchases (a x b)
No chance	[ ]	2200	0.0	0
Slight possibility	[ ]	900	0.2	180
Fair possibility	[ ]	700	0.4	280
Good possibility	[ ]	600	0.6	360
High probability	[ ]	400	0.8	320
Certain	[ ]	200	1.0	200
Total				1340
Percentage of the sample				26.8%

Hence it would forecast that roughly twenty-six point eight per cent of the target market represented by the sample of 5000 would be likely to purchase a refrigerator in the next six months.

At some time you will attend an organized activity, socially, at work or at college. In such a case you usually know in advance all the people who will be invited to the event (they may bring friends as well).

Construct a simple questionnaire similar to the one in the inset above in which you ask people to say how likely it is they will be coming to the event and how many people they are likely to bring with them. Collect in all the questionnaires and use them to make a prediction of how many people are likely to attend.

Make a careful note of how many people actually do attend the event and how this compares with your forecast. Account for any differences between the two.

Composite of sales force opinion
The sales force is in constant contact with the market and is in an excellent position to provide estimates of potential sales demand. In using the estimates of the sales force we have to take into account any bias that may exit. For one reason or another the force may be biased either in the direction of pessimism or optimism. We also have to take into account that the sales force is often comparatively unappreciative of the larger economic factors which may influence sales. Providing one can identify sources of bias and adjust for them in interpreting predictions it is possible to make use of these estimates.

Expert opinion

Another method of forecasting involves getting the opinions of experts. Experts may include dealers, distributors, suppliers, marketing consultants and even trade associations. The government also produces its own forecast for the economy and various European bodies make similar predictions for European countries.

 Everyone is an expert at something

Ask a group of people to estimate what percentage of them would be prepared to attend an event which you are actually organizing (a party, dance, outing, etc.). Get them to write down their answer on a piece of paper and hand it to you. Write down a list of the percentages: 0–9%, 10–19%, 20–29%, etc, and against each one write down the number of people who predicted percentages in this range. This is a **frequency table**. Get them to discuss the assumptions they were making in producing their estimate.

Next ask them if they wish to revise their estimates. Collect in any revised estimates. Use the original estimates plus any revisions to them to obtain a best estimate of the percentage of people who are likely to attend the event.

Compare the estimate with the number who actually attend the event and account for differences between the two figures.

Analysing past data

This applies to environmental forecasts, industry forecasts and company sales forecasts. Here, however, we will comfine our observations to the latter two of these. Many firms base their forecasts on the basis of what they have achieved in the past. This **incrementalist approach** to forecasting offers few opportunities for mistakes except where there are large swings in sales from one year to the next. There are two basic methods, each of which has a number of variants.

Methods which adopt a solely time-dependent approach

The first set of methods is referred to as the **solely time-dependent** approach. Here, it is assumed that sales simply vary as a function of time. The effects of time are divided into:

- a **cycle**: fluctuations every few years (e.g., the effect trade cycles as various major economies in the world are hit by booms and slumps)
- a **trend**: a general upward, downward or static (no trend) pattern (e.g., upward trend of sales of video recorders during the growth phase of the life cycle)
- a **seasonal effect**: systematic variations at certain times of the year (e.g., additional sales of bathing costumes in the summer months)
- **erratic variation**: unpredictable or random variations (e.g., demand interrupted by an industry-wide strike)

▶ Expert opinion can be used in both long-term and short-term forecasting.

Salespersons' opinion

Thompson	1756
Keenan	3664
Jefferies	1432
Clarke	1698
Barry	184...

'Never mind what Keenan says he's going to do. You simply multiply his figures by 3 and divide by 8½.'

▶ Sales force estimates can be used as a basis of short-term forecasts.

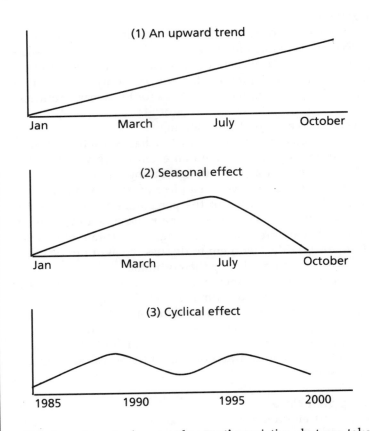

We do not try to forecast the **erratic** variation, but we take it into account when making forecasts and express it as the error attached to the sales forecast. **Erratic** variation comprises such things as strikes, fashions, and other unforeseen circumstances. These factors are unpredictable and need to be removed from past data in order to inspect the other three elements. Clearly, this approach to forecasting has to be used with products where unexplained variation is only small.

The **trend** (1) component comes about as a result of developments in a population, the formation of capital and developments in technology. It is evidenced by a general upward or downward shift in the pattern of sales. If there is no such pattern then there is assumed to be no trend.

The **seasonal** (2) component refers to recurrent sales patterns that may exist within the period of a single year. This will reflect things such as weather, holidays, seasonal buying habits and so on.

The **cycle** (3) depicts the wavelike flow of sales over a number of years and is most useful when examining data for use in intermediate range forecasts (three to seven years). Traditionally, the cycle represents swings in economic activity.

Time series analysis consists of analysing the original sales data into its trend, cyclical, seasonal and erratic components. The series is then recombined to produce a sales forecast.

Time series forecasting

A company sells fish and chips all the year round but sales are highest during the summer months because of the holiday trade. In both July and August sales amount to fifteen per cent of the annual turnover. Sales (in terms of weight of fish and chips sold) last year were ten per cent up on the previous year and twenty per cent up on the year before. The summer weather in both cases was regarded as average or below average. Assuming an average summer, weather-wise, for the coming year, the firm would expect sales to rise by another ten per cent for the year. However, because of a current economic slump in the country there is a general belief in the town that summer visitors may only amount to eighty per cent of the previous year's record breaking total. Last year the firm had a sales turnover of £240,000 equivalent to 180,000 kilos of fish and 360,000 kilos of chips.

The firm is currently trying to work out its purchasing requirements for the coming year and is in the midst of making forecasts. The July and August requirements are of considerable interest and the firm makes its estimates as follows:

Total requirement of Cycle x Season x Trend x Previous year total
(a) fish for
July/ August: 0.8 x .015 x 1.10 x 180,000 = 23,760 kilos
(b) potatoes for
July/August: 0.8 x .015 x 1.10 x 360,000 = 47,520 kilos
for each month.

▶ Time series analysis requires series of past data. It divides data patterns up into trend, seasonal and cyclical patterns and assumes that past patterns (modified by the trend) will be repeated.

Exponential smoothing

This technique assumes no knowledge of industry sales/market share nor presumes the need to forecast sales for many hundreds of items. It applies to forecasting sales of individual product items. **Exponential smoothing** is basically a technique which requires the minimum amount of data and is calculated by means of a simple equation. Many firms produce many hundreds or thousands of products. Notable examples are the firms operating in the pharmaceutical industry. For such firms a simple forecasting technique is required which requires the minimum of data. In its simplest form exponential smoothing requires only three pieces of information:

1 The current period's actual sales Q_t
2 The current period's smoothed sales q_t
3 A smoothing parameter a, a value between 0 and 1

The sales forecast for the next period t+1 is given by the formula:

$$q_{t+1} = aQ_t + (1-a)q_t$$

► Exponential smoothing methods are most often used where there are hundreds or thousands of items to be forecast. They work best where there are no obvious patterns in the data.

Such forecasts are handled by computer which, using an iterative procedure (trial and error), can regularly determine that value of *a* which gives the most satisfactory results in making forecasts. The value is the one which gives the best fit to past sales. Once the system has been set up, all that has to be done is to add new sales figures to the database as and when they occur.

There are a number of more sophisticated variants on this approach, for example, double exponential smoothing, exponential smoothing incorporating seasonal and trend factors, etc.

Statistical demand analysis

The method is suitable for forecasting environmental changes and industry sales but can be used to predict changes in market share. So far, the statistical or mathematical approaches we have considered treat the factors which seem to influence sales as regularly re-occurring phenomena. The difficulty with this approach is that some patterns do not re-appear at regular intervals. For example, while there are economic booms and slumps from time to time their patterns are not so precise as to enable accurate forecasts to be made.

Statistical demand analysis tries to identify the source of all influences on demand so that more accurate forecasts can be made. The basic statistical method to take account of such factors is **multiple regression analysis**. Multiple regression is a statistical tool which can be applied to past data to discover the most important factors influencing sales and their relative influence. Experience seems to indicate that the factors most commonly considered are price, income, population and marketing promotion. The first stage in a regression analysis is to build a causal model in which we try to explain sales in terms of a number of independent variables. For example, we might conjecture that industry sales of umbrellas (S) are related to their relative price (P), personal disposable income (I), relative advertising expenditure (A) and the absolute level of rainfall (R). What we have to do is to estimate the parameters a,b,c and d and apply them to quantifications of P,I,A and R for the period of the forecast. We would express this relationship in the form of an equation:

$$S = aP + bI + cA + dR$$

In principle, demand equations of this variety are acquired by fitting the best equations to historical or cross-sectional data. The coefficients of the equation are estimated according to what is called the 'least squares criteria'. According to this criteria the best equation is the one that minimizes a measure of the error between the actual and the predicted observations. The better the fit the more useful will be the equation for forecasting purposes.

Whilst regression analysis is a popular technique it must be used with care. There must always be an adequate number of observations – in making annual forecasts ten to fifteen years data is not

► Multiple regression analysis is used very widely by economists to analyse economic data. It is a sophisticated tool of analysis and requires computer assistance. There are a variety of different packages that can be used in conjunction with a microcomputer. Lotus 123 (spreadsheet) has a regression feature and a powerful version of the technique is found in SPSSPC.

► Statistical demand analysis tries to account for past data patterns in other ways than trend, seasonal or cyclical factors. It assumes that there are rational explanations for dips and surges in demand and tries to identify the factors which account for them.

unreasonable, where there are four independent variables. Another problem is what seem to be independent variables sometimes turn out to influence each other and are not really independent at all. For example, relative price and relative advertising expenditure may well influence each other, since advertising costs can be reflected in the selling price.

Forecasting sales of new products

To forecast sales of new products one needs some initial sales figures to play with. Given that some early sales data is available it is then generally possible by using other mathematical models or **curve fitting routines** to make some prediction for sales over a specified period of time. Alternatively, it may be possible to look at sales histories of similar new products and make predictions by analogy.

> ► Simulated data can be obtained experimentally by giving shoppers the opportunity to buy the product.

Forecasting sales of new products in retail outlets

Large retail chains often add new lines to their stock. Most of these retailers have benchmarks against which to judge whether a product is likely to be successful or not. A common practice is to offer the product for sale for a limited period in just one of its shops. If the product fails to achieve level of sales within the specified period it is withdrawn from sale and not put on sale in other outlets.

> ► Kotler P. and G. Lilien (1983), *Marketing Decision Making: a model building approach.* New York. Harper and Row

CHAPTER SUMMARY

1 Marketing planning requires the size of current and potential markets to be carefully measured and estimated. A company's production schedules, planned manning levels and financial budgeting are all related to the sales forecast that is made. Inaccurate forecasts have a negative effect on the efficient operation of a company.

2 Firms adopt a variety of approaches to obtain a sales forecast but the basic approach is to:

a Make an environmental forecast
b Make an industry forecast
c Make a company sales forecast, using the data in (b) and assuming a given market share.

3 There are methods which rely on asking people questions and those which involve the statistical analysis of historical data. The sales force and expert opinion are ways of getting subjective estimates about future demand. The other approach relies on statistical analysis of data – time series analysis and regression

analysis are ways of making estimates. For firms producing hundreds or thousands of products, a simple forecasting technique such as exponential smoothing is appropriate. Such forecasts are handled by computer.

► Now that you have reached the end of the chapter, turn back to the objectives and make sure you have achieved each of them.

4 To forecast sales of new products we need some initial sales figures to play with. Given that some early sales data is available it is then generally possible by using mathematical models or curve fitting routines to make predictions for sales over a specified time period. Alternatively, it may be possible to look at sales histories of similar new products and make predictions by analogy.

(10) The life cycle concept & product portifolio models

Chapter objectives

By the end of this chapter you should:

■ be able to understand the concept of the product life cycle

■ know how firms can use the product life cycle concept to analyse products and services

■ understand that firms need to have a balanced product/service portfolio with elements at different stages in the product life cycle to ensure long-term survival and growth

■ know how to use the Boston Consulting Group (BCG) model to assess the health of a firm's product mix and to suggest strategies as well as understanding the limitations of this approach

■ know how to use the GE-McKinsey matrix to assess the health of a firm's product mix and to suggest strategies as well as understanding limitations of this model

■ be familiar with the following terms as used by marketers: product life cycle, product/service portfolio, growth share matrix, Boston Consulting Group (BCG) matrix, stars, cash cows, dogs, problem children, GE-McKinsey matrix.

Introduction

This chapter looks first at the concept of the product life cycle and examines its usefulness as an aid to analysing marketing situations. We then go on to discuss the development and use of portfolio models as aids to understanding how well the firm's products or services are performing. These analytical methods are useful in developing marketing and business strategy.

The fit between strategy and the firm's capabilities

If an organization is to perform well, then the fit between the types of products and services it offers and the resources and other capabilities it can put together has to be good. Organizations are comprised of individual people with special interests. Over time such interests show themselves in the development of specialized skills and become a notable feature of the organization. Eventually, this means that organizations will be in a better position to produce and market one product rather than another. This can lead to an imbalance in the portfolio of product-market offerings of the organization and a change in strategy may be necessary.

First, let us look closely at an important basic idea in marketing that has implications both for the strategy needed to market products and the profitability of the products themselves. The idea is the **product life cycle**.

THE PRODUCT LIFE CYCLE

▶ The product life cycle tries to identify distinct stages in the sales history of a product. Distinct opportunities and problems exist with respect to marketing strategy and profit potential at each of these stages.

There is evidence to show that most products go through recognized stages during the course of their lives. Each stage in the life cycle brings with it environmental threats and opportunities that require changes to be made in marketing strategy. In general, life cycles exhibit the following features:

- products have a finite life span
- the sales history of a product follows a path which can be described by an 'S' shaped curve until finally levelling off. At this point market maturity occurs. When the maturity phase has run its course there then follows a period of decline
- the stages in the life cycle are known as introduction, growth, maturity and decline
- the life cycle of a product may be extended by discovering new uses or new users for the product, or getting present users to increase their consumption
- as the product passes through the various stages in the life cycle the average profitability per unit of the product sold at first increases and then eventually begins to decline.

A graphical representation of the life cycle of a typical successful product appears in the figure below:

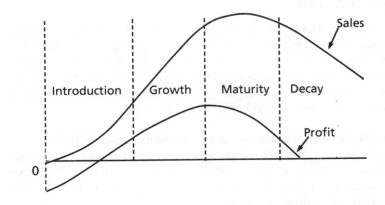

A difficulty encountered in trying to make use of the product life cycle concept is that many products do not appear to act as it suggests. They seem to by-pass some stages while getting stuck in other stages. Moreover, they may even bounce back after a period

The length of the product life cycle

The length of the product life cycle can vary enormously. Steam trains first appeared on the railways in Britain in the early nineteenth century. They were withdrawn from regular service during the 1960s but enthusiasts run them on private railways in the 1990s. Moreover, in some parts of the world steam trains are still in regular service.

The hula hoop had an initial life cycle which lasted a matter of weeks. Interest in it is revived from time to time, even now.

Clothes change fashion with the seasons so they appear to have relatively short life cycles. However, fashions come back in vogue again from time to time and old products are introduced as new ones.

Some fast moving consumer goods products may have relatively short life cycles. Others, such as the Mars Bar, seem to go on forever.

Cinemas appeared to be dying out in the 1960s but revived in the 1980s and now appear set to go on forever in a more contracted and changed form.

of downturn. These observations have brought about criticisms of the product life cycle as a useful concept.

The relationship between sales and profit varies at every stage in the life cycle. In addition, the comparative significance of and interrelationship between price, promotion, distribution and the actual specification of the product itself alter over the life cycle. Product quality is significant during the introductory stage, since failings that become apparent during trial of a product can lead to

Products bounce back

'I think Granddad is enjoying his second childhood!'

buyer rejection. Marketing communications, especially advertising, needs to be enlightening during this period. At a later stage widening distribution or reducing prices may become more important. Besides giving pointers to the most fitting strategies for products or services, the product life cycle concept can assist the firm to take better advantage of the market position of the product or service. It can provide directives for new launches, moves to new markets and the need for diversification.

The product life cycle concept can be used to analyse:

- product category (for example, microcomputers)
- product forms (for example, desk top microcomputers)
- product brand (for example, IBM)

Of these perhaps the most useful application is for product forms.

 Obtain a copy of of one of the popular used car price guides such as *Parkers*. Choose two different makes of car, say Volvo and Ford. What evidence of the product life cycle can you find by studying the product introduction, modification and withdrawal patterns of these two manufacturers?

Why do you think that these two manufacturers exhibit different patterns?

The introductory stage

Profits are low or even negative during the introductory stage. Sales are low and promotion and distribution costs are at their highest in relationship to sales. Throughout this phase firms are often trying to recover research and development expenditure. In addition, extensive advertising is required to secure distribution at the retail level. High margins can provide the cash for heavy promotional expenditure and this in turn produces high initial prices that may discourage rapid adoption of the product by certain customer segments.

Growth stage

This coincides with a more rapid growth in sales. In addition new competitors come on the scene attracted by the prospect of large scale production potential and the large profits to be made as the market grows in size and economies of scales come into operation. Prices and promotional expenditure remain relatively unchanged from the introductory stage, though they may reduce slightly. The amount of money spent on promotion in relationship to the amount sales generated – the promotion to sales ratio – declines. All this produces increased profits as costs are spread over a larger volume and unit manufacturing costs decrease owing to the effects of the experience curve.

The rate of growth eventually slows down as fewer new buyers

▶ Product life cycle consists of: introductory stage, growth stage, maturity stage, decline stage.

▶ This occurs because it is desirable to tell potential customers about the new product and encourage them to try it out.

enter the market for the first time. A firm may employ several strategies to keep up market growth as long as possible. These include:

- improving product quality
- adding new features
- refining styling
- bringing in new models and flanker products
- going into new market segments
- changing the emphasis of advertising from creating product awareness to bringing about conviction and purchase
- reducing the price to bring in price sensitive buyers.

▶ Through such strategies a business will not only strengthen its competitive position but will also increase its costs. The maximization of current profits is relinquished in the expectation of making even greater profits in the next stage. All this means that the firm needs considerable funds to invest up front.

Refer again to the used car price guide suggested above. This time select a different make of car. See what evidence you can find of the manufacturer making any of the following changes over the time period shown in the guide:

- improving product quality
- adding new features
- refining styling
- bringing in new models and flanker products
- going into new market segments
- reducing the price to bring in price sensitive buyers (holding the price steady in the face of inflation has the same effect).

Maturity stage

The stage of maturity follows the decline in the rate of sales growth. The slow down in the rate of sales growth leads to overcapacity in the industry that in turn leads to increased competition.

In the course of the maturity stage firms make frequent price reductions and increase advertising and consumer promotions. Research and development are activated to create product improvements and flanker brands. The weaker competitors may well leave the market but the better established ones prosper. The latter's products generate cash that can be put into products that are at earlier stages in their life cycles.

▶ This assumes that other firms are offering the same product or service

Decline stage

Sales of most products eventually start to decline. There are several reasons for decline, including technological headway, shifts in consumer tastes and increased domestic and foreign competition. Decline leads to overcapacity in the market, price cutting and lower profits. Some firms may withdraw from the market. Those who remain may reduce the number of products that they offer;

give up smaller market segments and weaker trade channels; cut the promotion budget; or reduce prices even further.

Firms will consider dropping products during this stage unless there are good reasons for retaining them. Weak products may take up a disproportionate amount of management's time and resources. They may demand frequent price and inventory adjustments, short production runs and expensive set-up time. In addition, they may require the kind of advertising and sales-force attention that could lead to greater profitability if spent on vibrant products.

► Evidence indicates that products and services have distinct life cycles with identifiable stages. At each stage there are implications for the most suitable marketing strategy to adopt.

 Over a five year period the change in UK household penetration of a selection of consumer durables was as follows:

	% in 1984	% in 1990
washing machine	83	89
clothes drier	42	44
dishwasher	5	13
freestanding gas cooker	49	43
freestanding electric cooker	40	36
microwave oven	11	52
fridge freezer	31	50
separate freezer	35	38
vacuum cleaner	95	98
central heating system	69	80
shower fitment	29	46
oil/paraffin heater	9	3
colour television set	31	94
video recorder	28	62

(*Source:* adapted from the *Marketing Pocket Book* of the Advertising Association, 1992)

What do these figures actually tell us in terms of product life cycles?

THE PRODUCT/SERVICE PORTFOLIO

Management needs to establish an attractive balance among its products and services. Some products or services produce considerable amounts of cash. In many instances the cash is more than is essential for operational expenditure and for additional investment in facilities and staff. There will also be other products and services that will fall far short of requirements in this respect. The purpose of **product portfolio** models is to provide a means of rating products and/or services in order to assess the future, cash contributions and cash demands of each product or service. This leads on to investigating the competitive situation of a product or

► Inevitably some of the products in a firm's product mix are stronger than others. This may reflect their positions in the life cycle. On the other hand it may reflect the fact that they are products which do not match with the firm's capabilities.

service. We will look at various analytical approaches to the task.

Portfolio analyses start by looking at the positions of products. They consider the attractiveness of the market and the ability of the business to operate competitively within the market. The first of the portfolio models to be used extensively was the **growth-share matrix** – sometimes called the cash-quadrants model. In this model market growth rate was employed as the indicator for market attractiveness and relative market share was used to indicate competitive position.

The Boston Consulting Group (BCG) model

The **Boston Consulting Group (BSG) model** assumes that there will be a close connection between market share and market growth rate, and profitability or cashflow. It is argued that these are the most important criteria on which investment decisions should be based. Market share and the growth rate of the market are the two dimensions of the BCG matrix. This is shown in the figure below. The four partitions of the matrix are labelled to represent the type of products or services that may be located within each one of the four squares.

► Boston Consulting Group (1970) 'The Product Portfolio', pamphlet no 66, Boston.

The Boston Consultancy Group Matrix

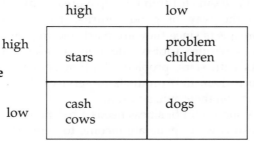

The figure shows products/services classified under one of four headings:

1 **Stars** are products/services which have a significant share in a swiftly developing market (product life cycle growth stage). They take up considerable resources but have substantial prospects for growth and profitability. They often show a rapid growth in sales and profits and produce good cashflows. Growing markets attract competitors and stars demand constant cash resources (for marketing purposes) to keep their position in the market throughout the growth stage. As a result, perhaps all the positive cashflows generated by stars will be needed for reinvestment purposes to

preserve their positions in the market. It is possible that extra cash will be required from other sources to boost continued growth.

2 **Cash cows** are products or services which may at one time or another have been stars but have now reached a point where there is little growth in the market (product life-cycle market maturity) stage. They give significant profits and cashflows but have reached their peak. Since the markets are mature and not growing in size there will be no need for cash for reinvestment purposes. The cash generated by these products and services is a number one resource for funding products or services falling into the category of stars or problem children.

3 **Dogs** are products which demand little in the way of resources but also produce poor profits and are inferior providers of cash. Firms should look closely at dog business to consider whether or not it is attractive to retain such products within the portfolio. We have to differentiate between stronger dog products and weaker ones. The stronger ones are likely to make reasonable contributions to the profitability of the business while the weaker ones will be making little in the way of net contribution. The general opinion is to divest weak dogs as soon as is possible. However, dog products or services may be essential purchases for certain customers who also buy a firm's more lucrative products or services. We therefore have to consider whether the firm's other products or services would suffer a serious drop in sales if the dog products were to be withdrawn.

4 **Problem children** take up a great deal of resources but offer little in the way of good returns. They frequently have attractive prospects since they are marketed to growing markets. However, they require a lot of attention in order to build up market share. As with stars, problem children demand a good deal of cash to turn them into products or services that will eventually produce cash on their own account.

A successful business needs a balanced portfolio containing a few cash cows to generate income to support stars and problem children in its portfolio. Organizations also need to be continually innovating and on the look out for new products. Cash cows do not last indefinitely since products and services, like people, have life-spans and life cycles. A constant supply of new products and services is essential for the long-term success of the organization.

Let us now evaluate the usefulness of the BCG matrix. A major disadvantage of the BCG model is its reliance on market share and market growth as the only factors to be used in appraising product portfolio strengths and weaknesses. The current market share held by a product tells us very little about the prospects for increasing or maintaining that market share. Experience shows that some high growth markets are not always preferable for they may well lack size (current or potential) and stability. The BCG model does not take account of the expertise in the organization. Given that one can obtain the relevant measures of market share and market

► New products and services may start off as problem children (during the introductory stage of the life cycle) and ones that make out become stars and eventually cash cows. The shaky ones become dogs and may become failures.

► The BCG matrix locates a product according to the market growth rate and the market share held by the product. Low growth market–high market share products generate cash to help sustain future breadwinners.

growth, it tells us nothing about the fit between the organization's capabilities and the products or services that it offers. The latter in fact are taken for granted.

Several other portfolio models have been formulated to overcome the various shortcomings of the growth-share model.

 A firm has analysed its product portfolio using the BCG matrix and plots its products as shown in the matrix below (the + sign denotes the actual point on the grid). The firm has six products, indicated by the letters a to f. The number appearing next to each letter shows the percentage contribution each product is making to the companies overall profits.

Relative Market Share

	high	low
high	+ b:12	+ c:0 + d:1
low	+ a:80	+ e:3 + f:4

(left axis label: **Market Growth Rate**, with "high" and "low")

What action would you advise the firm to consider? Why? What reservations might you have?

The GE-McKinsey matrix

The **The GE-McKinsey** model was developed cooperatively by McKinsey and General Electric in the early 1970s. It is more complicated to use than the Boston Consultancy Group matrix but it does have the benefit of giving greater flexibility regarding the factors it can include. It enables assessment of the fit between organizational competences (business strengths) and market attractiveness.

► See 'The GE Portfolio Matrix', *Business Week*, 28 April, 1975.

The GE-McKinsey Matrix

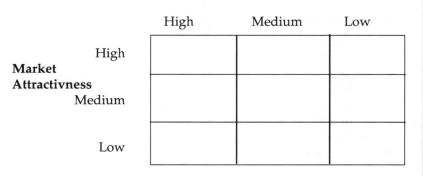
Business Strengths
(columns: High, Medium, Low)
(rows under **Market Attractivness**: High, Medium, Low)

▶ GE is a multi-business organization which recognized the value of the BCG matrix for assigning priorities to each business and making systematic and rational investment and allocation decisions. GE felt that other additional factors should be considered. GE therefore requested McKinsey and Company to develop the industry attractiveness business strength matrix.

Business strengths reflect such things as skills, competences, operating strengths and resources. Market attractiveness comprises anything which suggests that that the market is likely to lead to good profits for a firm and be relatively easy to exploit. A composite score for each of the two dimensions can be obtained by listing attributes of the two dimensions, scoring products or services along these attributes and assigning weighting. For example, we might decide that the dimension of business strength is best represented by the attributes:

1 Managerial skills
2 Strength of customer base
3 Technological competence
4 Cost structure

And the market attractiveness dimension may comprise:

1 Market sales growth rate
2 Market size
3 Competition
4 Fit with overall definition of business

The nature of the attributes will vary with the situation. A product or service is rated against each attribute on a nine point scale. Next a composite score for that dimension is obtained by assigning different weights to the various attributes and aggregating the weighted ratings for each dimension. These weighted, aggregated ratings can then be plotted on a two dimensional grid.

GEC McKinsey Matrix

We will work through the rating of a single product or service and use each one of two sets of four attributes for the two dimensions of business strength and market attractiveness mentioned above.

Firstly we would need executives in the organization to indicate weights that should be attached to the two groups of attributes. This would be done by requesting the executives to take each set of four attributes at a time and divide a hundred marks between the four attributes to reflect the degree of importance of each one. For example one executive might allocate the marks as follows:

Business strength	Market attractiveness
attribute (1) 22 marks	attribute (1) 47 marks
attribute (2) 24 marks	attribute (2) 11 marks
attribute (3) 33 marks	attribute (3) 16 marks
attribute (4) 21 marks	attribute (4) 26 marks
Total 100 marks	**Total** 100 marks

We will assume that there are five executives in the organization, and that each one is requested to do the exercise. When the task is completed, we aggregate the marks given by each executive for each of the attributes in turn. Next the total number of marks allocated to each attribute is divided by 5 so the average number of marks allocated by the executives to each one of the attributes can be established. Suppose this turns out to be:

Business strength
attribute (1) 18.5 marks
attribute (2) 26.6 marks
attribute (3) 31.8 marks
attribute (4) 23.1 marks
Total 100 marks

Market attractiveness
attribute (1) 36.6 marks
attribute (2) 15.5 marks
attribute (3) 15.2 marks
attribute (4) 32.7 marks
Total 100 marks

To obtain the weights for individual attributes we have to divide by 100, since the weights by definition must add up to one.

Business strength
attribute (1) 0.185 marks
attribute (2) 0.266 marks
attribute (3) 0.318 marks
attribute (4) 0.231 marks
Total 1

Market attractiveness
attribute (1) 0.366 marks
attribute (2) 0.155 marks
attribute (3) 0.152 marks
attribute (4) 0.327 marks
Total 1

The next step is ask each of the five executives to rate the product against each one of the two sets of four attributes on a scale running from 0 to 9. We then work out the average rating (by dividing the aggregate ratings for each attribute by 5) for the product against each of the two sets of attributes.

Suppose this turns out to be:

Business strength
attribute (1) 3.2
attribute (2) 4.8
attribute (3) 6.7
attribute (4) 5.7

Market attractiveness
attribute (1) 5.6
attribute (2) 8.2
attribute (3) 7.3
attribute (4) 8.2

We then obtain the weighted scores by multiplying by the relevant weight assigned to every attribute.

Business strength
attr. (1) $0.185 \times 3.2 = 0.59$
attr. (2) $0.266 \times 4.8 = 1.28$
attr. (3) $0.318 \times 6.7 = 2.13$
attr. (4) $0.231 \times 5.7 = 1.32$
Total 5.32

Market attractiveness
attr. (1) $0.366 \times 5.6 = 2.05$
attr. (2) $0.155 \times 8.2 = 1.27$
attr. (3) $0.152 \times 7.3 = 1.11$
attr. (4) $0.327 \times 8.2 = 2.68$
Total 7.11

The product's position on the grid can them be plotted as follows:

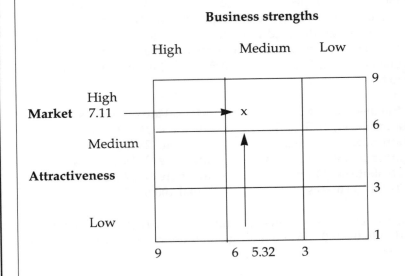

The three cells at the upper left of the matrix are ones in which a company should invest. The diagonal cells extending from the lower left to the upper right indicate products or services that are mediocre in terms of overall attractiveness. In this case a company should pursue selective earnings (for example, concentrate investments in segments where profitability is good and risk is relatively low). The three cells at the lower right indicate products or services that are low in overall attractiveness. In this last case a company should consider 'harvesting' or 'divesting' these products (that is either minimizing investment and rationalizing operations or cutting fixed costs and deferring investment in the meantime).

The business strength score reflects an enterprise's capacity to work towards building or maintaining market share. In addition to taking a snapshot of the business as it is at one moment in time an estimate of the prospective position of each product or service of the firm should be made. The time span should be over the next three to five years and be based on the assumption that the present strategy is pursued.

► For further ideas on the BCG and GE models see: R. A. Proctor & J. S. Hassard, 'Towards a new model for product portfolio analysis', *Management Decision*, Vol 28, Issue 3, pp. 15–17, and, R. A. Proctor & P. J. Kitchen, 'Strategic Planning: an overview of product portfolio models', *Marketing Intelligence and Planning*, Vol 8, No. 7, 1990, pp 4–10.

► The GE-McKinsey matrix takes into account business strengths of the firm and market attractiveness. Products scoring well on both dimensions should be retained for investment. Low scores on both dimensions suggest that these items should be considered for divestment.

 Take any organization or society of which you are a member and try, with a group of other people, to apply the GE-McKinsey matrix to the activities of the establishment. Evaluate your results.

Other Portfolio models

The **ADL** (Arthur D. Little) **multifactor portfolio** model is another extensively used model. It is a mixture of the BCG growth share matrix and a multifactor matrix. It employs two dimensions to evaluate each business or segment. These are industry maturity and competitive position:

- **Industry maturity** – which comprises four classifications:

1 Embryonic
2 Growing
3 Mature
4 Ageing

A business is judged according to its growth rate, growth potential, the distribution and stability of market shares, the number of competitors, technological stability and ease of entry to the market.

- **Competitive position** – which comprises five classifications:

1 Dominant
2 Strong
3 Favourable
4 Tenable
5 Weak

A businesses is classified according to such factors as how well it performs relative to optimum capacity utilization, how satisfactory its current level of profitability is and how distinctive its product advantages are.

  The ADL suggests strategy guidelines for each combination of industry maturity and competitive position. For example:

Industry maturity – ageing
Competitive position – tenable
Guideline: phased withdrawal or abandon

The **Shell Chemical directional policy matrix** is like the GE-McKinsey matrix. It differs from the latter in that it possesses greater precision in the estimation of factor ratings. Its strategy guidelines are also more clearly explained. Hughes (1981) describes an application of the matrix.

► Hughes M. (1981), 'Portfolio analysis', *Long Range Planning*, February pp101-103.

Comments on portfolio model usage

Portfolio models are easy to use. They help organizations to gain some idea of the profile of strong/weak products or services in the mix. They may, however, cause an organization to put too much stress on market-share growth and entry into high growth businesses. They may also cause firms to pay insufficient attention to managing the current business. Another problem is that the results can be manipulated to produce the desired results by adjusting the weights and ratings. Since an averaging process is taking place, several businesses may end up in the same cell location, but vary considerably in terms of their ratings aginst specific factors. Moreover, because many products or services will end up in the middle of the matrix it is difficult to suggest an appropriate strategy. The models do not accommodate the synergy between two or more products/services and this suggest that making decisions for one in isolation from the others may be shortsighted.

CHAPTER SUMMARY

▶ Now that you have reached the end of the chapter, turn back to the objectives and make sure you have achieved each of them..

1 The product life cycle presents a useful conceptual framework within which to study how firms should apply their marketing strategies. At different stages in the cycle some strategies are more appropriate than others. The life cycle also points to the different earning patterns through the various stages and suggests that it is necessary to have a balanced portfolio of products and services to ensure steady sales and profits at all times. This means that the firm has to prune its product lines and introduce new products to stay on course.

2 Several product portfolio models, the best known of which are the BCG (Boston Consulting Group) matrix and the GE-McKinsey matrix, were developed to aid firms assess the balance of the product mix. The BCG approach has limited applicability in so far as it can only be applied in those instances where there is a definite correlation between market share and profitability. The GE-McKinsey matrix overcomes such difficulties.

11 Product strategy

Chapter objectives

By the end of the chapter you should:

▋ know how marketers can change the nature of the product mix by:

1 adding new lines and thereby widening the product mix
2 lengthening existing product lines
3 adding new product variants to deepen the product mix
4 altering product consistency depending upon whether a firm wants to acquire a strong reputation in a few or many different areas

▋ know how product quality can be changed

▋ know how firms can discontinue products by harvesting, line simplification and line divestment

▋ be able to describe how marketers use branding as a strategy to market their goods and services

▋ be able to describe how firms make use of brand names and trademarks.

▋ know how firms position their products in the marketplace, especially how positioning fits with branding strategy

▋ know how firms make use of design as part of their product strategy – especially how they use standard and customized products.

▋ know how firms use packaging as an important element in product strategy

▋ know how firms deal with the risk of product liability

▋ be able to describe the various ways in which marketers can provide product guarantees

▋ be able to describe the various elements of customer service.

Introduction

The most tangible sign of the nature of a business is the products and services it is producing or marketing. They help to create the image of the firm in the mind of the customer. Moreover, the impression that the customer will have of the firm will rest upon his or her perceptions and feelings about its products or services. This is important since experience with only one of a firm's products or services can affect a person's attitude to the firm's other products or services. This can apply even if the customer has never used the other products. From the point of view of the firm, current products and services not only account for current sales and profit but will also be important contributors to future income. To

► Shops, stores, firms and other organizations which are open to the general public can do much to protect their image by ensuring that their toilet facilities are clean, hygienic and easily found. After all they form part of the image of the organization in the users mind.

ensure future success firms have to adapt their products or services to changing wants and needs in the marketplace.

A definition of a product or service

A product is not simply a tangible object nor a service or visible activity. People buy products or services to satisfy their needs or wants. As a result of satisfying these needs and wants they obtain benefits. Firms have to understand the nature of the needs and wants and appreciate the kind of benefits people expect to obtain. There are different kinds of benefits that people can obtain from buying goods and services. These include:

- good value for money
- novelty
- availability
- good design
- ease of use
- safety
- economy in use

The customer's decision to buy one firm's product over another will depend on his or her perception of the benefits of using one product versus another.

► The topic of analysing the **product mix** is more fully discussed in Chapter 10.

PRODUCT MIX

The product mix comprises the group of products sold by a company. It has:

- width – number of lines the firm carries e.g., washing machines and spin driers
- length – total number of items in the product mix e.g., three kinds of washing machine and four kinds of spin drier
- depth – number of variants of each product are offered in the line, e.g., front loaders, top loaders, twin tub, etc.
- consistency – how closely related the various product lines are in terms of the use to which they are put, e.g., all domestic appliances.

The four dimensions indicated above provide a means for defining the company's product strategy. The company can expand its

► A product line comprises of a group of similar products targeted at a broadly similar group of consumers who will use them in a broadly similar manner. The nature of the product lines can be changed by altering the nature of the items.

1 **New lines** can be added thereby widening the product mix, for example a manufacturer of washing machines could introduce a line of tumbler dryers.

2 Existing product lines can be **lengthened** by introducing additional items, for example the washing machine manufacturer may

introduce larger or smaller washing machines than are currently being offered.

3 New **product variants** can be added to deepen the product mix, for example the washing machine manufacturer may introduce new models which are the same size as as existing items but which have different features.

4 **Product consistency** can be made more or less depending upon whether a firm wants to acquire a strong reputation in a few or many different areas.

Malcolm runs a small stamp collectors business in Liverpool. Some of the items he gets are quite valuable while others are not. On some days, while his wife manages their small shop on Lord Street, he visits stamp fairs in different parts of the Midlands and North of England to find interesting items. Occasionally he has a stand himself at one of the fairs. Once every six weeks he goes to the NWP auctions in Liverpool and bids for lots of stamps which attract his interest.

Malcolm's business attracts a wide variety of customers ranging from well to do business people with thousands of pounds to spend on stamps to young children starting their first collection. He carries a wide range of stock, covering all countries in the world.

He earns an adequate income from the business but would like to improve his position. What factors do you think Malcolm should take into account in trying evolve a product strategy which would enable him to improve his own financial prospects in the stamp collecting business?

Product-line decisions

Items within a product line make different contributions to sales and profits. If only one or two items make up the bulk of the contribution then this means that a product line is vulnerable should competition intensify and sales for these items plummet. Products which make very low contributions might be better dropped from the product line unless there are substantial reasons for not doing so.

The firm needs to keep an eye on what competitors are offering (see Chapter 5 on competitor analysis). Gaps in the product line may become apparent when product offerings are compared to competitors, product offerings.

If a product line is too short a firm may be able to increase its profits by adding items to the line. On the other hand, if it is too long, profitability may be increased by dropping products. There is a tendency for product lines to grow longer over time. This may result from excess production capacity at various times and the need to introduce new items to take up this excess capacity and increase overall profitability. However, as items are introduced to the line costs may rise. When eventually a product line is reviewed for its profitability, it may become apparent that profits can be improved substantially by pruning less profitable or unprofitable products and shortening the line.

Product quality

► Product quality is reflected in: performance, features, reliability, durability, serviceability, aesthetics, reputation, match with specifications. D. A. Garvin, 'Product quality: an important strategic weapon', *Business Horizons*, Vol 27, 1984.

Product quality is an important contributor to business profitability. Quality has been found to be positively related to market share and return on investment over a wide range of products and in different market situations. Moreover, high quality is usually associated with premium prices.

Product quality can be enhanced in a number of ways:

- by improving product performance
- by including new improved product features
- by increasing product reliability
- by ensuring that a product corresponds closely with its specification
- by making a product more durable
- by improving the serviceability of a product
- by improving the product finish and appearance

The firm's task is to build sufficient quality into the goods and services it has to offer to satisfy customer requirements. If quality levels are set too high or too low, under-or over-engineering as it is called, this can result in failure to maximize profitability or can leave customers disgruntled.

 Obtain a recent copy of a *Which?* report from the commercial reference section of your local library. Choose a consumer durable product and see how one of the reports defines the following:

- performance
- features
- reliability
- conformance to specifications
- durability
- serviceability
- product finish and appearance

Product Decisions

There are three broad categories of action that can be taken with respect to product: it can be introduced to the market, it can be given a 'face lift' and it can be withdrawn, discontinued or eliminated. The first two of these topics are discussed in Chapter 12. They relate to the introduction of entirely new product lines into the product mix, to the introduction of new items within a product line and to major changes to existing product items within a line. Here, we will briefly review **product discontinuance or elimination.**

Product elimination

A firm can benefit from discontinuing a line or product. It may free up resources which can be assigned to more viable or profitable products. The resources comprise money, staff and machine time. Warning signals that indicate that a product should be withdrawn are as follows:

- absolute decline in sales volume
- sales volume declining as a percentage of total sales
- declining market share
- volume sales not meeting with anticipated projections
- future sales projected lower than requirements
- return on investment falling below minimum acceptable
- variable costs more than sales revenues
- consistently rising costs as a percentage of sales
- products taking up more and more executive time and attention
- regular cut in price required to maintain sales
- regular increase in promotional budgets to maintain sales

▶ This is a complex decision. It could be that resources are required to launch new products or to support stars or problem children. Firms may be reluctant to discontinue products while they are still making profits.

There are three courses of action which can be taken with respect to the product elimination strategy:

1 **Harvesting**. This involves getting the most from the product while it lasts. Efforts should be made to cut product costs to help improve cash flow. Alternatively, prices may be increased without a simultaneous increase in costs. Harvesting produces a slow decline in sales. When the product no longer provides a positive cash flow, it should be dropped.

2 **Line simplification**. Here a product line is trimmed by pruning the number and variety of products or services on offer. The aim is to keep the falling line stable and to restore the health of the line. It is a strategy which becomes especially relevant during times of rising costs and resource shortages.

▶ The profitability of the product mix may be improved by adding products to the product line or by deleting them.

3 **Total line divestment**. In this case the whole product line is discontinued.

Brand strategy

A **brand** is a name given by a producer to one or a number of its products or services. It could be the producers' own name or it could be a name unconnected with the producer. The British Alcan company, for example, uses the Alcan name with many of its industrial aluminium products but uses the brand name Bacofoil with aluminium food wrapping foil for consumer markets. Brand names are used to differentiate products from their competitors and to make it easier for customers to recognize them. People come to associate a given level of service or quality with a brand name and can buy in the confidence that quality or service will be provided wherever and whenever the product is purchased.

Branding's ability to enhance a product's saleability varies with the product and company. In cases where price is virtually the sole factor upon which firms compete then branding is not an important issue, for example an agricultural producer selling farm produce to a food processor. However, in the same instance, a food processor may develop consumer preference for a brand by differentiating and promoting it. The producer tries to convince buyers of the product's superiority over other brands.

Brand identification is necessary for the firm which wants to differentiate its product from competitors' products. It provides the company with some control over the resale and marketing of the product by wholesalers and/or retailers and simultaneously enhances promotional effectiveness. In making use of brand identification a company is taking important steps towards competing on a non-price basis.

The branding decision is critical in the case of products where the potential effectiveness of brand identification to secure product differentiation is uncertain. For example, at one time experts contended that branding women's dresses was of minimal value because women bought according to criteria unrelated to the brand – such as colour, design, styling and fit. Nowadays, the industry not only uses brand names but promotes them heavily. Manufacturers came to understand that variations in women's shapes not provided for in different standard sizes provided opportunities for real product differentiation and profitable branding. For example a woman could be a size 12 but might need a slightly larger waist measurement than is provided in the standard measurements for size 12. A brand may establish a reputation for giving that little bit of extra size in the waist.

Branding has the best potential pay-off where it is possible to differentiate the product effectively with respect to features that consumers consider important. It also has potential pay-offs where products or services have features for which shoppers are actively searching. It reduces the searching time shoppers have to spend in finding products or services with the desired features.

Family brands

A firm which is marketing more than one product or service has to make up its mind whether to sell each one under a separate brand

► Agricultural products, and products of fisheries, forests, and mines are difficult to differentiate because of their unprocessed form. However, brand identification and clever packaging and promotion can achieve some degree of product differentiation. On the whole, it is fair to say that product differentiation through brand identification and promotion is easier to obtain for consumer than for industrial products.

It's all in the brand

'Les Grandes do a medium-sized dress madam, but it's designed for the woman with the fuller figure.'

name or to use a **family brand** to cover all offerings. Both of these approaches have benefits but their respective appropriateness depends on circumstances. Three factors should be taken into acccount when making such choices. These are the nature of the product line, the promotional policy and the desired market penetration.

The nature of the product line is perhaps the key issue. Products which seem similar to one another in the mind of the customer – such as items of underwear – benefit particularly from the family branding. However, while the effect of providing a family brand name may be positive it can also be negative. It is important to make sure that all items carrying the family brand conform to the consumers' standards of acceptance. Quality has to be similar across the products marketed under a family brand name. The consumer also has to believe that the quality the manufacturer has achieved with one product can be carried over into another: Yamaha motor cycles and organs for example. Products should really be sold to the same kinds of markets, for example the St. Michael products are sold to the fast-moving consumer goods markets, there is no attempt at the moment is to sell St. Michael refrigerators or cars.

► Marks and Spencers' St. Michael brand is an example.

Products without common marketing attributes are perhaps best marketed under individual names. In addition family branding can produce adverse effects: soap, with its unpleasant taste, would be a poor companion in having the same brand name as food products.

The promotional budget tends to be less in the case of family branding. Promotion can be directed toward the entire line and

**An unfortunate choice of
brand name**

'Would you like sugar on your
Fairy, sir?'

► In the wristwatch market Rolex
has a cheaper brand label, Tudor,
which is directed towards a market that wants all the quality of
the Rolex product but does not
want to pay the price for actually
having the Rolex brand name on
the product.

promotion of a single item can increase recognition or demand for
the whole line. On the negative side, however, family branding
can restrict opportunities for emphasizing individual differences
in items.

The desired market penetration is important because individual
items in a product line meet with varying degrees of competition.
A producer of kitchen and washer appliances may encounter only
weak competition on dishwashers and electric ranges. However,
one of its competitors may make only washing machines and,
through aggressive promotion, may have captured a large market
share. It may be extremely difficult to compete with this competitor. In such instances, where the same degree of market penetration does not exist for all items in the line, individual branding
permits greater promotional flexibility. In addition individual
branding can enable a producer to achieve greater market penetration by marketing similar but brand-differentiated products which
appeal to different market segments.

Multibrand products

Producers of specialty goods often market their goods through a
limited number of selected retail outlets in order to gain dealer
cooperation in aggressively promoting the goods. This can limit
the total sales potential because in any one market no single
retailer or even a small group of retailers can normally attract all
the buyers. In such a case market penetration can be increased by
offering identical merchandise under a different brand name to a
second group of selected retailers.

Separate brands may also be appropriate where products have
been developed for and positioned on clearly defined target market segments and marketing policy is directed towards developing
a clear and identifiable brand-segment relationship.

Multiple brands are often produced as a result of mergers
between firms. Whether all the brands are retained may depend
on the extent to which different brands have developed dissimilar
images that appeal to different market segments. Or whether they
have developed strength in different regional markets with well-
known names that management is reluctant to abandon.

Manufacturer's brand and retailer's own brand

Private brands are those owned and controlled by middlemen
rather than by manufacturers. Alcan, for example, produce aluminium wrapping foil and sell it through retailers under the brand
name Bacofoil. Alcan also sells aluminium foil to the same retailers
to be offered for sale under the brand name of the retailer, for
example Sainsbury or Tesco.

A producer's decision concerning the acceptance of private brand
orders should depend on the probable effect on the sales and profits of its own brand. If these turn out to be detrimental then accepting the private brand order may not be such a good idea.

However, the producer may have to take into consideration the fact that a large retailer may not be prepared to place orders at all with a firm unless it can sell at least some of the goods that it purchases under its own brand name.

From the point of view of the middleman the private branding decision should be based on the likelihood of obtaining greater profits or greater control over the market.

Contracts relating to private brands may allow the producer to build up production volume, result in cost reduction and bring in contributions to profits and overheads. They may also bring about stable production planning and long production runs. Products may then be sold without incurring much marketing or promotional expenditure. Some large retailing chains such as Sainsbury and Marks and Spencer may actually insist on using their own brand and it may be the only way for producers to supply to such chains.

There are difficulties for the producer in supplying own brands. The retailer is put in a powerful position since it controls the marketing of the product. The retailer may also even end up determining and controlling the producer's costs. Moreover, the manufacturer will have to conform to the specifications, stock levels and delivery patterns laid down at the time it entered into the agreement with the retailer. Not only can the supplier lose control over the marketing of the products but it can also lose control over the running of its whole business if it becomes too dependent on the retailer. Moreover, if the private brand under which the product is labelled takes up all or a large part of the production then the manufacturer is in the position of having all its eggs in one basket. Should the firm suddenly decide to go elsewhere for the product then the supplying firm will run into considerable difficulties.

(ACT) Make a list of consumer branded goods under the following headings:

- single brand
- multi-branded goods
- multi-product brands
- own label products

Product Names

In addition to brand names, products may also have **product names**. Ford may be the brand name but Sierra is the product name for a particular range of cars. The use of such a name reinforces the product differentiation value of the brand and makes it easier for the customer to recognize and recall the product.

Marketers suggest that a product's name, where it has one, should be appropriate for the product and the image it is trying to communicate to a potential purchaser. Nevertheless, one does wonder just what images car product names such as Astra, Violet, Bluebird and Cherry are trying to conjure up for the motorist. It is further suggested by marketers that the name should contain some hint of the benefit to be gained from the purchase. Sometimes it is difficult to see any imagery or benefits associated with product names. Under these circumstances the benefits of the product have to be more fully communicated through promotion and expenditure incurred.

 Suggest possible reasons why the following product names were introduced:

- Jaguar (cars)
- Daz (washing powder)
- Senior Service (cigarettes)
- Bacofoil (aluminium wrapping)
- St Michael foods (Marks and Spencer)
- Typhoo (tea)
- Lucozade (soft drinks)
- Fairy (washing powder)
- 7up (soft drinks)
- Green Giant (tinned sweetcorn)
- Oxo (stock cubes)
- Golden Wonder (crisps)
- Brillo (pan cleaner)
- Alcan (aluminium producer)
- Ewbank (carpet sweeper)
- Creda Cavalier (electric cooker)
- Wispa (chocolate bar)
- Head and Shoulders (shampoo)
- Tipp-Ex (correction fluid)
- Domestos (toilet cleaner)
- Lemsip (cold remedy)
- Filofax (diaries)
- Pot Noodle (snack meals)

Trademarks

Brands and product names have to be registered as **trademarks** to protect them from unauthorized use. However, names that deliberately confuse or mislead customers are not permissible. There are also other restrictions such as not allowing female names to be registered for cosmetics in the UK. A registered name or trademark of a successful product or service can become a valuable or appreciating asset to a company.

▶ Branding is a way of distinguishing a product or service from other offerings in the market. Brand names come to be associated with an expected level of quality which extends to all products bearing the brand name.

PRODUCT POSITIONING STRATEGY

The term **positioning** applies to marketing a brand to a part of the market where it fares favourably in comparison with competing products. In view of the fact that markets comprise different wants and needs, one brand cannot serve the requirements of the entire market. Any strategy should aim to match a product with that segment of the market where it is most likely to succeed. The product should be positioned in such a manner that it stands apart from competing brands. A product's positioning indicates what the product represents, and how customers should evaluate it.

Positioning is accomplished through the use of the marketing-mix variables, particularly through product design and marketing communications. Positioning to achieve product differentiation applies equally to consumer and to industrial goods. In some cases product positioning can be achieved on the basis of tangible differences (i.e. product features), however, in many instances customer perceptions about products are used to differentiate and position them.

Product positioning is accomplished in the following way:

1 Find out and explore the nature of the product attributes that are considered important by customers.
2 Establish how the importance of these attributes varies among the different market segments.
3 Examine the best position for the product with respect to each attribute, taking into account the positions of existing brands.
4 Work out an overall position for the brand (based upon the overall match between product attributes and their distribution in the population and the positioning of existing brands).

For example, the product positioning of a brand of personal computer for students could be based on portability and affordability. It could be ascertained that price and portability are two important product attributes in general but that in the case of the student market segment they are *the* most important attributes. It might be discovered that in the student segment of the market there are already cheap microcomputers – but only one of them is really portable. The task then might be to offer a cheap portable computer which would be:

a cheaper than the existing product
b more portable than the existing product
c both (a) and (b) and also have more features than the existing product.

There are six different ways of positioning a product:

► Blue Nun wine has had several successful positioning strategies. At first it was the wine which was 'perfect' with every dish. Next it was the wine that 'goes everywhere'. Then it became the wine 'sold by the glass'. The wine can be seen to represent different things with each of the three changes.

1 Associating a product with an attribute, feature or customer benefit, for example a particular model of car as 'the most economical way to get to work by car'.

2 Positioning by price/quality, for example cheaper than competing products or more features than competing products.

3 Associating the product with a use or application, for example 'the wine you have on special occasions'.

4 Associating the product with a user or class of users, for example 'the car for the business executive'.

5 Positioning with respect to a product class, for example a soap as a bath oil product rather than a soap, or 'not just another night club but a new experience'.

6 Positioning with respect to a competitor, for example 'an IBM compatible microcomputer'.

Choose five of the following products and list as many attributes as you can which you think potential users will consider important. Note how people will have different specifications for the attributes according to their needs. For example, in the case of caravans, roominess may be important – but it will mean something different to a family with three children plus a dog, to a childless couple.

- caravans
- chocolate
- microcomputers
- houses
- clothes
- alcoholic drinks
- soft drinks
- holidays

- television programmes
- dry cleaning
- watches
- furniture
- public transport (buses)
- public transport (trains)
- public transport (airlines)
- restaurants

Positioning a single brand

In order to maximize its benefits with a single brand, a firm should try to associate itself with a core segment of the market where it can play a dominant role. It may also be able to attract customers from other segments outside its core.

Another single brand strategy would be to consider the market undifferentiated and cover it with a single brand. This strategy only tends to work in the short run. In order to gain entry to a market, competitors segment and challenge the dominance of the single brand by positioning themselves in small viable niches.

To protect the position of a single brand a firm may introduce other brands. For example, if its original brand is challenged by a competitor with a cut-price alternative product it might increase the price of the original brand. This strategy will take the challenger's brand out of direct competition with the existing brand. At the same time the firm might introduce a new brand priced to

▶ BMW cars are positioned mainly in a limited segment – high income professionals.

compete directly with the competitor's brand.

There are two crucial requirements for the successful management of a single brand in the marketplace:

1 The brand has to be positioned in the marketplace so that it can stand competition from the strongest rival brand
2 Its unique position should be maintained by creating the appearance that it is in fact a different product.

Positioning multiple brands

Multiple brands are introduced to the market for two major reasons:

1 To seek growth by offering varied products in different segments of the market.
2 To avoid competitive threats to a single brand.

To enable a firm to achieve growth targets profitibility and increased market share, multiple brands should be carefully positioned in the market so that they do not compete with each other. If this is not done effectively then **cannibalism** can occur. Unfortunately cannibalism will always occur to some extent and the aim should be to minimize its effect.

► Cannibilism occurs when sales of one brand take sales away from sales of another brand marketed by the same company.

Product repositioning strategies

In order to maximize its market share, a product will require **repositioning** from time to time. Repositioning becomes necessary if:

● a competitor's new product or service has been positioned next to the brand and this is having an adverse effect on the product or service's share of the market
● consumer preferences with respect to the product or service have changed
● new customer preference clusters have been pin-pointed that suggest promising opportunities
● the original positioning was incorrect.

Positioning or repositioning a product or service carries high risks. The technique of **perceptual mapping** can be applied to reduce those risks. A perceptual map is a grid which shows how people perceive products to be positioned in relationship to one another. The technique may be illustrated with a hypothetical example relating to the car market. The map helps the marketing strategist to assess whether the company's cars are on target. The concentration of dots representing competing models shows how much opposition there is likely to be in a specific area of the map.

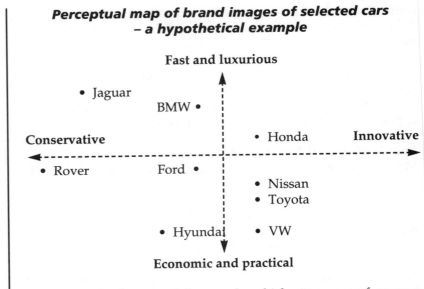

Perceptual map of brand images of selected cars – a hypothetical example

Cars towards the top of the graph, which stresses performance and luxury, should fetch a higher price than cars towards the bottom, where the emphasis is on economy and practicality.

Products may be repositioned in three ways:

1 **Among existing users.** Here the marketer promotes more varied use of a product by its existing users. A table wine may have been positioned as a wine for 'special occasions', repositioning might suggest its use as 'being suitable for every occasion'.
2 **Among new users.** Here the product is presented with a different image in order to appeal to the people who have so far rejected it. It is important to make sure that its current customers of the product are not alienated.
3 **For new uses.** Here the marketer has to search for latent uses of the product. New uses for nylon sprang up in the form of varied types of hosiery, tyres, bearings, etc. It was the new uses that kept nylon on the growth path; wrap knits in 1945, tyre cord in 1948, textured yarns in 1955, carpet yarns in 1959, and so on. Without the new uses nylon would have hit the saturation level as far back as 1962.

Product design strategy

A firm can offer **standard** or **customized** products. Standardized products are built to a single design specification though they are usually offered in different grades and styles with varying prices. Customized products are ones which have been made to the specifications of an individual buyer. Between these two a firm may also offer standard products with modifications.

> ► Product positioning refers to how firms signal a product's differential advantage to the market. The relative positions of brands within a market are often shown in a grid. Positioning reflects the relative importance that the marketer puts on consumer benefits associated with the brand.

Standard products

There are two benefits associated with standard products. Firstly there are the benefits accruing from the effects of the experience curve. Secondly, such products can be marketed nationally with more efficiency. A disadvantage of standard products lies in the fact that it orientates management thinking toward unit cost savings and inhibits even small changes in production design to accommodate shifts in market requirements.

Larger firms tend to obtain the most benefits from standardization. These take the form of extra profits generated as a result of economies of scale and long production runs. Large firms are able to produce at low prices. Small companies fare better as job shops, doing customized work for individual buyers where there are higher profit margins. By and large, small firms cannot obtain the advantages of economies but do have the advantage of flexibility.

▶ See Chapter 5 for the effects of the experience curve.

Customized products

These are marketed on the basis of the quality of the finished product. That is the extent to which the product meets the customer's specifications. Usually the producer works closely with the customer reviewing the progress of the product until completion. Unlike standard products, price is not usually an important factor. Customers anticipate paying a premium for customized products.

Some large companies do get involved in producing customized products. It depends very much on the nature of the product. There is also a spin-off from developing customized products in that it sometimes leads to the development of new standard products.

Standard products with modifications

This represents a compromise between the two previous strategies. With this strategy the customer is offered the standard product but is able to specify a limited number of modifications.

In producing a standard product, a firm is looking for economies of scale. At the same time, by permitting modifications, the product is individualized to meet the specific requirements of the customer. The strategy makes it easy for the firm to keep in close contact with market needs. This enables it to identify how those needs may be satisfied through product improvements and modifications. It also enhances the organization's reputation for flexibility in meeting customer's requirements.

▶ Firms can opt to produce standard or customized products. They may produce products which have an element of both. The former leads to lower costs while the latter is more likely to meet customers' exact requirements.

Packaging

In addition to protecting a product, **packaging** is also an important form of promotion. In the first instance, it calls shoppers' attention to the product in retail stores – particularly important in super-markets. Secondly it carries messages and other items of information to assist the shopper in making purchase decisions.

Davos

A greek chocolate firm, Davos, was having trouble with one of the first chocolate products it launched in that it was not achieving the kind of success the firm desired. The firm could not stop its production since the product was one of its major chocolate lines. Instead the firm removed the product from the market. Production continued but from then on the firm marketed it with a different packaging and under a different brand name. Sales increased sharply and the product became one of the firm's best selling ones.

Source: 'Target marketing of consumer products', unpublished MBA Thesis, Mattheos Mansolas, Keele University 1990.

Package design has to be capable of drawing the shopper's attention away from an enormous selection of other competing products and brands. Good packaging involves using colour, design and style which is suited to the product's intended market segment and its retail environment.

Candid Canda

The Irish sweet manufacturer Clara Canda indicated that it was using design to launch a commando raid on the international confectionery market. The company intimated its intention of exporting its first branded sweets to the UK, the Continent, Australia and New Zealand under the Cleeves name. Exports were to be in packs which make a stark contrast to the sector norm. A company spokesman was quoted as saying ' If you are a minnow and have no money you have to go in obliquely like a commando raid to get distribution '.

Adapted from : *Marketing* 7 November, 1991 p. 15

► Packaging not only protects goods but it also promotes them.

PRODUCT LIABILITY

At one time there was a saying 'Let the buyer beware'. Things today have changed and product liability suits emerge very much in favour of the plaintiff. Design deficiencies which allow a product to malfunction with detrimental effects can bring in claims from users for substantial damages. This is something which pharmaceutical companies know to their cost. Many products, however, do have the potential to produce unfortunate results if they are used incorrectly. The labelling and packaging of a product must clearly specify how the product should be used.

To overcome potential problems firms have instigated a variety of action plans. Some refer to actions which can be taken by the firm's employees to ensure that goods leaving the factory are safe. Others refer to actions that can be taken to monitor how the products are used by customers. Actions which can be taken include:

- producing a list of legal safeguards and making sure that employees know about them
- ensuring employees are aware of their potential culpability which results from product modifications, unsafe packaging, absence of warnings to users, etc
- ensuring that all products in stock are safe products
- checking all doubts with legal advisors
- setting up and reviewing risk management policies to ensure that products needing disclaimers and warnings about misuse and abuse are identified and properly catered for
- telling salespeople to investigate reported product use that could lead to potential risks.
- putting on seminars for customers on the use of hazardous equipment and materials.

> ► The onus is on the supplier of goods to ensure that users are aware of the consequences of misuse of a product.

 Make a list of products (e.g. medicine) which you think could, if misused by customers, lead to 'unfortunate' circumstances. Check the labelling and/or instruction given with these products to see whether adequate warnings are given to customers about the possible misuse of the products.

Product guarantee

A **guarantee** is a statement or promise to the customer that a product being offered for sale is fit for the purpose being claimed by the producer. The promise indicates what the seller will do if the product performs below expectations or is defective. The provision of guarantees accomplishes several things:

- provides lower risks for the user
- signals high product reliability
- reduces buyer complaints and dissatisfaction with the product
- generates feedback on products or services from the user
- indicates an emphasis on product quality within the company
- signals to the market the company's belief in customer satisfaction
- provides an additional incentive for the customer to use the product correctly.

How long should a guarantee last?

Nearly all products and services that you can obtain have some kind of guarantee attached to them. Guarantees usually are for a given period of time and relate to parts and materials and to defective workmanship. The product may be replaced or repaired depending on its nature.

Bearing in mind these comments, list the kind of guarantees you would expect to find offered for five of the following products. If you can, find out what guarantees are actually given. Can you account for the variance (where it exists) in the guarantees given?

- video recorders
- car batteries
- shoes
- holidays (foreign)
- typewriter ribbons
- beer (at a pub)
- cans of baked beans
- horse-racing bets

- fresh fruit and vegetables
- video cassettes (unrecorded)
- surgical operations
- airline trips
- football matches
- cigarettes
- books
- washing machines

Customer service

In some markets customer service has become extremely important and has become part of the value added or what is known as the **augmented** product. Consumer target markets like the car and the electronics markets require a high level of customer service. It includes delivery, liability, technical advice, discounts, credit, guarantee, and so on.

> One example of customer service provided by nearly all jewellers shops relates to setting the time on watches. The complexity of the task varies with the nature of the watch and, of course, instructions do accompany watches. In some cases, however, the task can be quite complex.
>
> While owners of watches may take pleasure in learning how to set the time on their watches initially it is nicer to have the watch telling the correct time, date, etc., from the moment it is purchased. Amongst other possibilities, it might allay the onset of cognitive dissonance.

► Cognitive dissonance, see Chapter 7

CHAPTER SUMMARY

1 Marketers can change the nature of the product mix by adding new lines and thereby widening the product mix; by lengthening existing product lines; by adding new product variants to deepen it or by altering product consistency depending upon whether a firm wants to acquire a strong reputation in a few or many different areas.

2 Product quality is reflected in such things as performance, features, reliability, conformance to specifications, durability, serviceability, product finish and appearance. Marketers have to tailor products to meet the wants and needs of customers.

3 Profitability can often be improved by discontinuing products. This can take the form of harvesting, line simplification and line divestment.

4 Branding is an important aspect of product strategy. Important decisions relate to whether to make use of multi-brand products, multi-product brands and where appropriate providing distributors with their own brands. Part and parcel of the branding issue is the question of use of brand names and trade marks.

5 Product positioning is a key element in marketing strategy. Firms position their products in the marketplace in such a way to make best use of their differential advantage. Fitting in product positioning with brand strategy is especially important.

6 Product design can have a substantial impact on both sales and profitability. Getting the mix between standardized and customized products is they key.

7 Many products 'sell themselves in supermarkets' and often the only tangible evidence of their nature is to be seen in the packaging. Getting the packaging right so that it promotes the product is all important.

8 Customers may misuse a product in a way which can have unfortunate or dangerous consequences. The onus is on the producer of the products to ensure that they are properly labelled to ensure that users know the dangers of misuse.

9 People need some kind of guarantee that a product will work for an acceptable period of time or will work for an indefinite period of time. Often one cannot tell whether or not this will be the case from simple inspection of the goods at the time of purchase.

10 Customer service has become an integral part of the product in many instances. Providing installation help or technical advice with some products is almost essential.

▶ Now that you have reached the end of the chapter, turn back to the objectives and make sure you have achieved each of them.

⑫ New product strategy

Chapter objectives

By the end of this chapter you should:
▮ know how marketers define a new product
▮ know how to describe new product failures, understand the factors which contribute to failure and know how to try to avoid failures
▮ know how marketers get new product ideas
▮ be able to describe the new product screening process
▮ be able to describe what is involved at the business analysis stage in the process of new product screening
▮ know how firms undertake product development
▮ know when and how marketers undertake test marketing prior to launching new products
▮ be able to describe the consumer-adoption of innovations process
▮ be familiar with the following terms used by marketers: new product, new product failure, new product success, new product screening, idea acquisition, initial screening, business analysis, product development, market testing, commercialization, morphological analysis, test marketing, sales wave research, simulated store technique, controlled test marketing, consumer diaries, consumer-adoption process, innovators, early adopters, early majority, late majority, laggards.

Introduction

New products are a key element in the continued survival of an organization. Firms which do not innovate and market products which meet with the changing expectations of customers may soon go out of business. The search for new products is a continuous one. The nature of the product life cycle ensures that new products are needed to replace profitable existing ones which will eventually die off. This chapter explores how firms can try to make sure that successful new products are found.

WHAT IS A NEW PRODUCT?

A new product is something which is new to a company. Heinz, for example, was not the first company to bring canned soups to the market , but the product was certainly new as far as Heinz was concerned. Additions to existing product lines and improvements of an existing product may also be thought of as 'new products'.

▶ In practice only about one in ten of new products are actually new to the firm *and* new to the market. Booz, Allen and Hamilton (1966), *The Management of New Products*, and Booz, Allen and Hamilton (1982), *New Product Managements for the 1980's*.

DEFINING NEW PRODUCT FAILURES

Innovation is considered to be the cornerstone of success in many industries. The importance of innovation in the marketplace was stressed by Theodore Levitt nearly thirty years ago when he warned against the dangers facing firms which did not respond to new developments in the marketplace and which lurked in the shadow of product obsolescence.

New products can contribute to nearly one quarter of a firm's profits over a five year period. Michelin for example, captured eleven per cent of the US tyre market when it introduced radials, which produced longer tyre life. Between 1968 and 1984 Lever introduced twelve new brands of soaps and soap powders to UK national markets. Five of these introductions became brand market leaders and three others became sectional leaders (Hardy, 1987). Nevertheless the incidence of failure in introducing new products is extremely high.

Failure for one firm may very well be a successful product for another firm. It all depends upon the financial expectations of the firm. A good yardstick when evaluating the comparative success of a new product is the return on investment it generates but we have to bear in mind that what will satisfy one company will not necessarily satisfy another. A company accustomed to earning an overall after-tax rate of return on capital employed which exceeds thirty per cent per annum will on average need to introduce new

▶ Hardy L. (1987), *Successful Business Strategy*, Kogan Page

▶ Many large firms working on the frontiers of technology often come up with good ideas but because the initial market size or even long-term market size is small they may not choose to develop the product. Instead they may 'transfer the technology' to a smaller firm, for a royalty payment. The smaller firm is better able to exploit the opportunity. Of course, the reverse can happen, too. When a small firm is unable to exploit a new product idea it may call upon the help of a larger firm which has the resources required.

Relative theory

Parishoner – 'I think the fete was a huge success. Mrs Brown said she's never enjoyed herself so much.'
Vicar – 'Who's talking about enjoyment? I'm trying to save the church spire!'

products which will generate at least this level of after-tax return on investment in order to maintain long-term profitability.

Firms with different rates of return on capital may have different expectations, reflecting the nature of the industry in which they operate. In addition, firms of substantially different size, yet considering the same product-market opportunity, will also have different expectations.

Forecasting sales, profits and costs for new products is extremely difficult and the estimates made can sometimes be wildly inaccurate. Unsatisfactory new product opportunities which are likely to incur heavy research and development (R&D) costs need to be screened out at a very early stage to avoid unnecessary losses. In 1985 General Motors, IBM and Ford collectively spent more than $6.8 billions on R&D.

In 1982 spending in the early phases of new product development accounted for ten per cent of the total cost of bringing out the product. By 1992 this figure had risen to twenty per cent. In the face of uncertainty and escalating costs, firms would benefit from examining ways of screening new product opportunities.

► During the early stages of the product life cycle of the tumbler drier the larger firms, such as Philips, were deterred from entering the market because they thought they would be unable to generate sufficient profits in order to earn the level of return on investment they required. It was only later when the market had increased in size that they felt the market was attractive.

The advantages of screening

3M spends over six per cent of turnover on research and believes in creating many new products, accepting that the good ones will win through and that fall-out rate will be high at the low-investment stage (McBurnie T and D Clutterbuck (1988), *The Marketing Edge*, Penguin).

Reasons for failure

Some of the major reasons for new product failure are:

- products are lacking in useful or meaningful uniqueness
- poor planning during the introduction phase
- poor timing of the introduction, for example, before the market is ready for the product
- over-enthusiasm leading to oversight of key points
- poor marketing after launch
- lack of backing from top management in the organization leading to the product never really standing a chance of being a success
- company politics, for example between various brand managers
- unanticipated high product costs

► A product is new if it is new to a company. What is a failure for one company may well be a success for another. It all depends on the expectations of the organization. There are many different reasons for failure.

The reasons for failure are many and are often associated with a firm's inability to use common-sense reasoning, or inattention to the management task of marketing the product.

A SYSTEMATIC APPROACH

A systematic approach to finding and evaluating new product ideas can enable a firm to avoid developing products which are unlikely to be winners. We can all use our common sense but often we benefit enormously by having aids that structure our thinking – it is so easy to overlook a critical detail. The first aid to structured thinking about new products concerns the adoption of a six phase development programme:

> 1 Idea acquisition
> 2 Initial screening
> 3 Business analysis
> 4 Product development
> 5 Market testing
> 6 Product introduction to the market

The first three of these phases are vitally important in view of escalating costs during the early stages of product development. The sooner that potentially poor product ideas can be screened out, the better for the company.

The C5

Clive Sinclair's answer to traffic problems was unveiled on the 10th January 1985. The C5 was a low slung, lightweight, single seat, 31 inch high, battery and pedal-powered tricycle. It had a range of 20 miles before recharging and was priced at £399. Some motoring correspondents were less than enthusiastic about the product. One described it as a 'fun machine that can hardly be regarded as a serious, everyday, all-weather transport'.

Production of the C5 was suspended on the 29th March 1985 and TPD, makers of the C5, called in a receiver on the 14th of October 1985.

Adapted from : *Chronicle of the 20th Century*, Longman 1988

Idea acquisition

New product ideas can be acquired or generated in different ways. Feedback from customers, contact with R&D establishments, a firm's own R&D department, monitoring competition, reviewing trade journals, etc., can all give rise to new product ideas. However, such ideas arise only one at a time and cannot be evaluated against a large set of alternative ideas for new products. A powerful idea-generating device would therefore seem to be a useful thing to

▶ P. Kotler, *Marketing Management: Planning, Analysis and Control*, Prentice-Hall, 1988, p. 407, predicts a shortage of new product ideas in certain areas.

have so that lots of new product ideas can be generated and evaluated simultaneously. **Morphological analysis** is such a device. Its basic premise is the idea that a product is an entity which has different dimensions. It may come in different shapes and sizes, appeal to different target markets, be made of different materials, etc. It is the combination of attributes which go into creating the product entity itself. A toy may be constructed of wood, be relatively large, have the shape of an elephant and appeal to the toddler market. We can even go beyond tangible dimensions. A product may be a perfume extracted from flowers, taking on the metaphorical shape of youth and appeal to those who value natural products.

Morphological analysis involves first identifying the most important dimensions of a product – usually three or four – and then generating a list of attributes relating to the identified dimensions. The next step is to take combinations of the attributes generated (one for each dimension) and ask ourselves whether or not we already market this kind of product. For example, taking the perfume example, one combination might be:

> ► In such a case the use of a random word generator to produce possible attributes can be very useful (see for example Proctor R. A. (1989), 'Innovations in New Product Screening and Evaluation', *Technology and Strategic Management*, Vol 1 no 3, pp 313-323).

	Dimensions	
	Source	Image	Target Market
attributes:	extracted from flowers	youth	users of natural products

If the combination we generate does not represent a current product offering and we feel that it could constitute an attractive product market opportunity then we might retain it as a possible idea to be progressed to the next of the six phases – screening.

 Take any fast-moving consumer product that you find on the shelves of a supermarket and undertake a morphological analysis of the product.

Screening

Without undertaking desk and/or field research it is difficult to quantify what we might expect to sell. Pooled estimates of subjective expert opinions, however, can sometimes provide remarkably close estimates. It is therefore a good idea to involve members of the firm who have some idea of the quantities of the various new product ideas that the firm might expect to sell. Based on these predictions it will then be possible to do some rough estimates of likely profits to be generated. This can, however, be very time consuming and may not produce useful information at this stage in the process. It is perhaps better left to the third phase – business analysis – where a full quantitative analysis and evaluation can be made.

New product failures can arise because management simply overlooks some of the qualitative dimensions involved in developing the product. A good idea at the screening stage is to use a checklist against which to evaluate the product ideas. Experience seems to indicate that successful products:

- fit with the internal functional strengths of the business
- fit with market needs.

The checklist should therefore be a list of questions which address these two requirements, such as:

- is it possible to reach the market through present distribution channels?
- is the product complementary to current products?
- can it be priced below competing products of a similar quality?
- will it be easy to promote the product?
- is it a product for which there will always be uses?
- is there a wide variety of potential customers?
- can it be produced/marketed with existing resources?
- will it fill an unsatisfied need in the marketplace?
- will the market grow in size?

The checklist can be extended and modified. New product ideas can be rated against the items on the checklist and those satisfying key criteria can be passed on to the next phase – business analysis.

 Phil is considering starting a club for disabled people at the local church hall. Suggest a checklist of points he might have to take into consideration before taking the matter any further.

Business Analysis

The business analysis phase involves making sales, costs and profit projections to determine whether it will be possible to satisfy company's objectives. The key elements of the task are:

- predicting sales over a specific period
- estimating cost behaviour over the same period.

There are expert ways to estimate sales: expert opinion was one method mentioned above. Other approaches include:

- examining sales histories of similar products
- surveying market opinion.

If we are surveying market opinion, it has to be remembered that we are dealing with a 'concept' and not a finished product. We therefore have to find some way to represent the product or service concept so that the interviewees can say whether or not they would buy the product. We might ask the following question:

- Would you (the interviewee) buy the product?

▶ See survey of buyers' intentions in Chapter 9.

Tick one of the following – definitely ( ), probably ( ), probably not ( ), definitely not ( ).

Based on previous experience we could assign probabilities of purchase to the descriptors 'definitely, probably', etc. and then forecast sales. The concepts can be presented symbolically or physically. At this stage a word and/or a picture description will suffice. In addition to getting some idea of the quantity we can expect to sell we should also be looking for qualitative feedback. It is possible that with some adjustment the product or service will sell better. It is important to get this right at the outset. The kind of qualitative questions to ask here are:

- are the benefits of using the product clear to the user?
- does the product solve a problem or fill a need?
- do other products already fill this need and give satisfaction?
- is the price right in relationship to the perceived value?

Whatever approach is taken, minimum and maximum sales estimates should be obtained so as to gain some idea of the amount of risk involved.

The method of forecasting depends on whether the product is a one-time purchase, an infrequently purchased product or a frequently purchased product. For infrequently purchased products attention has to be given to predicting first time sales and replacement sales. For frequently purchased products attention has to be given to first time buyers and repeat purchases. In using any of the three identified methods of forecasting it is essential to gain a separate estimate of:

- first time purchase
- replacement purchase
- repeat purchase.

In estimating costs we must bear in mind that present costs may change over the time span of the sales forecast. Costs, like sales, have uncertainties attached. Escalating prices of raw materials can play havoc with any projected profitability subsequent to the launch of a product.

▶ Putting a value on the financial appeal of a new product is of course very important but we do have to bear in mind the uncertainty that surrounds these estimates. There is always the danger that once numbers are put down on paper they will be treated as if they represent certainties. It is therefore a good idea to keep in mind the more qualitative aspects of evaluation as defined in the checklist of criteria used at the screening stage.

When making a financial evaluation of the new product ideas carried forward to this stage one should examine the following factors:

- estimated after-tax return on investment
- payback period
- variance in the estimates of return on investment and payback between the best scenario and the worst scenario (to indicate risk).

Products which pass through the criteria set for this phase may then move on to the product development phase.

Product development

Some products are obviously more complex than others. Product development can be an extremely lengthy business or it can be reasonably short. As a stage in the new product development process, it is important for all products. This is the stage where the product moves into R&D and engineering (in the case of a complex technological product) and it is here that the really heavy costs can start to mount up. It is at this stage that a firm determines whether the product idea can be turned into a technically and commercially feasible product. Turning an idea into tangible reality involves what is known as **prototyping**. The aim is to develop a physical version of the product (a prototype) which:

- consumers will recognize as fitting their expectations
- will perform safely under normal use and conditions
- can be produced for the budgeted manufacturing costs.

Prototyping can take days, months or years according to the nature of the product. Commercial aircraft take several years to develop. On completion, the prototype must be subjected to rigorous functional and consumer tests. Functional tests are carried out in the laboratory and in the field to ensure that the product performs safely and effectively. **Consumer testing** can in fact take a variety of forms. Consumers may be wooed into the laboratory to try out the product or be given models or samples to try out in their own homes. In-home placement tests are conducted on a wide variety of products.

► Domestic appliances such as washing machines undergo a long programme of physical testing in the laboratory to iron out the operating bugs. Once they have completed this stage, a number of machines are put into the homes of employees of the company who volunteer to test the machines under normal working conditions.

Test marketing

Not all products are test marketed. Some firms may reason that to test market the product may be to provide precious business knowledge to competitors. Test marketing, on the other hand, can avoid disasters and save firms millions of pounds. The amount of test marketing that a product requires is affected by the investment cost and risk on the one hand and pressure of time and cost of research on the other.

The greater the investment the more need there is to proceed with thorough testing. The same is true of high risk new products, particularly those with original features.

There is a variety of test marketing methods and there are differences between test marketing industrial goods and consumer goods.

Test marketing – consumer goods

Several approaches are found:

Sales wave research

Sales wave research amounts to persuading people to try a product at no cost and then re-offering them the product, or a competitor's product, at a somewhat lower price. They may be re-offered the product as many as three to five times (sales waves), and the researchers note how many customers pick the product again, together with their reported levels of satisfaction with the product. The researchers can work out repeat purchase rate in settings where consumers spend their own money and choose among competing brands.

Simulated store technique

Simulated store technique involves inviting a large group of shoppers to a brief screening of some television commercials. They are shown a number of well-known advertisements together with a number of new ones. One of the advertisements promotes the new product but this is not specifically brought to the attention of the audience.

Group members are given money to spend and invited into a store where they have the choice to buy any items they may choose or alternatively to hold on to the money. A note is made of how many people buy the new product and how many buy competing brands.

The group is then asked to explain their reasons for purchase or non-purchase. Some weeks later, group members are contacted by telephone to assess their attitude, usage and satisfaction with the product. They are also offered the chance to repurchase products.

► Shocker D. and Hall W. G. (1978), 'Pretest market models, a critical evaluation', *Journal of Product Innovation Management*, 3 1986, pp 86–7.

Controlled test marketing

Here a number of stores agree to carry a new product for a price. The company introducing the new product can nominate the number of stores and the geographical areas it requires. The firm supplies the product to participating stores and oversees shelf location, number of facings, displays and point of purchase promotions, and pricing. Sales are later assessed both from movement off the shelves and from inspecting consumer diaries. A sample of consumers is interviewed later to gain their impressions of the product.

This kind of test marketing can be criticized for its lack of reality in so far as the firm with the new product does not have to sell to the stores in the first instance. Secondly, there is considerable opportunity for competition to interfere and distort the results.

Actual 'test marketing'

Test markets are the best way to find out about the consumer acceptability of a new product. A few representative towns and cities are selected. The company has to sell to the trade as it would do following a national launch. Full advertising and promotion campaigns, similar to the one which would be used in national marketing, are conducted in the areas involved. Test marketing can be expensive but its costs are a fraction of the amount involved in a full scale national launch. In addition to predicting sales – perhaps the key function of the test market – it also allows firms to test out various marketing plans.

Industrial goods market testing

Test marketing is not commonly used in the case of industrial goods. This is because it is too expensive to produce a sample of products such as machine tools or ships' propellers. Instead, industrial firms may use what is known as a product use test which is similar to the in-home use test in the case of consumer products. The manufacturer picks potential customers who agree to use the product for a limited period of time. The technical staff of the manufacturer then observe how the customers use the product. This can lead to the exposure of unanticipated problems of safety and servicing. Moreover, it gives the manufacturer a good idea of the amount of customer training and servicing that is required. After the test period the customer is asked to express how likely they are to purchase the product and any other reactions to it.

▶ J C B excavators loan out their new excavators to civil engineering contractors and other large builders for product testing. Often the products are tested to breaking point under extreme operating conditions. The results fed back to the company are extremely helpful.

Trade shows are another way open to industrial manufacturers to introduce new products. Manufacturers try to assess how much interest visitors to the trade show express in the new product and whether or not they intend to buy. Dealer and distributor showrooms are another situation in which the product can be tested.

Controlled test marketing is occasionally used. Under these circumstances a limited supply of the product is produced and the sales force is instructed to sell it in a limited geographic area. The campaign is given full promotional support.

Commercialization

If a company is a manufacturer then commercialization will involve the heaviest expenditure of the whole process of introducing a new product. Production costs alone are huge, but another major cost is marketing. The cost of introducing major new consumer packaged goods into the market can run into millions of pounds or roughly half sales earnings during the first year of operation.

Timing the introduction of a new product is extremely important. Not only does the firm have to keep an eye on what the competition is doing and pace its strategy accordingly, but it also has to bear in mind the effect of a new product on its other products. The introduction has to be timed so that sales of a similar product are not suddenly stifled by undesirable side effects.

▶ It may be possible to avert the risk of failure by adopting a systematic approach to evaluating ideas. This would include initial screening and business analysis. Product development and market testing prior to introduction to the market can also assist.

Deciding where to launch a new product can also be extremely important. Very few companies undertake to launch a product into full national or international distribution. Firms develop a planned market roll out over time. The smaller companies select perhaps one city at a time and instigate blitz campaigns to secure footholds in the surrounding territories. Once these have been secured they then move on to new cities. Larger companies tend to operate on a region by region basis. Where a company has a national distributor network then it may introduce its product nationally for example in the case of car manufacturers.

Organizing for new products

▶ Companies such as Schreiber Furniture, Hovis and Lockwoods Foods have all employed this type of approach or a simple variant on it. Sowrey T. (1987), *The Generation of Ideas for New Products*, London: Kogan Page.

Effective innovation needs effective organization. Traditionally, innovation has tended to stem from production departments carrying out research and development. When a prototype is produced it is shown to top management for approval. This type of arrangement is still common in many companies. A major weakness of this approach is that it does not arise from market-oriented planning and as a result the products developed may not be directly related to consumer needs. A natural progression from a production oriented type of organization structure is to put responsibility for new product development into the hands of some kind of committee. Usually the committee comprises members who represent the major functional areas of the business. Because of other commitments (the members of the committee are usually very senior staff), this sort of arrangement may not be very effective if many new ideas have to be considered.

▶ It has been used by Lever Bros, Lyons Bakery, Whitbread, Fisons, Van den Berghs, Pedigree Foods and many other well-known companies (Sowrey, 1987).

Placing responsibility for the development of new products with product managers in marketing departments has become a popular way of handling new products in UK based companies. A difficulty that may arise in using this kind of approach is that, since product managers are responsible for existing products, they may not have the time to attend to new products. An extension of having product managers in charge of new product development, and one which makes inherently more sense, is to have a new products department. Such departments usually have line responsibility for the new products until the test market stage.

▶ Cadbury-Typhoo, Findus, Quaker Oats and United Biscuits number among the firms to have adopted this kind of approach (Sowrey, 1987).

THE CONSUMER-ADOPTION PROCESS

How do potential customers learn about new products, try them, adopt them or discard them? In order to get a new product off the ground successfully a firm's marketing management has to understand this process.

Adopters of new products have been found to move through the following five stages:

1 **Awareness** – where the consumer becomes aware of the innovation but has no information about it
2 **Interest** – where the consumer is stimulated to find out more information about the new product

3 **Evaluation** – where the consumer is weighing up whether it is worthwhile trying the innovation

4 **Trial** – where the consumer tries out the product on a limited basis to assess its desirability

5 **Adoption** – where the consumer decides to make full and regular use of the innovation.

Rogers (1962) explored how people come to adopt innovations over time and discovered that there were five categories of people:

1 **Innovators** – willing to try out new ideas and take risks

2 **Early adopters** – opinion leaders in their sphere of social intercourse, who take innovations on board after due consideration

3 **Early majority** – adopt new ideas early in the cycle but are not usually opinion leaders

4 **Late majority** – these people tend to be sceptical and adopt an innovation only after the majority of people have tried it

5 **Laggards** – tend to be suspicious of change and only take on an innovation when it has been tried and tested.

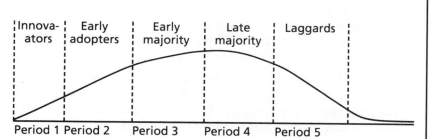

Adapted from E.M. Rogers (1962), *The Diffusion of Innovations*. New York: Macmillan.

Rogers' typology suggests that in launching new products a firm should carefully research the characteristics of innovators and early adopters along with their media characteristics. Unfortunately, this is not straightforward task since people may fall into one typology for one product and another for a different product. Rogers argued that there was a tendency for early adopters to be younger, have a higher social status, a more favourable financial position and a different type of mental ability from later adopters. He saw them making use of more impersonal and cosmopolitan information sources that were in closer contact with the origin of the new ideas.

Link with the product life cycle concept

The theory of the diffusion and adoption of innovations and the life cycle concept are linked. On the launch of a new product a

► See Chapter 7 for more on the product life cycle

► The idea of the consumer adoption process provides a framework within which to understand how consumer new products and services may come to be adopted.

company seeks to stimulate awareness, interest, trial and purchase. This is a lengthy process and during the introductory stage only a relatively few people will buy it (the innovators). Later, if people find that the product gives satisfaction, larger numbers of buyers will be attracted to purchase (the early adopters). The emergence of competition speeds up the process by increasing awareness and causing prices to fall – the early majority are drawn in. Eventually the growth rate of the market declines as new buyers approach zero and sales become steady at the replacement rate. Sales start to decline as new product categories, forms and brands appear and cause consumers to shift allegiance.

CHAPTER SUMMARY

1 The simplest way of defining a new product is as anything which is new to an organization and which amounts to more than a simple modification of an existing product.

2 Defining new product failure depends upon the criteria by which we are assessing success or failure. Put simply, a new product failure is a product which fails to live up to the organizations's expectations (usually expressed in financial terms). It follows that what may constitute a failure for one firm could be considered a success for another firm.

3 Many factors contribute to new product failure. However, failures may be avoided if the organization carefully states its expectations on key criteria in the first instance and then evaluates the new product ideas against these criteria.

4 Ideas for new products arise in many ways. Suggestions may come from competitors, distributors and the organization's own employees. In addition there are creativity techniques which can be used to help generate new product ideas. One of the best known of these is morphological analysis.

5 The new product screening process is intended to help eliminate new product ideas that are unlikely to be successful in the firm's terms. Initial screening involves constructing a checklist against which to rate any new ideas. Those that pass the checklist stage go on to further analysis.

6 Business analysis is part of the new product screening process. Estimates are made about the feasibility of developing and marketing a product to meet with the firm's required sales and profit targets. Costings and market research data are used to make projections and reach conclusions.

7 If firms are reasonably sure that a product idea is a good one

they can go on to the product development stage. This can vary enormously in length of time and in cost, according to the nature of the product.

8 It is generally agreed that all products should be test-marketed prior to commercialization on a national or international basis, unless there are strong grounds for not doing so. Test marketing cannot save heavy research and development expenditure but it can avoid wasting money on expensive marketing and production of initial stock if it proves that products are unlikely to be successful in their current form.

9 New products are at the very first stage in the product life cycle. To get new products off the ground we have to understand the process by which new products come to be adopted. Key people in the adoption process are the innovators and the early adopters. Organizations need to be able to identify these people and persuade them to adopt the product if they are to stand the best chance of getting the product off the ground.

► Now that you have reached the end of the chapter, turn back to the objectives and make sure you have achieved each of them.

Pricing decisions

Introduction

In this chapter we will explore key pricing phenomena and their consequences. Firstly we will look at aspects of classical economic theory and what it does and does not explain. Secondly we will look at pricing in practice and point to the differences between theory and real world problems.

Definition of price

Buyers, distributors and producers are all interested in **price**. One way of looking at a price is as the amount of money for which a product or service is exchanged, or offered for sale to potential purchasers , irrespective of its value or worth.

OVERVIEW OF PRICING POLICIES AND STRATEGIES

Pricing policies and strategies vary extensively and there is no single best method to set prices. In a perfectly competitive market a producer has almost no control over prices: they are determined by market forces brought about by competitive pressures and patterns of consumer expenditure.

Pricing takes on its greatest importance in a business when:

- a new product is being introduced
- a competitor increases or reduces its prices
- a change arises in the economy that will influence demand
- business moves influence demand
- there are changes in government regulations
- a technological breakthrough happens which influences production costs
- the firm changes its strategy or tactics.

► Perfectly competitive markets demand that there is an homogeneous product, complete information among buyers, rational buyer behaviour and large numbers of producers. There are extremely few such markets in reality.

Classical economic approach to pricing

Classical economics takes the view that price determines the supply of goods and services and the demand for goods and services in the marketplace.

The law of demand

The **law of demand** states that the quantity of a good demanded per period of time is inversely related to price. That is, as the price of a product increases so demand decreases and as price decreases demand increases. This pattern is illustrated by the figure shown below. The typical market demand curve slopes downwards from left to right, indicating that as price falls more is demanded. Thus, if the price falls from OP_1 to OP_2, the quantity demanded will increase from OQ_1 to OQ_2.

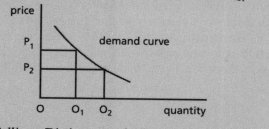

Source: *Collins Dictionary of Economics* (1988), London: HarperCollins Publishers.

► Utility is the consumer's estimate of the goods or services'
capacity to satisfy his or her needs.

The law is based upon the assumption that a consumer is logical and has full knowledge of the available goods and services
and their substitutes. Moreover it assumes that a consumer has
a limited budget and motivation to maximize utility. If relative
prices of goods and services change, the consumer will normally substitute less expensive for dearer goods thereby
increasing his or her utility.

Price elasticity is a key concept in understanding how demand
shifts with respect to changes in price.

$$\text{price elasticity of demand} = \frac{\% \text{ change in quantity demanded}}{\% \text{ change in price}}$$

It will be appreciated that the ratio is usually negative – this is
because as price rises demand usually falls. It is customary, moreover, in illustrating elasticities, to drop the negative sign. When
price elasticity is 1 it means that demand rises (falls) by the same
percentage that price falls (rises). We should note that in this case
total revenue is not affected by changes in price. However, when
the elasticity is above or below 1 then total revenues will be
affected by changes in price.

Price elasticity of demand	Effect of a change of price on total revenue
1	None
>1	Demand rises or falls at a greater rate than rate of price change.
<1	Demand rises or falls at a lesser rate than rate of price change.

Calculating price elasticity of demand enables us to determine
whether a product's price is too high or too low. If a firm is trying
to maximize its revenue then the price for a product or service will
be too high if demand elasticity at that price is greater than 1 and
too low if demand elasticity at that price is less than 1.
Unfortunately it is not possible to generalize this rule to profit
maximization since we have to take the behaviour of costs into
account.

The concept of elasticity of demand can be extended to consumer income. When an item is substantially reduced in price, there is, in effect, an increase in real income of households which consume the item. With the additional purchasing power, these households may elect to change to buying more expensive products instead of consuming more of the former product. In this case the effect on income outweighs the substitution effect. For example, if a poor family consumes a lot of potatoes and if the price of potatoes falls, then this family might use the increase in real income to buy more meat and reduce its consumption of potatoes. This brings us to measure called **income elasticity of demand (IE)**:

▶ Income elasticity of demand:

$$\frac{\% \text{ change in quantity demanded}}{\% \text{ change in income}}$$

Income elasticity:
>   IE <1 = normal goods
>   IE >1 = superior goods
>   IE <0 = inferior goods

In the case of **inferior goods**, where a rise in consumer affluence is expected, the business can expect a decline in sales. As a consequence, the firm might reduce investment plans for the product and diversify into products with positive income elasticity coefficients (superior or normal goods). It could also change the image of the product by giving it an up-market appeal to attract better-off customers. Luxury goods are **superior goods** and when consumer affluence increases producers of these products can expect to do well and it may be desirable to have investment plans. **Normal goods** are necessities and these exhibit relatively little response to changes in income.

▶ In times of consumer affluence, superior goods fare better. In times of recession, inferior goods do well. Firms which can shift the direction of their investments from inferior to superior goods, and vice versa, as economic climates change are in a strong position.

Another useful measure of demand sensitivity is the relationship between the price of one good and the quantity demanded of another. This measure is known as the **cross-price elasticity of demand (CPE)**. In this case:

● products are substitutes for one another if CPE >0
● products are complements to one another if CPE <0

▶ Cross-price elasticity of demand:

$$\frac{\% \text{ change in quantity demanded of x}}{\% \text{ change in the price of y}}$$

Price elasticity varies over time and according to the stage in the product life cycle. In addition, price elasticities are likely to be different for price increases and for price decreases. They will also be influenced by the extent to which a given price deviates from the average market price. The following case study will illustrate price elasticity of demand:

The demand for theatre tickets

A particular theatre, which can seat up to 1000 people wanted to maximize its revenues from sales of tickets. The managers undertook a survey of theatre-goers to determine whether or not people would continue to come to the theatre if the price was fixed at various levels. Based on the survey the managers were able to produce the following table:

Price (£ per ticket)	Quantity of tickets demanded
12.50	0
10.00	200
7.50	400
5.00	600
2.50	800
0.00	1000

From the table the theatre managers deduced that the demand equation was:

$$D = 1000 - 80P$$
where D is the demand and P is the price.

Let us see how they might have arrived at this equation.
  One way would be by drawing a graph and reading the equation from it. The graph is shown below:

Theatre tickets: price and quantity demanded

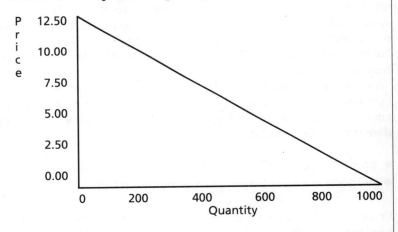

The point at which the line (curve) cuts the horizontal axis is 1000. For every drop of £2.50 in price, 200 additional people will come to the theatre. 200/2.50 = 80. Because the line is backward sloping, the slope will be −80.
  The price elasticity of demand for tickets at each price can also be calculated. For example, the percentage price cut from £10 to £7.50 is −25%. At the same change in price there is an increase in demand from 200 to 400 tickets – a rise of 100%. The price elasticity of demand at £10 is thus 100/−25 = −4. Price elasticity of demand at each price is therefore as follows:

Price (£ per ticket)	Elasticity of demand
12.50	−infinity
10.00	−4.00
7.50	−1.50
5.00	−0.67
2.50	−0.25
0.00	0.00

By definition revenues will be maximized when the price elasticity is −1. From the table we can calculate that this is when the price of a ticket is £6.25.

This amount could be calculated using differential calculus, thus:

the revenue (price mutiplied by demand) equation is:

$$P \times O = P(1000 - 80P)$$
$$= 1000P - 80P^2$$

differentiating the equation gives:

$$= 1000 - 160P$$
$$P = 1000/160$$
$$= 6.25$$

▶ A good introduction to differential calculation is to be found in J. Curwin and R. Slater, *Quantitative Methods for Business Decisions*, Chapman and Hall, 3rd edition 1991.

or it can be obtained graphically thus:

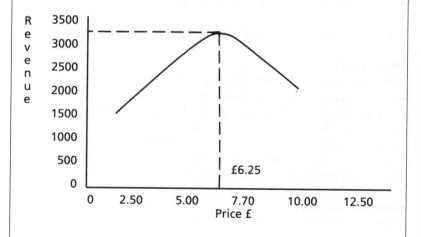

▶ Price elasticity is central to economic notions about price. Sales of products with a high price elasticity of demand fluctuate the most with price changes. Elasticity also varies at different prices and revenues are maximized when it is equal to (−)1.

The analysis therefore shows that in order to maximize revenues the theatre managers should charge £6.25 for a seat. Since the demand equation is: D = 1000 − 80P then:

$$D = 1000 - (80 \times 6.25)$$
$$= 500$$

This means that 500 people will come to the theatre – which will leave half the seats empty!

The revenue generated will be 500 x £6.25 = £3125.

The theatre managers might think in terms of having a smaller auditorium and putting the additional space to some other resource-generating use, for example installing a bar. Alternatively, the managers might try to find ways of attracting more people to the theatre by changing its product positioning.

Limitations of using the classical approach

There are several key assumptions which limit the practical applicability of the classical approach. These include:

- that the firm's objective in establishing its price for a product is to maximize short-term profits
- that the only parties to take account of in setting the price are the firm's immediate customers
- that price can be set independently of the other marketing variables
- that the demand and cost equations can be estimated with some degree of precision
- that the firm has true control over price
- that market response to price changes is well understood.

Let us now look at each one of these in turn.

Objectives

The economic model assumes there is a single product with the seller setting a price which maximizes immediate rather than long-term profits. In reality demand and costs do change over time because of changes in taste, population and income on the one hand and changes in technology and input prices on the other. In addition to these factors one would have to take into account the position of the product in its life cycle.

► Theory suggests that firms seek long-term profit maximization.

Multiple parties

There are a number of other participants to consider:

- intermediate customers – a variety of relationships may exist. The producer may set a price to the distributor and allow the latter to charge whatever price it likes. On the other hand the producer may determine both the final price to the consumer and the distributor margin necessary to create an incentive for the distributor
- competing firms – the pricing policy adopted by a firm has a profound influence on the rate of entry of new competitors and the pricing policies of existing competitors

- government – from time to time government may intervene to control prices.

Interaction with other elements in the marketing mix

Not taking account of the interaction with other elements in the marketing mix is a substantial failing of the classical economics approach. The classical approach assumes that the variables of the market mix other than price are held at a constant level.

Estimating demand and cost functions

Demand functions are very difficult to work out and must be based on historical data or survey estimates. In the case of cost data, econometric analysis may prove more successful but the reliability of the estimates used in making future projections is questionable.

Price discretion

The amount of discretion that a seller may have in setting price is largely influenced by the buyer's concern with price and the amount of product differentiation that exists in the market. Where product differentiation is prominent and the buyer's concern with price is inconsequential then the marketer will have a high measure of discretion on setting the price. In other instances, especially where concern with price is high, there is much less discretion open to the marketer.

► Price is often taken as a marker of product quality. A high price is associated with high quality. In the case of consumer goods this is often accompanied with advertising through glossy magazines and and distribution through selective quality image retail outlets.

► Petrol is a case where consumers are price conscious. Many people are prepared to queue for cheap petrol rather than be served quickly at a petrol station nearby where it is a few pence dearer.

Varying buyer reactions to price changes

Classical economic theory shows an inverse relationship between price change and demand: a reduction in price being associated with an increase in demand and an increase in price with a fall in demand. In practice, however, this may not necessarily be the case. A price decrease, for instance, could signal to the market:

- the product is about to be supplanted by a later version
- the product has bugs in it and is not selling well
- the firm is in financial trouble and may not remain in business to provide spares when they are needed
- the price will come down more and it will pay to wait
- there has been a decline in product quality

Any of these factors may lead to a fall in demand. On the other hand a price increase might suggest:

- the product is in strong demand and may soon become unobtainable
- the product represents exceptionally good value for money
- the seller may charge more if the buyer waits too long

► Economic theories of pricing have their limitations when it comes to applying them in practice. However, they provide a framework within which to evaluate pricing in the real world.

► Older houses present a good example of this. If the price is too high potential buyers may feel as if they are being taken advantage of or else they simply may not be able to afford the asking price. If the price is too low they tend to assume that there is something wrong with the house.

These factors may, of course, lead to an increase in demand.

In addition there is an expected range of prices which people anticipate having to pay for a product. If the price lies outside the range – above or below – then it is likely that purchases will not be made.

ACT Make one list of consumer durables and another of fast moving consumer products which you can buy at the supermarket. Take a look around you local town or city over a period of a few days and see what evidence you can find to show that products are priced in bands.

Price setting in practice

While the classical economic approach to price setting is valuable there are many difficulties in putting it into effect. Economic pricing models oversimplify reality and cannot be readily implemented. Nevertheless, pricing rules of thumb and guidelines used in practice also tend to emphasize one factor such as cost, demand or competition to the neglect of the other factors.

Cost-oriented pricing

Many firms set their prices largely or even entirely on the basis of their own costs. Frequently all the costs are counted, including a general arbitrary allocation of overhead made on the basis of expected operating levels. **Standard cost pricing** and **mark up pricing** are the most basic types of cost-oriented pricing. Both of them comprise appending some fixed percentage to the unit cost to arrive at a preliminary price. The preliminary price is then compared with the going market price for a similar product and adjusted slightly if necessary.

Standard cost pricing

A microcomputer manufacturer estimates that the average variable costs and fixed costs associated with producing a particular model of a given specification, assuming unit sales of 100,000 over five years, amount to £500 per unit. The average cost per unit is found by adding up all fixed and variable costs (see page 214 for a more detailed description) and dividing by the number of units to be produced. The following costs are included:

● design and development costs
● production costs
● depreciation
● overheads
● rent
● insurance

- handling and packaging
- storage
- cost of inventory
- advertising
- delivery
- installation
- warranty service
- patent royalty

Selling, merchandizing and administration expenses usually add another thirty per cent on to the costs and the firm would want to make £200 profit per machine. The preliminary price then becomes:

£500 + (0.30 x 500) + 200 = £850

The manufactuer notes that dealers would normally expect to pay around £840 for such a machine, so it adjusts the product down to that level.

Mark-up pricing

In this case the manufacturer would proceed as above but would desire a specified percentage mark up on sales that it wants to earn. Let us assume this to be twenty-five per cent. Then the price to the dealer would be calculated as:

$$\text{Mark-up price} = \frac{\text{Unit costs}}{(1 - \text{desired return on sales})}$$

Unit costs were initially estimated at £500 but £150 has to be added for selling, merchandizing and administration. Hence the preliminary mark-up price to dealers would be:

$$\frac{650}{(1 - 0.25)} = £866.67$$

Such an approach does not really make for sound practice. Any approach that leaves out demand elasticity in setting prices is unlikely to lead to profit maximization either in the short run or the long run. Because demand elasticity changes – as it is likely to do seasonally, cyclically or over the life cycle – the optimum mark up should also change. If the mark up stays as a fixed percentage of the cost then it is unlikely under normal conditions to lead to profit maximization.

There are conditions when a rigid mark up at the right level may produce optimum profits. These are when average unit costs are fairly constant for different points on the demand curve and costs are constant over time.

▶ Both of these prerequisite conditions – constant costs and constant elasticity – have been found to exist in many retailing situations. This could account for why moderately inflexible mark ups are in broad use in retailing and why they may well lead to optimal pricing requirements.

Target return pricing

Target pricing is the situation where a firm tries to determine a price which will give a specified rate of return on its investment. Like the above approach it takes no note of demand and except by chance cannot lead to profit maximization.

$$\text{Target return price} = \text{unit cost} + \frac{\text{desired return x invested capital}}{\text{unit sales}}$$

► Approaches to pricing which involve adding up the costs and putting on an amount for profit are easy to do and are often encountered in business. Even when prices are adjusted to take account of what other firms are charging they may still not be optimal. Such approaches do not take account of demand.

Target return pricing – an example

A tumble drier manufacturer has £2m. invested in the business and wants to set a price to earn a return on investment of 25% – that is £500,000. The tumble drier manufacturer estimates unit costs to be £120 and thinks that it can sell 20,000 units. Using this information we can see that the target return price, using the formula above, would be:

$$£120 + \frac{0.25 \times £2,000,000}{20,000} = £145$$

As we can see from this example the manufacturer does not try to establish the relationship between price and demand. It simply assumes that 20,000 units can be sold and then sets a price afterwards. At the price of £145 it may very well be able to sell many more units of the product, or of course it may sell less than it expects. In either case it is unlikely to maximize profits, except by chance. A higher price may generate fewer sales but it could generate larger profits. A lower price could generate more sales and more profits. However, unless the firm tries to establish the relationship between price and demand it cannot really expect to maximize profits.

Demand-oriented pricing

As the name suggests **demand-oriented pricing** takes account of the strength of demand. Firms taking on this strategy exact a high price when or where demand is strong and a low price when or where demand is weak, even if there is no dissimilarity in fixed and variable costs in either case.

Differences in the strength of demand in the market permit firms to conduct a programme of price discrimination in different market segments. The ability to practice price discrimination requires that:

- the market is segmentable with evidence of different demand intensities in the segments
- there is no chance that buyers at a lower price are able to resell at a higher price
- there is no chance that competitors will undersell the firm in the segment being charged the higher price
- the cost of segmenting and policing the market exceed the extra revenue obtained as a result of price discrimination
- that price discrimination is allowable under the law
- higher paying customers are not resentful and do not react negatively to the company in the long run.

Penetration versus skimming pricing strategies

Firms are often eager to achieve early market **penetration** with a new product and will set a comparatively low price to instigate growth and to capture a large share of the market. Because of the effect of the experience curve long-term profitability will almost certainly rise with a large market share or a growth in market share. Such a strategy may be pursued if the market seems to be highly price sensitive, or whenever a product is favoured by economies of scale in production, or, where a low price discourages actual and potential competition.

In contrast to a penetration strategy other firms may try to take advantage of the fact that some buyers are prepared to pay a high price because they want the product very much. In the beginning, therefore, a firm may set a high price to gain a premium from these buyers and will progressively reduce the price to bring in the more price-elastic segments. This strategy is referred to as **price skimming** and is often used where there is an adequate number of buyers whose demand is relatively inelastic. It may also be used where the unit production and distribution costs associated with producing a smaller volume are not so much higher that they cancel out the advantage of charging what some of the market will buy, or where little danger exists that a high price will stimulate the emergence of competition.

Competition-oriented pricing

Here a firm sets its prices in line with what competitors are charging and keeps its price at the level charged by the industry. This is referred to as the **going-rate** price.

Going-rate pricing is used, as a rule, in homogeneous product-markets. The market structure in such cases ranges from pure competition to pure **oligopoly**. In a purely competitive market the firm can exercise little choice in setting its price. In the case of pure oligopoly , in which a few firms control the industry, firms are apt to charge the same price as competitors, but for different reasons. In this case, in view of the fact that there are only a few firms, each one of them knows the other's price. Moreover, the buyers are also

► Pure competition exists where many competitors offer the same product or service (for example a commodity market). An oligopoly exists where a few firms are producing essentially the the same commodity, for example oil, steel, etc.

The psychology of pricing

'They're the first pair I've spotted for around twenty quid.'

Pricing a new product – skimming

Philips shocked the consumer electronics industry by introducing its proposed mass market Digital Compact Cassette (DCC) at an ultra high price. DCC was positioned as the replacement for the standard audio cassette and Philips had emphasized that it could be produced far more cheaply than products like Sony's Digital Audio Tape and Mini Disc.

A company spokesman stressed that prices would come down soon. He argued that launch operations were always expensive and that people try to market it at premium prices to get as much as possible paid for. He maintained that DCC sales would outstrip those of ordinary cassettes – a format which had peaked.

Source: *Marketing*, November 14 1991, p. 3.

well abreast of prices. Price differences are liable to favour the lower-priced firm, thereby discouraging increases by a single firm.

Where markets are inclined towards product differentiation, there is more scope for a firm in setting its prices. Product differentiation, whatever form it takes, serves to desensitize the buyer to price differentials . Products and marketing programmes are made compatible within a chosen pricing range, and firms respond to competitive changes in price to maintain their pricing range.

Psychological dimensions to pricing

Wandering around the shops you will notice that goods may be priced at £3.99 or £6.99 rather than £4 or £7. This is because research into consumer perceptions suggests that people tend to round prices down, so that the prices in fact are perceived to to be £3 and £6 respectively.

There are various other interesting dimensions to **psychological prices**. It was noted earlier in the chapter that raising prices can actually increase sales. We also saw that price is often seen as a surrogate for quality, and in the absence of information to the contrary, people will assume something is of better quality if it carries a higher price tag. This phenomenon can lead to absurdities where two products which have the same intrinsic value may fetch vastly different prices because the consumer considers one to be more 'special' than the other. Good examples are to be found in the purchase of perfumes and quartz watches. In the case of perfumes, the ingredients of a very expensive perfume may cost exactly the same as those in a very cheap perfume. In the case of quartz watches the same principle may apply and the more expensive watch may be distinguishable from the cheaper one only by its brand name.

Pricing points

In many industries firms make use of what are known as **pricing points**. A producer may get a retailer to agree to a point of sale in the shop price of say 79p. At this price the retailer and the producer may both be happy because the retailer is obtaining a satisfactory margin and the producer will receive a satisfactory price. If, however, the producer wants extra shelf space then it will probably have to offer the retailer more promotional discount so that it can sell the product at 69p. The retailer will not agree to sell it at 70p or 75p. Such a reduction in price to the user would cut into the price received by the producer and might not be worth the extra sales volume to the retailer that the extra shelf space generates. One way round this problem, of course, is to produce products in different packet sizes to meet with retailers' specific pricing points.

Price-quality relationship

Quality is something which by and large is in the eye of the buyer. It has long been recognized that products which have a higher quality can fetch higher prices. Many firms these days are basing their prices on the product's perceived value. Buyers' perceptions of value rather than the seller's cost are seen as the key to pricing. Moreover, firms employ the non-price variables in the marketing mix to build up the perceived value in the buyer's mind.

The concept of perceived value fits in well with the modern approaches to product positioning. The idea is to identify key dimensions upon which the product will be judged by end-users. For example, let us consider a microcomputer. The price may be:

+ £2400 if it is only equivalent to the competitor's microcomputer
+ £1000 – the price premium for superior performance
+ £500 – the price premium for superior service
+ £200 – the price premium for longer warranty on parts
+ £4100 is the price to cover the total value package

Clearly this kind of pricing strategy requires a knowledge of how much customers are willing to pay for these additional value characteristics.

BREAKEVEN ANALYSIS

A much-used tool in setting prices for new products is **breakeven analysis**. The idea is that production and marketing of every product involves a cost on the one hand but yields revenue on the other. As long as revenue exceeds cost the product will be profitable and it is at least useful to consider keeping the product in the product line. Of course, there are exceptions: profitable products may be dropped because they are not profitable enough, for instance if the firm might earn more profit by diverting its resources to different products or different projects. Similarly, apparently unprofitable products may be retained because they help to sell other very profitable products.

There are two kinds of costs associated with a product: variable

► Demand-oriented pricing offers the best opportunity to optimize profits. Furthermore it is making use of price as a strategic tool within the marketing mix. Firms should not overlook the importance of psychological pricing.

► Price is often taken as a surrogate for quality.

► See page 208.

costs and fixed costs. **Variable costs** are so called because they vary according to the amount of the product produced. Generally speaking, these costs are readily identifiable and can be costed against definite output of the product. The costs include labour and materials. Many firms have sophisticated costing systems which can allocate variable costs to individual products. The second kind of costs are called **fixed costs**. This means that these costs are fixed regardless of the output of the product. Fixed costs include overheads. So if a firm produced only one product then all of the fixed costs would be charged to it. Firms normally produce many products and so a fair system of spreading or allocating fixed costs has to be found.

In assessing the profitability of a product we are therefore interested in two things: firstly, whether the product covers its variable costs and, secondly, what contribution it makes to fixed costs and profits. Products and services which cover their variable costs and then make large contributions to fixed costs and profits are generally regarded as the more desirable.

The classical breakeven model assumes that there are distinguishable fixed costs associated with a product and, in addition, that there are variable costs. The idea is to estimate how much sales revenue is needed to recover the fixed costs associated with the product and at the same time cover variable costs. The sales revenue at the point where this occurs is known as the breakeven point – it is easily changed to unit sales by dividing sales revenue by the unit price. In the area above the level of sales revenue indicated by the breakeven point the firm is in profit, while below the breakeven point the product is not recovering all its costs. This is illustrated by the graph shown in the inset on page 215.

Breakeven point then is where the total revenue = the total cost. A selling price of £10 and an average variable cost of £5 results in a per unit contribution to fixed cost of £5. Breakeven point in units (BPU) is then:

$$BPU = \frac{\text{total fixed cost}}{\text{per unit contribution to fixed cost}}$$

If total fixed costs are £50,000 then:

$$BPU = \frac{50,000}{5} = 10,000$$

Breakeven point in money (BP£) is

$$\frac{\text{Total fixed cost}}{1 - \frac{\text{variable cost per unit}}{\text{price}}} = \frac{50,000}{1 - 5/10}$$
$$= £100,000$$

▶ Fixed costs are also known as **overheads**. Fixed costs include rent, heat, interest, executive salaries, etc.

An example of breakeven analysis

A firm is putting a new product on to the market. The product has fixed costs of £50,000. In addition, there are unit variable costs of £5 per unit. The firm envisages a selling price of £10 per unit. £10 appears to be the going rate.

The chart below shows how the sales revenue and profits generated by this product will vary with the amount sold. We can read off from the graph that breakeven point is where the sales in units = 10,000 units and sales revenue = £100,000.

Breakeven chart

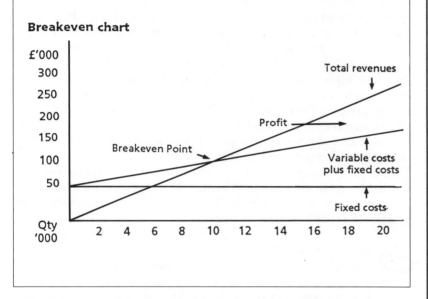

Profit is the excess over breakeven point.

Profit = (selling price – unit cost) x $\dfrac{\text{quantity}}{\text{breakeven}}$

Thus if sales are 12,000 units the profit =(10–5) x (12000 – 10000)
= £10,000

Breakeven analysis is most useful for testing out different assumptions. We can assume different ranges of prices, costs and sales figures and derive associated levels of breakeven, profitability and loss. In this context a spreadsheet can become an indispensable tool.

In using breakeven analysis we have to be aware that it is based on three major assumptions:

1 A fixed relation between sales volume and returns.
2 That the firm can accurately predict the demand curve.
3 That the firm has a true appreciation of the cost situation.

► Breakeven analysis is a useful tool to use when considering the setting of prices for new products. It enables a firm to associate various levels of profits with different prices assuming different costs and volumes of sales.

The fixed costs associated with a new product are £150,000. In addition, there are unit variable costs of £6 per unit. The firm envisages a selling price of £12 per unit, which appears to be the going rate. Calculate the breakeven point in units and in money terms.

PRICE LEADERSHIP STRATEGY

► The advantages are brought about by economies of scale and the experience curve.

A market leader should have all the advantages over its competitors that coincide with higher volume sales and should be able to set the price structure for the market. In the event that the market leader resolves to take a low unit profit margin, then because of the volume of sales achieved, profits generated should be substantial. This will not be the case with competitors who do not enjoy the same high volume of sales. In fact, the competitors will have higher unit costs, higher distributor margins and probably lower selling prices to the trade. Life will not be easy for competitors.

► Price leaders can provide other firms with the opportunity to differentiate their products if they price too highly for the market.

If the market leader decides to take a higher unit profit margin, this will give the whole market a price '**umbrella**'. All firms can charge higher prices and profitability all round can be increased. This allows competitors to introduce product improvements, funded by retained additional profits. Competitors can also invest in more aggressive marketing. The net result will probably be to weaken the market leader's position.

 Pricing umbrella
Xiang Tsang runs an umbrella manufacturing business in Taiwan and supplies to markets all over the world. Xiang has the largest share of the world market and achieves considerable economies of scale with high volume sales. The firm originally belonged to Xiang's uncle and he has only just taken it over after his uncle's death. He has no previous experience of the umbrella business. He notes that the profit margins on all the products are very low but that the company still makes a good profit. Anxious to do well in his new position as chief executive, he is wondering whether a price rise in real terms might be in order to increase profitability. If he were to couple this with improvements in product features he feels that that customers would be prepared to pay more for the improvement in product quality.
Do you think Xiang is right?

Stage in the product life cycle and leader's strategy

The phase of development attained by the market is of major concern to the market leader in making pricing decisions. If the market is in the growth stage then extra sales volume is available. The objective of the leader will be to earn a major share of the new business and so it will want to discipline competitors' actions and deter others from seeking entrance to the market. The leader can achieve this by keeping the unit margin of profitibility low.

With the increase in volume of a market the effects of the experience curve are felt and product unit costs should tumble. The dilemma facing the market leader relates to whether to bring prices down and if so how speedily this should be. The answer is to be found in the leader's designs with respect to the next stage in the product life cycle – the maturity stage. If it is the market leader's intention to lead in this phase then it will have to maintain its leadership through the transition phase. It must ensure that its prices move downwards as the volume moves ahead and unit costs decline. If it does not do this then there is always a chance that competitors will take advantage of the position and increase capacity and market share. It is probably advantageous for the leader to maintain its position since the additional volume of sales generated can mean that total margins will increase despite the lower selling prices.

▶ Other firms will not enjoy the same cost advantages as the leader and operating on tight profit margins are not in a position to achieve great improvements in differentiation. A potential entrant on seeing this situation may feel deterred from entering the market.

Once a static market position or one of decline is reached then the horizon for the market leader can be altogether different. There will be little chance of a new competitor entering the market and brand loyalty will have been established. In such circumstances the leader should be able to take higher margins without taking excessive risks.

The general counsel for firms possessing a lower level of market share is to follow the leader when it comes to changes in prices. There is a fundamental assumption in this that the marketers of such brands do not want to engage the leader in direct price competition. Their direct and indirect costs of production are probably higher than the leader's and price to the trade is probably lower. In such a situation the marketer is not in a good position to take on the leader with a pricing challenge.

▶ Other firms are recommended to follow the moves of the leader as far as price changes go.

Price wars

Price war is defined as any competition between rival suppliers centred on aggressive price cutting. Price wars often break out when demand for a product is depressed and there is excess supply capacity in the market. If fixed costs are a high proportion of total costs, suppliers may be tempted to cut their prices to maintain full capacity working.

Price warfare is beneficial to the consumer and to resource allocation within the market in so far as it serves to eliminate inefficient high cost suppliers. The problem from the suppliers' point of view is that cut throat price competition reduces the profitability of the market and everybody ends up worse off. For this reason suppliers, and particularly oligopoly suppliers, will normally try to avoid price wars and direct their competitive efforts into product-differentiation activities.

Go to the commercial section of any public lending library and ask for ask for the last two year's copies of the publication *Marketing*. See if you can find any examples reported of price wars.

CHAPTER SUMMARY

1 Pricing is a very important element in the marketing mix. It takes on its greatest importance when a price change is instigated.

2 A good deal of basic microeconomic theory is devoted to examining the relationship between price and demand. While many of the principles which have been developed have relevance to what happens in the real world, there are nevertheless many other factors that have to be taken into account. In reality, many differences can be found between theory and practice.

3 In practice firms use a variety of price setting methods. These may be cost oriented, demand oriented or competition oriented.

4 Understanding the principles of breakeven analysis and how this relates to price setting is important. This is particularly the case when setting prices for new products.

5 Price leadership has many advantages including high turnover and good profitability based on low margins. Firms exercising price leadership need to be wary of raising price margins since they can provide an umbrella for competitors to develop a differential advantage for their products.

6 Firms are advised to avoid price wars since they can lead to a stalemate position for all parties involved. But, where competition is keen, products homogeneous and economic times gloomy, price cutting and price wars may become inevitable.

► Now that you have reached the end of the chapter, turn back to the objectives and make sure you have achieved each of them.

14 Distribution strategies

Chapter objectives

By the end of the chapter you should:

▌ be able to describe the various channels of distribution through which firms can reach the market – direct through wholesalers and retailers, through agents and distributors, etc.

▌ be able to describe the different kinds of wholesale and retail establishments

▌ understand the advantages of franchising

▌ know the various channel decisions that have to be taken, i.e. whether to distribute direct to the customer or indirectly through middlemen, whether to adopt single or multiple channels of distribution, how long the channel of distribution should be, the types of intermediaries to use, the number of distributors to use at each level and which intermediaries to use – together with the criteria required to make such decisions.

▌ be able to describe the various ways in which producers can motivate intermediaries to promote their goods

▌ be able to describe the various elements that go into making up a physical distribution system

▌ know the impact that good inventory management can have on profitability and how it relates to customer service

▌ know how marketers evaluate different transportation methods and the advantages and disadvantages of the various methods

▌ understand the nature of the logistics concept and how this can lead to maximizing overall efficiency and effectiveness even if some of the elements of the distribution mix are not being optimized.

▌ be familiar with the following terms as used by marketers: mail order, brokers, wholesalers, retailers, factors, supermarkets, hypermarkets, multiples, superstores, chains, merchandisers, symbol groups, discount stores, department stores, co-operative stores, franchising, vending machines, telemarkets, viewdata systems, distribution programming, just in time (JIT) management, inventory management, level of service, product availability, stock-out, containerization, freightliner, logistics concept.

Introduction

Distribution is the element of 'place' in the four Ps. It actually involves all those activities to do with transferring the goods from the producer to the customer. It also includes the strategic decisions which determine the best way to make goods available to customers. A distinction is often made between these two dimensions of distribution by referring to them as **physical distribution** and **channel management** respectively. Physical distribution includes such things as warehousing, transportation and inventory management. Channel management concerns choice of suitable middlemen to act as intermediaries in the distribution process.

► See Chapter 2 for a full appreciation of the four Ps of the marketing mix.

CHANNELS OF DISTRIBUTION

Producers/suppliers have up to four methods of making goods and services available to the customer. These are discussed below:

1 Producer/supplier ————->customer

Both industrial goods and consumer goods may be distributed direct to customers. While it is common to find industrial goods distributed in this manner it is less common for consumer goods. In the case of industrial goods the size of the order in money terms is often sufficient to make it economical for the producer to supply direct to the customer. GEC, for example, distributes its transformers direct to customers. This does not necessarily mean that the producer will supply the transport. Specialist delivery firms may do this.

► Firms only take on those activities which they consider to be an economic proposition.

Many different types of consumer goods are sold direct to customers, for example encyclopaedias, cosmetics and vacuum cleaners. In such cases the producer chooses to take on the distribution function and, through specialization and experience, is able to do it as well as a middleman would do.

► There is an innovative element in distributing direct and firms can often steal a competitive advantage through adopting innovative strategies.

Mail order is another way of selling and distributing direct to customers. A wide variety of consumer goods are distributed in this way and once again the producer is able to specialize in this method and become efficient and effective.

► Well-known mail order houses include Great Universal Stores, Littlewoods, Freemans and Grattans.

2 Producer/supplier——> wholesaler——> retailer——>customer

Here, the producer supplies to a wholesaler who in turn supplies a retailer. The retailer then makes the goods available to the customer.

This is a method used by producers of both consumer goods and industrial goods. Consumer goods producers will use this method when they want to make their goods available through a large

Distributing direct to the consumer

For many years a number of firms have specialized in selling and distributing consumer goods direct to the consumer. They have made extensive use of catalogues and the development of 'clubs' run by neighbourhood agents. Representatives call on people at home during the day. Target areas have usually been large council states with a preponderance of non-working housewives. Prospective customers are asked if they would like to take the catalogue for their own personal use. The advantages of doing this are that goods can be bought on credit, the purchasers can browse through the offerings at leisure in their own homes and do not have to make on the spot decisions. Moreover, goods are delivered to the door and are returnable if found to be faulty. In addition catalogue holders can become agents. They will receive a discount on any goods which they wish to buy for themselves calculated according to the orders they bring in.

The agents have traditionally been housewives who have initially bought goods from the catalogue for themselves and then started a club among their friends and neighbours. Members of the club take it turn to borrow the catalogue and place orders through the agent. The marketing strategy, from the point of view of the companies concerned is to identify people who are socialites and likely to have a neighbourhood circle of friends.

number of small retail outlets which may be geographically dispersed. Under such circumstances it is not cost effective for them to supply direct to such a large number of retailers because orders are small and are placed relatively frequently. Wholesalers specialize in handling just this kind of distribution.

In the case of industrial goods firms it is likely that there are a sizeable number of customers (firms) dispersed over different parts of the country. Again the order sizes tend to be small making it more economic for a specialist wholesaler to undertake the distribtion rather than the producer.

3 Producer/supplier ———> retailer ———> customer

This approach applies to consumer goods marketing. It takes place where retailers can place orders in sufficient sizes to make it worthwhile for the manufacturer to supply the retailer directly. Department stores and retailing chains such as Tesco, Sainsbury and so on, are among the kinds of retailers who are equiped to do this. These retailers can then buy goods at the same price as wholesalers. The removal of the wholesaler's margin can then be partially passed on to customers in the form of lower prices. However, it does have to be borne in mind that that large retailers do incur higher costs as a result of carrying out the wholesaler's

► Producers can bring goods to the market directly or they can do so through one or more intermediaries.

There is an innovative element in distributing direct

'Take it easy Ginger, those pine trees can be heavy.'

function, for example, carrying higher levels of stock requires additional storage and display space. Higher stock levels also tie up a retailer's cash and prevent it from being put to more profitable use.

Large retailers operate on high volume sales and this enables them to achieve satsifactory profits with lower profit margins. The net effect of all these factors is often lower prices to the customer, than would have been the case if wholesalers and small retailers had been involved in the distribution chain.

4 **Producer/supplier ————> merchant ————> customer**
This method is often adopted in the case of industrial goods. It is a cost effective method for the producer/supplier. Merchants buy goods in bulk and break them down into smaller lots for resale to the customer. Merchants tend to sell a complementary range of products and are often described by a trade name, for example builder's merchants.

Producers/suppliers can, of course, use more than one of the methods outlined to distribute their product.

Services can be supplied in one of three ways:

1 Direct to the customer, e.g. accounts.
2 Through an agent, e.g. insurance.
3 Through a retailer, e.g. developing photographic films.

Types of distributor: wholesale

Wholesalers are often referred to as middlemen. They buy in bulk from producers and sell in small quantities to retailers. They specialize in a class of goods such as fish, vegetables, newspapers, etc. Some operate from central markets while others maintain warehouses and employ representatives.

Brokers

Brokers are similar to wholesalers except that they do not hold stock. Brokers operate in commodity markets such as metals and tea. They also sell insurance and financial services and deal with share transactions on the stock exchange.

▶ Commodity markets comprise products and services which are highly standardized. Chemicals, cement and refuse collection are examples.

Types of distributors: retail

In the case of consumer goods, distribution was traditionally through middlemen or wholesalers who then broke up orders into smaller lots and shipped them off to hundreds of small retailers. The wholesaler provided a useful function of breaking bulk and holding stock. Wholesalers maintained their own sales force and, because they specialized as distributors, were able to perform the task much more cheaply than a producer. However, over the last twenty years massive changes in retailing patterns have emerged. In particular, the development of self-service methods accompanying supermarkets and hypermarkets have led to massive sales volume being conducted through these kinds of outlets. Supermarkets and hypermarkets have developed as chains with centralized buying departments. It is this type of retailer which has made it more attractive for the producer to supply direct to the retailer.

Estimated UK shop numbers and turnover shares by type of organization.

	Number of shops		% per cent share of all commodity turnover	
	1971	1990	1971	1990
Co-operatives	7,745	2,614	13.2	10.8
Multiples	10,973	4,296	44.3	74.2
Independents	86,565	42,941	42.5	15.0

Source : *Marketing Pocket Book*, 1992 p.52

ACT Firms other than co-operative stores with ten or more shops are known as **multiples** or **chains**. Examples of multiples are:

Trade	Multiples
Bakers	Greggs
Butchers	Dewhurst
Grocers	Tesco

Off-licence	Thresher
Clothing (men)	Burton
Clothing (women)	Richards
Knitware	Edinburgh Woollen Mill
Footwear	C & J Clark
DIY	Texas Homecare
Booksellers	Blackwell
Jewellers	Ratners

Can you identify any other multiples in connection with the above trades? Can you identify any other trades and example of multiples?

Supermarkets

Supermarkets are usually found in chains of several hundred stores but do occur as single units. They offer a wide variety of fast-moving consumer goods such as food, drink and other household items. They feature self service with a number of checkout points. **Hypermarkets** are very large supermarkets, usually located out of town. They carry a much wider range of goods than a normal supermarket and sell clothing, gardening goods etc.

Superstores

Fairly recent developments include mass merchandisers which supply more specialized goods such as DIY items and car accessories. Smaller stores may be found in town centres and much larger ones are often found in retail parks on the edge of towns and cities.

Cash and carry

The **cash and carry** warehouse is effectively a wholesaler who provides for small retailers. Often bulk supplies may be bought at the wholesale price but no credit or transport facilities are provided. Individual consumers may also buy from this source.

Symbol groups

Symbol groups comprise a wholesaler and a number of retailers which enter in a specific kind of business agreement. Symbol groups developed to help smaller retailers compete more effectively with supermarkets. Wholesalers were keen to support the idea since they too were losing business. Spar is an example of a symbol group. In return for buying almost everything from a single wholesaler, special trade terms are offered to the retailer. Each shop displays the wholesaler's symbol and the wholesaler provides advertising support. Spar shops are not confined to operating in the United Kingdom.

► Spar outlets can be found in Spanish towns and cities.

Discount Stores

Discount stores buy in bulk and are able to sell expensive consumer durables such as washing machines at cut prices. Such stores do not often provide servicing, but larger firms such as Comet provide this as well.

Department stores

Department stores are large stores with numerous departments, usually including furnishing, soft-furnishing, clothing and household goods. Many have amalgamated into large national chains such as Debenhams. Like supermarkets, they usually buy direct from producers since they can negotiate advantageous terms through bulk buying.

Co-operatives

Co-operative stores were originally based on customer ownership and profit sharing organized by means of dividends proportional to purchase. Dividends have now been replaced by trading stamps and some local societies have amalgamated under national ownership. The co-operatives have their own wholesaling organization and own some factories.

Some products may be sold through every possible outlet while other products of a more specialized or high class nature may be sold through selected or appointed dealers. This usually means that the dealer does not sell competing products and thus gives an exclusive sales outlet to the producer. The dealer of course can sell complementary products.

 Suggest (a) appropriate channels of distribution and (b) appropriate types of retail establishments for the following products:

- tins of baked beans (producer branded)
- tins of baked beans (private/own label)
- matches
- children's toys
- novels
- newspapers
- machine tools
- agricultural implements
- cosmetics
- insurance
- postage stamps (current unused)
- postage stamps (used/unused current and obsolete for collectors)
- cling film
- motor cars

- electric locomotives for the railway
- power stations

(Note: more than one method may of course be appropriate)

Franchising

Franchising allows a distributor to be independent and control the business to his or her own liking. It usually requires an investment and a commitment to buy the franchiser's product and in return the retailer receives advice or assistance in managing or promoting the business. Some franchises operate under a common name with a standard corporate identity, such as Wimpy bars or the Body Shop. Others, such as laundrettes, may make use of a certain make of machine.

▶ Another form of franchise is to be found in the large-scale distribution of beers and soft drinks where branded products such as Guinness are distributed by bottling companies worldwide.

Some Franchising Operations	
Name	**Operation**
Hertz	Vehicle rental
Body Shop	International cosmetics and beauty products
ANC Holdings	Parcel and courier service
Mr Softee	Mobile ice cream sales
Spud-U-Like Ltd	Baked potatoes, fast food
Safeclean	Carpet cleaning
Tie Rack PLC	Ties, scarves, accessories

 The Metco company supplies metal alloys to foundries for industrial castings. Along with the alloys it also supplies know-how as to which alloys to use for different applications. Recently there has been a drop in orders despite a continued growth in the industry. Rumour has it that many of the foundries are buying alloys from other companies at lower prices and using these to produce castings for client customers. Metco is particularly bothered about the situation since it finds many of the foundries customers for them through its marketing department. Metco meets the BSI standards for alloys. Alloys obtained by the foundries from other sources do not do so.

What action do you think Metco should take?

Other retailing methods

Differing degrees of success have been achieved with **vending machines** which sell meals, drinks, cigarettes, etc. They are found in all kinds of locations, usually in the workplace or in public areas such as stations and airports.

 Draw up a list of products which you have seen offered for sale through vending machines.

Telemarketing is a broad term used to cover a range of distribution methods which employ television. For example, in the travel and tourism industry information on flight availability can be called up, so that travel can be booked via sophisticated viewdata systems (Prestel). Viewdata systems enable users to call up information and order goods with an answer back system and pay for them using a credit card.

Distribution strategy

There six basic channel decisions to make. These are:

1 Whether to distribute direct to the customer or indirectly through middlemen.
2 Whether to adopt single or multiple channels of distribution.
3 How long the channel of distribution should be.
4 The types of intermediaries to use.
5 The number of distributors to use at each level.
6 Which intermediaries to use.

Direct versus indirect distribution

The **advantages** of going direct are:

● it enables firms to exercise more control over marketing activities
● it reduces the amount of time spent in the channel.

The **disadvantages** are:

● it is difficult to obtain widespread distribution
● more resources are required to maintain distribution

The method is widely used by industrial goods producers and examples are to be found in consumer goods marketing, for example, cosmetics and encyclopaedias.
  Using intermediaries has the following **advantages**:

● it leads to increased marketing activities
● it produces wider distribution potential

► Wholesalers traditionally were the buffer between producer and retailer. They performed useful functions for the producer such as breaking bulk and holding stocks. Very considerable changes have taken place in retailing in the past thirty years and with it have emerged well-resourced retailer chains capable of buying in large quantities direct from producers.

The **disadvantages** are:

- firms have less control over marketing activities
- firms are more 'distanced' from the customer
- the product spends more time in the channel

Single versus multiple channels

The **advantages** of using a single channel are:

- it guarantees a minimum level of sales
- the exclusivity of using a single channel guarantees attention to the product

On the other hand, the main disadvantage is:

- it limits sales.

The advantages of multiple channels are:

- increased sales
- potential for wider distribution

On the other hand, there are disadvantages

- greater investment is required
- it can lead to detrimental rivalry

Channel length

In determining the best channel length to adopt the following five factors have to be taken into account:

1 The financial strength of the producer – those in a strong position can carry out the functions provided by intermediaries.
2 Size and completeness of the product line – the costs of carrying out the distribution function can be spread across the various items in the product line. The more items, the more economical it might be to consider a shorter distribution channel.
3 The average order size – large orders may be distributed direct to customers.
4 The geographical concentration of customers – geographically dispersed customers merit a longer distribution channel since servicing them requires substantial investment of resources.
5 The distance of the distributor from the market – geographical distance makes it less attractive for the producer to supply direct.

The above are guidelines and exceptions may be encountered in practice.

► Looking at the wristwatch market we find Seiko distributing its watches through many different channels whereas Maurice la Croix is much more selective.

The number of distributors required at each level in the chain of distribution

More distributors are required if:

- the unit value of the product is low – the physical quantity of stock held is likely to be high
- the product is purchased frequently.
- the product is technologically complex
- the service requirement is high
- the inventory investment is high
- geographic concentration is low
- total market potential is high
- the market share of the producer is high
- competition is intense.

▶ For products which are very much in demand it is essential to maintain adequate stock levels from which to supply customers. Specialist intermediaries having warehouses close to such markets are key factors in this process. Technical products which require spares or servicing can also benefit from an abundance of distributors.

The portable refrigerator

Alice runs a small electronics company manufacturing desk top computers. She is a very innovative person and has a wide range of interests. Alice has patented a design for a small portable refrigerator. The refrigerator will operate from conventional dry cell batteries, can be installed to make use of the electrical system in any vehicle with the aid of an adapter, and can also be plugged into a conventional electrical mains system.

Alice has undertaken market research to estimate customer demand for the product and has found this to be extensive. However, she is puzzled as to what is the best way to distribute the product once it goes into production.

What factors do you think she should consider?

Producers and intermediaries a cooperative effort

Channel management should be seen as a cooperative effort in which both distributor and producer are working together. Cooperation can lead to mutual benefits. Producers can help intermediaries by:

- providing a desirable assortment of products which are well designed, properly priced, attractively packaged, delivered on time and in adequate quantities
- building up consumer demand for these products by advertising them
- furnishing promotional assistance
- providing managerial assistance

● honouring product warranties and providing repair and installation services.

In return intermediaries are expected to increase product sales by:

● carrying adequate stocks
● providing effective promotional displays and undertaking some advertising
● providing services to customer – credit, delivery, installation, etc.
● honouring the product warranty conditions.

A key problem for producers is how to motivate intermediaries so that they always act in the best interests of the producer. Three approaches have been tried:

1 Cooperation

Here the producer uses the 'carrot and stick' approach. Positive incentives are given in the form of higher margins, special deals, cooperative advertising allowances, display allowances and sales contests. Negative sanctions are applied in the form of reducing margins, slowing down on deliveries, etc.

The weakness of this approach lies in the fact that the producer does not really study the needs, problems, strengths and weaknesses of the distributor.

2 Partnership

In this instance both producer and distributor agree on what the distributor should accomplish in terms of:

● market coverage
● product availability
● market development
● account solicitation
● technical advice
● market information.

It is common practice for the producer to pay sales commissions as follows:

● for carrying the proper inventory level
● for meeting the sales quota
● for servicing customers correctly and effectively
● for the proper reporting of customer purchase levels
● for the prompt payment of accounts due.

▶ Producers and distributors have expectations of each other.

3 Distribution programming

The previous methods all ignore one key point: the distributor's needs. Distribution programming identifies distributor needs and builds up merchandising programmes to help distributors operate optimally. Producer and distributor undertake joint planning of merchandising, inventory levels, space and visual merchandising plans, sales training and other promotions.

► Cooperation, partnership and distribution programming represent ways of providing motivation for distributors. The last of these is the best.

(ACT) Manoj is the owner of a clothes manufacturing enterprise in Greater Manchester. Situated in the Strangeways area of the city, it is close to a wide range of wholesaling and retailing companies which operate in the 'rag trade'.

Manoj offers discounts to wholesalers who agree to stock his lines. These take the form of standard quantity discounts off list price. In the case of the larger accounts, he offers additional discounts for early settlement of outstanding purchases.

Recently some of his longest standing customers in the wholesale trade have indicated that they are getting better terms from his competitors and the order book has fallen as a result. Manoj is reluctant to increase his discounts and wonders what else he can do.

What do you think he should do?

Choosing intermediaries

Selecting the right distributors for one's products is a key decision on which the success or failure of the company's marketing of products may depend. Factors which should be taken into account include:

- familiarity with the market
- coverage of the market
- interest or enthusiasm in the firm's product
- strength of marketing personnel
- product familiarity
- amount of contact with own customers
- previous track record
- cost of operation
- experience in dealing with competitors
- ability to provide customer service
- quality of service stock
- stock holding facilities
- credit worthiness
- image in the marketplace
- geographical location

- compatibility of distributor's marketing policies with suppliers
- strength of promotional activities and budgets
- whether the distributor is someone with whom the supplier can work.

Physical distribution

Physical distribution, as its name implies, is concerned with the physical movement of goods from the producer to the consumer. An uncoordinated physical distribution system can lead to a sharp increase in costs especially in consumer products' markets such as food items, where delays result in the goods being unfit for consumption.

Apart from being a marketing cost, physical distribution can be part of the firm's strategic marketing armoury. Efficient management of the physical distribution system can lead to lower costs which in turn can lead to lower prices on account of such things as better coordination, lower average delivery times and better service and quality. We look at this in more detail in the section headed logistics management below.

Warehousing, stock control and transportation

There is currently a trend towards what is called **JIT (just-in-time) management**. What this means is that producers try to minimize their holding of finished stock. They produce to order and just enough to meet expected demand.

Stocks are held by wholesalers and retailers. Holding stock effectively ties up the company cash. It means not only that the company does not have that amount of cash to spend on activities it may wish to pursue but it also means that the company is incurring costs. There are opportunity costs associated with the cash tied up in stock. The same cash would earn money if it were in an interest-bearing account. It is also likely that the firm has a bank loan or overdraft which is incurring interest. Clearly money which is tied up in stocks could be used to pay off such loans and decrease the amount of interest paid. Stock also takes up physical space and the more stock that is held the greater is the amount of space required to house it. Buildings cost money to put up and maintain and land has considerable value. Therefore there is every incentive for all businesses to minimize their stocks to such an extent that it matches demand. This is a difficult task since if too little stock is held customers' demands cannot be met. Not only is a sale lost but a frustrated customer is an unsatisfied one who might then switch to a competitor's product.

Inventory management and level of service

Inventory management is linked with the level of service decision and is therefore a rather complex subject. One of the principal factors which will affect the effectiveness of the marketing operation

▶ Christopher and McDonald, *Marketing: an Introduction*. London:Pan, p, 72. Rank Xerox have found that it pays to ship high value spares to European customers by air express, rather than by less expensive surface transport. The main benefits are faster deliveries with lower inventory carrying costs for goods in transit.

is the level of customer service that a company offers. Level of service refers to making the product available. It comprises delivery frequency and reliability, stock levels and order cycle time as they impact upon availability.

Product availability is usually measured in terms of the percentage of demand that can be met from stock. Clearly the larger the amount of stock that is held the greater the product availability. One problem, however, is that the cost of holding stock and making the product available rises exponentially (disproportionately) as the percentage of demand that can be met from stock rises. This is largely because additional safety stocks have to be carried to lessen the risk of running out of stock. The decision to be made relates to the trade off between the cost of holding stock and the cost of a stock-out. The company therefore has to balance the cost of a stock-out against the cost of holding stock. Unfortunately there is no precise way to measure the cost of a stock-out in terms of lost profitability. The consequences of a stock-out could be any of the following:

- loss of sale to competitor
- loss of customer to competitor
- loss of sale on related items
- loss of other customers who may learn of poor product availability
- additional cost of shipping goods from other depots
- having to expedite a rush order with heavy on-costs
- having to progress a customer's re-order

Somehow the company has to work out the probability of each one of these eventualities and then assess the financial impact on profitability. Market experiments to assess the precise impact of non-availability on market share indicate that, over a certain range, improvement in level of service does have an impact on sales. There also appears to be a saturation point beyond which the customer does not seem to distinguish between improvements in stock availability. Finding the point where trade-offs balance is a key problem for marketing management.

▶ Inventory management and level of service are linked to one another. The higher the stock the higher the level of service. Since there is a cost associated with holding stock there has to be a trade off between the two.

ACT Fernando has a busy city centre newspaper stand in Madrid on the Gran Via, a major thoroughfare close to offices and shops. Newspaper stands are situated every 400 metres or so along the Gran Via. Knowing how many copies of each magazine, journal and newspaper to order is a major job. If he orders too few he loses business to the other stands. If he orders too many then he will lose money on the unsold items.

Suggest a system that Fernando could set up to make the best out of this situation.

Transportation

Choice of method of transportation is a key element for all members of the distribution chain. There are numerous strategic decisions to be made with regard to transportation. These include:

- whether to use road, rail, sea or air transport
- whether a producer should have its own transport system.

Within the UK and Europe, **road** transportation takes the largest share of the work. Over the years there has been a gradual shift from rail to road transportation in the UK to such an extent that even if the railways were to double the amount of freight they carry, it would only reduce the amount of freight carried by road by ten per cent.

Road transport provides considerable flexibility because it offers a door-to-door service (few industrial companies have their own railway sidings). Goods can be loaded at the factory and delivered straight to the customer. There is no problem of changing from one form of transport to another with all the extra handling that this involves. Even remote rural areas can be reached by road. Some things cannot be delivered by rail, but special facilities can be provided by road hauliers to deal with exceptional loads.

Road transport is economical since the road haulage industry is very competitive. At the same, the continuing development of motorways in the UK and on the continent of Europe has linked up the main centres of population making transportation between them speedy.

Perhaps the most important advance has been in the use of **containers**. Freight can now be packed into large containers at the point where it is produced and sealed. Containers can be packed before lorries arrive. Furthermore they are of standard size and can be used with any operator's vehicles. When goods are sent overseas they can be easily loaded on and off lorries and ships. Firms using containers often make a heavy initial investment to acquire the containers. However, the goods are much safer in containers and the system has been developed to cater for all kinds of goods – including refrigerated goods and liquids.

Road transport is not suitable for transporting goods of great bulk. **Rail** transport can be speedier than road transport under some circumstances and British Rail has developed its own freightliner system which makes use of containerization. British Rail maintains its own fleet of lorries which picks up containers from customers, loads them onto trains, transports them to an intermediate destination and finally offloads them onto British Rail lorries for delivery to the customer. Containerization and the freightliner system are likely to pay an important role in distributing goods to Europe from the British Isles.

▶ Containerization and road transport are key elements of transportation within the U.K. The railway freightliner service can offer advantages and, of course, it is not possible to transport everything economically by road.

Suggest suitable transportation arrangements for the following:

- 5,000 tons of coal – from Newcastle-upon-Tyne to Birmingham
- 4 tons of furniture from Wycombe to Crewe
- 1 box of urgent medical supplies from Manchester to Edinburgh
- a very large electrical transformer from Stafford to Houston, Texas.
- a bus from Leyland to Doncaster.

International transportation

As far as trade with overseas countries is concerned, ninety-five per cent of the volume of trade (seventy-five per cent of the value) takes place by **sea transport**. Sea transport offers considerable flexibility and exporters can often find accommodation for goods fairly easily. The growth of containerization has been accompanied by the building of special container vessels. However, in recent years there has been a steady increase in **air freight**. In keeping with this trend, newer and larger aircraft have been developed which are capable of carrying heavier loads.

> The North West's second Channel Tunnel terminal is to be located in the Port of Liverpool's Royal Seaforth Dock, within the confines of the Freeport providing a vital land-bridge between Ireland, the UK, Europe and, ultimately, North America. The terminal is expected to be operational by May 1993 and it will triple rail freight running out of the Port of Liverpool through the UK.

Air transport is obviously most important where there is a need for speedy delivery. Mail, medical supplies and newspapers come into this category as do spare parts for industrial machinery, and components for cars and computers. The cost per tonne carried is higher in the case of airfreight but the cost of transport is built into the price the consumer pays for the goods. Low value items might increase considerably in cost if they were sent by air, whereas the price of diamonds would increase almost imperceptibly if they were airfreighted. Packing costs and insurance costs are often lower if goods are airfreighted.

► Air transport can be advantageous sometimes.

Logistics

Logistics is a concept which suggests that distribution, other elements of marketing, production and purchasing should be viewed as a total system. In order to optimize the output of this total system, it may be necessary for some or all its components to operate sub-optimally. Marketing may have to offer a lower level of customer service than the optimum level; production might have to schedule shorter production runs, etc.

The logistics mix is made up of :

- **facilities** – this is concerned with the location and number of warehouses and production plants
- **inventories** (see earlier in the chapter)
- **communication decisions** – accompanying goods as they flow through the distribution system is information. This information is part and parcel of the demand forecasting, order processing and invoicing systems. This is necessary to provide a satisfactory customer service at an acceptable cost.
- **utilization decisions** – this relates to the packaging of goods and their subsequent assembly into larger batches. The two have major implications for logistics economics.
- **transport decisions** (see earlier in the chapter).

Taken together, these five areas make up the total cost of distribution. Decisions taken in one area can have implications for one of the other areas. For example, transport costs and stock levels are obviously affected by the siting of distribution depots.

The management of logistics is all about looking for cost savings by changing the cost structure in one or more area. On the other hand, it may be possible to be show that a sufficiently profitable competitive advantage can be gained by investing in one or more of the areas.

▶ The logistics concept argues that the whole system can be made more efficient even though part of it is running below maximum efficiency.

CHAPTER SUMMARY

1 Distribution of stock to users is vitally important. The producer can choose from a number of distribution routes. He/she can reach the market direct, through wholesalers, retailers, agents, distributors, etc. In most cases, the producer can obtain a strategic advantage by selecting one method over another.

2 The pattern of distribution for consumer products has undergone many significant changes in the last twenty to thirty years this had led to the setting up of all kinds of different wholesale and retail establishments. Of particular significance has been the development of supermarkets, hypermarkets and superstores.

3 Franchising represents a particularly advantageous way of doing business with intermediaries in the chain of distribution. In return for agreeing to tie their business with a certain producer, intermediaries receive advantageous terms and considerable help in the marketing of the goods. Producers

also have much to gain from such an arrangement since they can be assured that the intermediary will not supply its customers with competitors' products.

4 Channel decisions are key strategic decisions. They involve deciding whether to distribute direct to the customer or indirectly through middlemen, whether to adopt single or multiple channels of distribution, how long the channel of distribution should be, the types of intermediaries to use , the number of distributors to use at each level and which intermediaries to use.

5 Franchising agreements go only part way towards motivating channel members to do their jobs well. Moreover, franchising may not always be possible or even desirable to both parties. Producers need to offer all their distributors the opportunity for motivation. Several approaches are used in practice but the method of distribution programming appears to be the most attractive.

6 Good inventory management and providing an adequate level of customer service are important contributors to the profitability of any firm. Achieving the right balance between the two is quite hard to achieve.

7 Transportation is a key element in achieving efficient distribution. Different methods of transportation have different associated costs, different levels of effectiveness and in some cases may not even be available. Containerization has done much to revolutionize the way in which many goods are transported.

8 Appreciating the nature of the logistics concept can lead to maximizing overall efficiency and effectiveness even if some of the elements of the distribution mix are not implemented in an optimum fashion. The distribution mix comprises facilities, such as warehouses and production plants; inventories; communications accompanying goods as they flow through the distribution system; the packaging of goods and their subsequent assembly into larger batches; and transport.

▶ Now that you have reached the end of the chapter, turn back to the objectives and make sure you have achieved each of them.

15 Marketing communications strategies

Chapter objectives

By the end of this chapter you should:
▌ be able to describe the basic concepts of communications theory and understand the relevance of the various elements to marketing communications

▌ be able to describe the stepwise models which relate to communications and to advertising

▌ know the kind of the objectives that can be set for marketing communications

▌ be able to describe how marketing communications have to be designed; specifically matters relating to the format and structure of the message and the information source

▌ be able to describe the advantages and disadvantages of using different types of media – newspapers, magazines, television, commercial radio, outdoor advertising, cinema advertising, etc

▌ know how marketers choose appropriate media, assess the cost effectiveness of media vehicles and, in conjunction with agencies, schedule advertising

▌ be able to describe the different methods of measuring advertising effectiveness

▌ be able to describe what is involved in sales promotion, public relations, direct marketing, direct mail, leafleting, exhibitions and sponsorship

▌ be familiar with the following terms as used by marketers: advertising, response hierarchy models, stepwise models, outdoor advertising, reach, frequency, impact, media vehicles, media scheduling, portfolio tests, samples, trial offers, lobbying, direct marketing, direct mail, telemarketing, leafleting, exhibitions, sponsorship, sales promotion.

Introduction

This chapter introduces the general concept of communication and then goes on to examine specific types of marketing communication. It considers advertising, direct mail, sales promotion, exhibitions and sponsorship. A separate chapter is devoted to selling (see Chapter 16).

COMMUNICATION

Communications can be described by the following model:

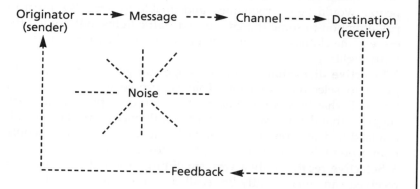

A person originates a message which flows down a channel of communication to its destination. The receiver of the message provides feedback to the originator with respect to the message that has been sent. The clarity of reception and feedback is distorted somewhat by 'noise' in the system. Noise can be caused by a variety of factors, amongst which are other communications to the recipient and communications between other communicators in the system.

Communication in marketing is a straightforward adaptation of this model. A company is the **originator**, source or sender of the message. The **message** itself consists of ideas, suggestions or requests. The **channel** is the medium used to transmit the message and can take the form of TV, journals, newspapers, billboards, etc. The **destination** or **receiver** in this instance is the potential customer or the target.

The key points in effective communication are:

- the originator or sender must know the destination or target to be reached and the kind of response required
- the originator or sender has to create a message in such a way that it will be readily understood by the receiver or target
- an efficient channel of communication that reaches the receiver or target must be used
- feedback channels have to be used to enable the receiver's response to the message to be understood by the sender.

Noise exists in the system which makes it difficult for the intended receiver to actually receive the message. People are constantly bombarded with all kinds of messages – visual, audio, sensual, olefactory, etc. from advertisements, announcements, incidents in the street or in the home, etc. and may not receive an intended

Identify the target audience

↓

determine communication objective

↓

design the message

↓

select communication channels

↓

allocate the promotions budget

↓

decide on the promotions mix

↓

measure the results of the promotion

message. The reasons are that people exhibit:

1 **Selective attention** – people do not pay attention to everything that is going on around them. Much has to be shut out, otherwise people would be overwhelmed and unable to cope. We learn to pay attention to some things, e.g. red traffic lights, but not to others, e.g. the clothes worn by someone crossing the road near to red traffic lights.

2 **Selective distortion** – what messages do get through are subjected to selective distortion. That is, people interpret them in terms of what they want to hear or see. For example, if a message suggests that driving while under the influence of alcoholic drink can lead to deaths on the road, there is a tendency for some people to interpret this as referring to highly intoxicated drivers only.

3 **Selective recall** – only a very small proportion of the messages received can subsequently be recalled. There is also selectivity in terms of what is recalled. People often recall a face but may have difficulty in fitting a name to the face. This has obvious implications for advertising where the visual image may well be recalled but not the brand name of the product!

The main task for a communicator is to create a message that is able to gain the person's attention and subsequent action despite the amount of noise in the system.

In the basic model of communication one looks for **feedback** from the receiver (target or destination) to establish that the message has in fact been understood. In marketing there is also feedback. Occasionally it possible to gain feedback through measuring the change in the level of sales following a marketing communications campaign. More often, however, it is not possible to relate

► The factors which cause people to buy particular goods or services are many and it is difficult to relate sales to advertising. Quite apart from the fact that there may be many other factors at work, advertising has a delayed effect. We might see an advertisement now and not act on it for several weeks or even months. On top of this, some magazines may circulate for months, for example in GP's waiting rooms. So this only compounds the matter.

Getting a message across through all the noise

'Try shouting "Fire, fire!". That usually gets everyone's attention.'

changes in sales to marketing communications campaigns because there are too many different factors influencing sales and there is a delay in the time it takes for the effect to work through.

Firms have to manage complex marketing communications with their distributors, consumers and various publics. Marketing communications can be in the form of advertising, sales promotion, and/or publicity. Selling is also another form of marketing communications. The basic steps in developing an effective communications programme involve:

- identifying the target audience
- determining the communications objective
- designing the message
- selecting the communications channels
- allocating the total promotions budget
- deciding on the promotions mix
- measuring the results of the promotion.

ADVERTISING

Advertising can be thought of as any paid form of non-personal presentation and promotion of ideas, goods, or services by an identified sponsor. Because it is not always possible to relate advertising campaigns or expenditure to sales a variety of different objectives might be set for advertising. These include the need:

- to create awareness of a brand, company or organization
- to keep a product or brand name constantly in the mind of the customer
- to stimulate interest in a product or brand
- to give out information about what a product or service can do for the customer.

Advertising can be at the corporate level, where it is used to promote the company name, or at the level of product or brand. There can also be differences in terms of the target audience. It can be aimed at the final consumers or alternatively it can be aimed at selected distribution channel members.

Advertising has an image of being expensive. It need not be expensive though almost inevitably some of the expenditure will be wasted. Large firms think in terms of advertising and even campaign budgets while small firms think in terms of modest sums spent to best advantage. Large firms use national newspapers, television and posters, small firms may be well served by local newspapers, local radio and trade journals. Large firms deal with well-known advertising agencies, small firms use local agencies.

Differences also exist between industrial and consumer goods

▶ Oil companies are well known for corporate advertising which stresses they care about preserving the environment. Advertisements showing unspoilt countryside with captions such as 'who would believe an oil pipeline runs through here' would be an example.

producers. Consumer goods producers need to address very large audiences with their marketing communications and advertising forms an excellent means of communication to achieve this purpose.

To be effective advertising has to target the right message to the right people.

How advertising works

A knowledge of how advertising works is basically a knowledge of how communications works. Psychologists have been studying the process for years but as yet no firm conclusions have been reached. The search continues, for it has been said that unless one has a reasonable understanding of what advertising can and cannot achieve, one has absolutely no way of deciding what role an advertising programme should take, what objectives should be set for it and how to measure whether it has achieved those objectives. Measurements of advertising effectiveness have, however, been developed and advertising strategies do contain objectives. It would seem therefore that there is some knowledge of how advertising works.

The stepwise models of the early 1960s

These models (also known as Response Hierarchy Models) suggest a simple relationship between advertising and the purchase of goods. Advertising was initially thought of as a method to get the product known to the customer. The idea was that as long as one delivered enough advertising to the right consumers, the results could be measured in sales.

The **stepwise model** is an accumulation of several theories developed since E. St Elmo Lewis first suggested ideas relating to a model for selling goods in 1898. His theory to suggested that there are four stages of consciousness through which a customer must pass before a purchase is made. Lewis concluded that a sales talk must be planned to arouse these stages in the customer.

E. K. Strong suggested the **AIDA** model in 1925. The model comprised four stages:

- attracting Attention
- maintaining Interest
- arousing Desire
- getting Action

Many similar models were developed by various psychologists in the early part of the twentieth century. Some suggested that an application could be in advertising but most of the work was general in nature and related to the whole area of selling.

In 1961, Lavidge and Steiner developed the **hierarchy of effects** model. This model contained many of the ideas discussed above and this time was directly related to advertising. The model suggested a six stage process where the customer moves through:

AWARENESS
↓
KNOWLEDGE
↓
LIKING
↓
PREFERENCE
↓
CONVICTION
↓
PURCHASE

Various promotional activities are considered appropriate to move customers through the stages. To create **awareness** teaser campaigns, sky writing, jingles, slogans and classified advertisements are considered appropriate. In order to convey **knowledge**, announcements and descriptive copy are suggested. Image advertising and status or glamour appeals are seen as ways of developing a **liking** while competitive advertisements and argumentative copy are seen as ways of developing a **preference**. Finally, price appeals and testimonials are seen as ways of developing **conviction**. Deals, last chance offers and point of purchase retail store advertisements are seen as ways of bringing about **purchase**.

▶ Descriptive copy informs the reader what the benefits of using the product will be.

Also in 1961, Colley produced a model called **DAGMAR** which stands for 'defining advertising goals, measuring advertising results'. It argued that a communication must carry a prospect through four levels of understanding:

▶ Colley, R. H. (1961), *Defining Advertising Goals for Measuring Advertising Effectiveness.* New York: Association of National Advertisers.

AWARENESS
↓
COMPREHENSION
↓
CONVICTION
↓
ACTION

In the following year, 1962, the **Innovation Adoption** model was published by Rogers. In this case the theory was not directed specifically at the relationship between advertising and sales but rather on the adoption of a new idea. Several stages were suggested in the model:

▶ Rogers, E. M. (1962), *Diffusion of Innovations.* Collier, Macmillan.

AWARENESS
↓
INTEREST
↓
EVALUATION
↓
TRIAL
↓
ADOPTION

All of these models seem to fit in well with the more general communications model of:

EXPOSURE
↓
RECEPTION
↓
COGNITIVE RESPONSE
↓
ATTITUDE
↓
INTENTION
↓
BEHAVIOUR

► Advertising models underline the theory that there are different stages in the buying process. They argue for different kinds of advertising messages to be directed to potential customers who may be at different stages in the process.

This general model of communication suggests that people have to be exposed to a message and receive it. The cognitive response stage refers to becoming aware and informed about the subject of the message – awareness and comprehension. The attitude stage corresponds to the development of a liking, interest, desire or preference for a product or service. Intention just precedes actual behaviour and corresponds with conviction or trial.

More recently interest has focused on the qualitative dimensions of advertising suggesting that advertising should be emotionally appealing and novel in nature.

 Collect some cuttings of advertisements from magazines and newspapers. See what evidence you can find in them of the advertisers trying to make use of the stepwise models. For instance, can you find examples where the advertisements are trying to create awareness of a product or service? Can you find examples where developing comprehension about the product or service is the key focus of the advertisement? Can you find examples where developing interest is the key focus of the advertisement?

Communication objectives

Advertising can have different communications objectives. Some of these are listed below:

- to create **awareness** of a product or service. This is an important task to be undertaken when a new product or service is first introduced to a market. Awareness features as the first stage in most of the stepwise models described above. This kind of advertising will continue until general awareness of the product achieves a satisfactory level
- to provide information about a product or service. Comprehension and **knowledge** about a product or service are seen as important early stages in the movement towards purchase. Clearly, before it is worth trying to give out more information about a product awareness levels relating to the product need to be substantial
- to generate enquiries. In some instances, advertisers seek to stimulate enquiries about a product through advertising. An advertisement may provide some information about a product or service but indicate that more detailed information is available on request. Holiday facilities are often promoted in this way. New sales leads for salesmen can also be found in this way
- to build recognition of a company name. This fits in with the notion of corporate advertising and is most relevant where a firm offers a wide range of products or services which are marketed under the company's name, e.g. ICI. It is not really useful where all the firm's products are sold under different brand names
- to reach those beyond the reach of salesmen. There may be occasions where a firm simply cannot get to people who are concerned in purchase decision-making process. This may be the case in industrial marketing where it may be extremely difficult to identify all the people who influence the buying decision

► See Chapter 7

- to evoke **desire** for a product or service. This is another of the stages in the response-hierarchy models – see the AIDA model above. People may have developed an interest in the product or service but not have developed a desire for it. Here, advertising attempts to stimulate desire
- to make the selling task easier. Intermediaries in the chain of distribution are more likely to agree to stock a product if they see the company selling the product engaging in advertising aimed at the users of the product
- to overcome prejudices. National prejudices may discriminate against imported goods even if the imports are actually encouraged by the government of the country. In such cases advertising can be used to create knowledge about the product or service and the countries from which they came. Prejudice often originates from ignorance

- to remind people about a product's benefits. People are apt to forget if they are not reminded regularly of the benefits of using a particular brand. In order to maintain a brand's share of the market it is necessary for a firm to remind people regularly of the benefits of using the product
- to allay cognitive dissonance. People need to be reassured that they have made the correct purchase decision when they have bought an expensive new item. Some advertising may be aimed at allaying any worries people may have about having made the wrong choice of brand or having made a mistake in purchasing the item at all.

► See Chapter 7

It will be seen that some of the objectives match with some of the stages in the models described above.

Designing the message

The appeal, theme , idea or unique selling proposition is what the communicator has to get over to the target audience in order to produce the desired response. Benefit, identification, motivation are all concepts that can be built into the message.

► Radio Rentals' 'There will never be a video that's easier to pro-gramme. Probably' – advertising message illustrates the point about benefits.

Messages can be built around rational, emotional or moral appeals, themes, ideas or unique selling propositions. Economy, value and performance are used in messages with a rational content. This type of message is often directed at industrial buyers and consumers purchasing expensive items such as cars, houses and substantial consumer durables. Emotional appeals make use of both positive and negative emotional appeals. On the negative side this involves fear, guilt and shame, while on the positive side it comprises humour, love, pride and joy. Too much fear in a message may cause the audience to reject it. The use of humour may generate noise and interfere with the message.

► Puns are quite popular. For example: 'Hot, not bothered'. Renault Clio, 16 valve.

Moral appeals appeal to people's sense of what is right and just. They can be used in green advertising or in promoting social causes or even in things for children, e.g. books and safety prams.

Message structure

Various research findings on message presentation can be used by advertisers to advantage. For instance recent research indicates that it is better to present questions in television advertisements to viewers and to allow them to reach their own conclusions.

► 'If you believe in a free society, why not join one?' Bradford and Bingley Building Society. Also includes a pun!

Message format

In a printed advertisement the headline, copy, illustration and the colours used all have an impact on whether and how the message is received. Voice quality is important for radio advertisements and facial expression, gestures, dress, posture and hairstyle are important in television advertising. Where the message is printed on packaging then size, shape and colour of the package are all important.

Message source

The credibility of the information source is a key influence on whether a message is likely to receive attention and be recalled. Expertise, trustworthiness and likeability are the descriptors most associated with the credibility of the information source.

 Find examples of advertising which are designed for the following purposes

- to create awareness of a new brand of soap powder
- to provide information about tooth decay prevention
- to generate enquiries about holiday flats
- to build recognition of a company name
- to create a favourable image of a political party
- to evoke desire for a brand of shampoo
- to overcome prejudices about foreigners
- to remind people about a product's benefits
- to relieve cognitive dissonance after the purchase of an expensive holiday package.

Indicate how these advertisements attempt to achieve their objectives.

► Advertisements have different objectives and messages have to be designed to help firms achieve these objectives. The structure, form and source of the message are all important considerations.

The advertising budget

Since advertising can have various objectives and it is relatively difficult to measure the relationship between advertising expenditure and the attainment of objectives, the method of setting budget expenditure is not very precise. There are a number of different approaches:

1 Deciding how much the organization can afford to spend on advertising in total and then assigning expenditure for different purposes on a 'best guess' basis.
2 Forecasting sales for the coming year and allocating a fixed percentage of expected sales as the amount to spend on advertising.
3 Taking the previous year's expenditure and adding a fixed percentage to it for inflation.
4 Allocating an amount which is a fixed percentage of the previous year's sales.
5 Systematically working through all the advertising objectives that have been set and trying to determine, as objectively as possible, exactly what is required in terms of advertising and hence expenditure in order to achieve the objectives.

► Not all firms set their advertising budgets in the same way.

6 As (5) but taking into account what competitors spend on advertising as well.

Advertising agencies

Very small firms may do some advertising for themselves in local media. Larger organizations, however, make use of advertising agencies. Users of the service liaise with an account executive who is responsible for ensuring that all aspects of a client's requirements are dealt with by the various departments in the agency. A typical agency has a variety of staff to work on the various requirements of the client. The creative section prepares the text and layout of advertisements; the studio deals with the artwork; media staff plan bookings and purchase space in appropriate media. In addition there are also staff who try to assess how successful advertising has been in terms of objectives set. Agencies receive payment for two main types of work:

► Advertising agencies handle the designing and placing of advertisements.

1 Commission on the advertising they place with the media.
2 Charges for copy preparation (text of an advertisement), artwork and campaign planning advice which they levy on the customer.

The media

The table below gives some idea of the amount of money spent on different media.

**Display advertising expenditure 1990
by medium (£m.)**

Medium	£m
Press	2,962
TV	2,325
Poster & transport	282
Cinema	39
Radio	163

Source : *The Marketing Pocket Book*, 1992

Newspapers

Newspapers enjoy a very wide circulation in the United Kingdom and in many other countries. One has to note the difference between national newspapers and local newspapers in terms of the catchment areas they cover. Different national newspapers attract different kinds of readers and hence this has to be taken into account when choosing which particular newspaper to use.

► Over the period 1984 to 1990 the readership of quality newspapers as a whole increased by ten per cent. Much of the increase however was brought about by the introduction of the *Independent* in 1986. Over the same period readership of tabloid newspapers decreased by ten per cent.

Local evening newspapers such as the *Liverpool Echo, Manchester Evening News* and the *Evening Sentinel* (Stoke-on-Trent) cater for people within roughly a thirty miles radius of the centres of the cities where they are published. They are used by firms wishing to promote their goods in those particular areas. Advertisements can be placed at relatively short notice and the circulation provides good penetration of the target audience. Free weekly newspapers also provide a good advertising in-road into local markets.

Many newspapers are prepared to include stories in their editorial review columns when a firm introduces new products or moves to new premises.

Circulation figures of selected national and regional newspapers in 1990 ('000)

Nationals	'000
Daily Express	1,585
Daily Mail	1,708
Daily Mirror	3,083
Daily Record	778
The Star	912
Sun	3,855
Today	540
Daily Telegraph	1,076
Financial Times	289
The Guardian	424
The Independent	411
The Times	420

Regionals:	
The *Evening Standard* (London)	502
Bristol Evening Post	102
Birmingham Evening Mail	219
Express and Star (Wolverhampton)	235
Liverpool Echo	194
Manchester Evening News	255
Yorkshire Post	89
The Scotsman	84
Belfast Telegraph	132

Source: *The Marketing Pocket Book*, 1992

(ACT) Obtain a copy of an evening paper and a daily newspaper. Compile a list of the different kinds of goods and services which are offered in both types of newspaper.

What differences do you observe in the kinds of items appearing in the two lists?

Magazines

Magazines represent a way of advertising both for consumer goods manufacturers and industrial goods manufacturers. To enable consumer goods manufacturers to promote advertising

► One has to be aware of the difference between **circulation** and **readership**. For example it is estimated that there are many times more readers of magazines than there are copies in circulation. The monthly publication *True Romance* has a circulation of 31,000 but the readership is put at 476,000.

messages direct to the customer there are general interest magazines and specialist magazines covering particular topics such as computers, cars, DIY, etc. Advertising in these magazines ensures that the message is reaching the target audience who have an interest in the product or service on offer.

Since most consumer goods are distributed through intermediaries, the availability of retail and trade magazines provides an excellent means of communication for producers who want to advertise to distributors.

In the case of industrial goods there are magazines aimed at people working in different industries. Purchasing officers and buyers in firms as well as technical specialists, read these magazines to gain up-to-the-minute information about what is going on in the industry. Since these magazines also carry advertising they represent a good means of bringing informative advertising to the attention of potential decision-makers in industrial buying groups.

Press advertising expenditure by medium 1990 (£m)

National newspapers	251
Regional newspapers	1,096
Consumer magazines	40
Business & professional	234
Directories	492

Source: *The Marketing Pocket Book*, 1992

 Make a list of all the different kinds of specialist magazines that can be found in a large newsagent's shop. Can you think of any hobbies, activities, etc. that are not covered by the range of magazines that are included in your list?

Television

Access to television is widespread throughout Europe and many developed countries. TV advertising operates on a regional basis so that it is possible to home in on geographical areas. Moreover it offers colour, sound and movement to illustrate advertising messages. In the UK the two commercial channels attract large viewing audiences but research indicates that these tend to be only particular social groups. Upper and middle-class social groups show a preference for watching the BBC channels. Another problem is that many viewers of the commercial networks have indicated that they do not watch the advertisements.

Commercial Radio

There are now many commercial radio stations operating within the UK. They tend to be situated in cities and provide local news and entertainment for the surrounding area. Reception varies according to the nature of the terrain over which they transmit,

► Stations such as Atlantic 252 have good reception in most parts of England.

but generally speaking reception is very good within a radius of twenty miles and they can be heard thirty miles away.

In comparison to TV advertising, radio is a cheap way of addressing target market groups. Research indicates that prime listeners are women at home, people driving to work and younger people. The audience is not therefore representative of the population as a whole.

An obvious weakness of this form of advertising is that it does not offer any visual image.

Outdoor advertising

Under the heading of outdoor advertising are posters, hoardings, neon signs, and mobile advertisements on buses, taxis and tube trains. The principal use of outdoor advertising is that of reminding people of a product or an advertising campaign or to reinforce a detailed TV or newspaper message. They are also used by firms to introduce their names to consumers for the first time.

This type of advertising is considered to be an inexpensive form of promotion.

Cinema advertising

Following a period of substantial decline in popularity attributed to the growth of TV ownership in the 1950s and 1960s, cinemas staged something of a recovery in the 1980s. Audiences tend to be in the younger age range, fifteen to twenty-four years. Advertising tends to concentrate on items which appeal to this age group.

 Over a period of time put together a list of the different products and services you see advertised on television, on billboards and mobiles, at the cinema and hear on commercial radio.

Do you perceive any difference in the kinds of products and services being promoted in the different media? If so, can you account for this difference?

Other advertising media

Other advertising media comprises:

- aerial banners
- airships
- balloon displays, tethered
- balloon releases
- electronic outdoor advertising display
- golf tee signs
- hot-air balloons
- inflatable portaboards
- litter bins
- motor poster

► Many different forms of media exist. Each one has its own advantages and disadvantages.

- post office nu-media (graphic display)
- post office continuous video tape
- post office leaflet dispensing
- taxi cabs
- teleguide (telephone recordings)
- video tapes

Media decision

Selecting the right media amounts to discovering the most cost effective media to deliver the desired number of exposures to the target audience. This involves examining the **reach**, **frequency** and **impact** of advertisements.

Reach is most important when a firm is trying to create initial awareness of a product. Frequency is most important for a complex product or for creating a brand image. The media planner has to be familiar with the reach, frequency and impact of the major media types. Each type has advantages and limitations in terms of reach, frequency and impact. Media planners match limitations and advantages with the requirements of the message. For example, a message announcing that a sale is taking place today may be given over the radio. The radio is an excellent medium for reaching people within the range of the transmission who are on the move or who need to be reminded about an event just before it takes place. It also facilitates the sending of short notice, urgent or last minute messages. The relatively high frequency with which such messages can be transmitted acts as a powerful reminder and reinforces the impact of the message. Obviously, the nature of the product, the nature of the message, the cost and the type of audience using the media are key factors in the process.

Assessing the cost effectiveness of media vehicles

Audience size, composition and cost are the indicators of effectiveness used by media planners. Circulation and type of audience are important measures taken into account by the planners. They calculate the cost per thousand of the target reached by a particular media vehicle. One should bear in mind that this is not the same thing as the cost per thousand reached with respect to users of the media. Many of these people may not be in the target group. Other things being equal, planners prefer media vehicles that have the lowest cost per thousand people reached of the **target** media group. Other considerations are the quality of the editorials and the extent to which people pay attention to the advertisements.

Media scheduling

A firm can vary its advertising expenditure to suit the seasonal pattern, or it can advertise throughout the year. Most firms do the latter. Kuehn (1962) showed that the appropriate pattern of timing should reflect how much advertising **carry-over effect** exists and

► **Reach** is the number of persons who are exposed to a media schedule at least once during a specific time period.

► **Frequency** is the number of times within a specific time period that an average person is exposed to a message.

► **Impact** is the qualitative value of an exposure through a given medium.

► Kuehn, A. A. (1962), 'How advertising performance depends on other marketing factors', *Journal of Advertising Research*, March 1962, pp. 2–10.

the degree of habit that exists in customers choice of brand. Where both are low it is appropriate to time the advertising so that it coincides with the seasonal pattern. Where carry-over effects and habit are high it is better to time advertising to lead the sales curve. The higher the carry-over then the greater should be the lead time. Steady advertising expenditure should be used when habitual purchase patterns are greatest.

Having decided how to vary expenditure a firm has to then look at advertising over a short period of time so as to obtain the maximum impact. More continuous advertising should be used when the rate at which new customers appear in the market is high. This should also be the case when the frequency with which people make purchases is high or the rate at which people 'forget the brand' is high.

Advertisers tend to use continuous advertising when the market is expanding with fast-moving items, in tightly defined customer categories. Concentrated advertising in a single period of time occurs when the product is sold in a single period. In the case of seasonal or infrequently purchased items or when limited funds exist, bursts of advertising are used. An alternative is to use continuous advertising at low weight levels reinforced periodically by waves of heavier activity.

▶ Carry-over effect reflects how long the influence of an advertisement will be felt.

▶ The choice of media should reflect its effectiveness to reach the target audience. Media scheduling should be related to seasonal sales patterns where they exist.

 Fred is the product manager for a range of aluminium wrapping foils. The trade is seasonal with peak sales at Christmas time when people buy the foil to wrap around turkeys.

Fred makes use of in store merchandising aids to help sell the foil and this year for the first time is contemplating TV advertising. This is in response to advertising started by a French manufacturer of foil who is keen to get in on the British market. The French competitors advertising schedules appear to be erratic and Fred needs to know how the his firm should schedule its advertisements to have an optimum impact on the market.

How would you suggest he should schedule the advertising?

MEASURING ADVERTISING EFFECTIVENESS

Effective advertising involves three essential ingredients.

1 Good copy – the wording and layout of the advertisement are critical.
2 Correct media selection.
3 Advertising at the right time and with the right frequency.

Most of the money spent on measuring advertising effectiveness goes into **pre-testing** advertisements. The accent is on trying to measure the communication effect of an advertisement, i.e. the potential effect on awareness, knowledge or preference.

There are a number of ways of pre-testing advertisements:

- **direct rating** involves showing a consumer panel alternative advertisements and getting them to rate them. Ratings are made according to: the attention-getting power of an advertisement; whether it encourages the recipient of the message to listen, watch or read further; the clarity of the message; the effectiveness of the appeal; and whether it suggests follow-through action
- **portfolio tests** provide the consumer with a collection of advertisements and ask them to recall their content. Recalling the advertisement indicates its ability to be understood and remembered
- **laboratory tests** are used to measure the consumers' physical reaction to advertisements. Pupil dilation tests, changes in heart beat, etc., reflect an advertisement's ability to attract attention.

Since campaigns will have a number of objectives advertisers are interested to find out how effective they have been in reaching these objectives. **Post-testing** involves questioning consumers in order to assess how effective advertising messages have been in achieving predetermined objectives. These objectives may have involved changing the level of awareness about a brand, for instance, or increasing knowledge or preference for the brand. Usually a random sample of the target market is questioned in order to ascertain such information.

> ► Measuring advertising effectiveness involves pre-testing and post- testing. Recognition and recall testing is commonly used and measures are taken of an advertisement's ability to achieve its objectives.

 Collect a number of full page advertisements from a range of magazines and get your friends to rate the each advertisement for:

- attention getting power
- whether it encourages the recipient of the message to listen, watch or read further
- the clarity of the message
- the effectiveness of the appeal
- whether it suggests follow through action.

Measuring effectiveness in relation to sales

Advertising expenditure can be related to market share. We might predict that advertising expenditure and market share would be directly proportional, i.e. the more money spent on advertising, the greater the advertised product's share of the market. However, some established products retain a large share of the market with minimal advertising. And, for obvious reasons, new products with little or no market share require disproportionate spending on advertising.

Some researchers try to relate sales directly to advertising by analysing historical data with the help of statistical methods, such as correlation and regression analysis. Another approach involves conducting field experiments in which the levels of expenditure are studied. In both cases, however, many factors intervene to influence actual sales and it is difficult to establish just how variations in advertising impact on sales. In special cases where advertisers seek to sell goods direct to customers, the latter are often asked to indicate to which advertisements they are responding. This last approach helps the advertiser to gauge the effectiveness of different advertisements.

Sales promotion

Whereas advertising provides reasons why a customer should buy a product or service, **sales promotion** provides the incentive to buy. Sales promotion can take many forms. For example:

- free samples
- price reductions
- trading stamps
- coupons
- free gifts
- competitions
- retailers' discount/commission
- special offers
- trial offers
- in-store demonstrations

It has been found that many purchase decisions are made in the shop where goods are displayed. Point of sale selling aids are therefore key elements in the sales promotion process and sales promotions are often carried out by teams of sales merchandisers in stores.

Some use of sales promotion is made by industrial goods producers. Trade-in allowances for old models, free staff training and special credit terms figure in the sales promotion mix.

Sales promotion is used to attract new triers, to reward loyal customers and to get occasional purchasers to buy again. It often attracts people who like to switch brands because they are usually looking for low price, good value or premiums. In these cases, sales promotion does not usually gain the brand loyalty of such customers and so increases in sales and market share are usually only short term.

Sales promotion operates at the level of the consumer, the sales force and the retailer. In terms of consumer behaviour it may have

▶ Sales promotions are offered at the level of the consumer, the sales force and the retailer.

Sales promotions in 1991

British Airways offered mobile phones to passengers at Heathrow. The new service, using the Vodaphone cellular telephone network was offered to all passengers calling to book a flight into Heathrow, but was geared specifically for business travellers.

Me magazine, IPC's young women's weekly, cut its cover price from 52p to 25p in a bid to encourage sampling. The promotion coincided with an editorial revamp.

Golden Wonder indicated it was to offer watches to consumers who purchased 20 lids from its 'Pot' range. It was to be supported by a TV campaign.

Brooke Bond indicated it was to run a competition on Choicest Blend packs in Tesco stores. The prize was to be an all expenses paid trip on Concorde to see the musical *Phantom of the Opera* in New York. Runners up were to get tickets to see the *Phantom* in London.

---

the objective of inducing trial or attracting brand switchers. In the case of retailers, it can have the objective of motivating them to carry new items or higher levels of stock, or to gain entry into new outlets. For the sales force, it may have the objective of encouraging it to do more prospecting or stimulate out of season sales.

 Visit a shopping centre and make a list of different sales promotional items.

What do you think the promotions are trying to achieve?

PUBLIC RELATIONS

A **public relations unit** is responsible for creating and maintaining a positive and beneficial corporate image both internally and externally.

Forces in the external environment influence a company's operations. The source of the influence may be competitors, government institutions, financial institutions, economic forces, political pressures, ethical considerations, and sociocultural or technological change. All of these represent **publics** to an organization. An organization has to deal with its various publics in such a way as to give the impression that it is acting in the best interests of them all. The public relations function in a firm strives to help the organization develop and maintain a climate or environment which is favourably disposed towards its operations.

Public Relations activities include

- identifying specific interest groups and determining how they are likely to influence the activities of the organization

- advising the management about what is happening with respect to its various publics
- product publicity
- media relations, i.e. securing newsworthy information about the firm in the public eyes. This can be used to attract public attention to a particular product, service, activity or enterprise
- corporate communications which concentrate on creating awareness, understanding and positive attitudes towards the organization itself
- lobbying legislators, influential government officials or professional bodies over matters that have direct consequences for the organization.

A chemical firm accidentally discharged toxic effluence into a local river. The firm is to be prosecuted and cannot escape a heavy fine. The chief executive of the company thinks that the firm ought to undertake some public relations activity since media reports may have created a poor public impression of the company.

What action do you suggest the chief executive should take?

DIRECT MARKETING

Where individual approaches are made to customers we refer to this as **direct marketing**. At one time this was the sole province of personal selling but nowadays other methods such as telemarketing and mail shots have become increasingly more important.

Direct marketing has become the major area of growth in the world of personal computers. More and more companies have come on the scene offering better support, more technical knowledge , better and cheaper products than the established dealer and channel has been able to offer.

Direct Mail

Direct mail comprises personalized sales letters sent out to individual prospects. People using direct mail can buy lists of mailing prospects from companies who compile them or alternatively they can put together their own mailing lists. Mailing lists are kept in large databases and are regularly updated. The usefulness of such a database is clearly defined by how up-to-date it is.

▶ Business people on average open and read 88% of the direct mail they receive, according to a survey from the Direct Mail Information Service (1991). But 49% is then thrown way and just 2% gets a direct response.

A college is trying to raise money from its old students to set up a new lecture theatre for general use. It is anticipated that the conference suite will pay for itself within a short period of time but the college lacks the initial capital to

▶ Expenditure on direct mail advertising was estimated to be £2,372 m in 1990. (Source the *Marketing Pocket Book*, 1992.)

Direct time

Time Computer Systems is a Blackburn-based direct marketing organization which started off as as an upstairs room operation dealing in Amstrads. Within a matter of a few year it has grown to a size where it has a annual sales turnover of £20 m.

The firm provides added value to the products it markets and, following the dictum of providing customers with what they want at the best price, offers only optional warranty schemes. The area where the firm is keenest to add value is the hardware. Enhancements to most of the key components of the major brands are offered in the form of faster hard drives or more main memory.

Adapted from *PC Direct*, January 1992, p. 274.

convert some of its existing rooms to the required standard.

The college has decided to send out a letter to all ex- students of the college and all employers sending students to the college asking for a donation to this project. In return the college is going to put a plaque on permanent display at the entrance to the lecture theatre on which will be listed the names of all those individuals and employers who have donated more than a specified figure.

Draft out a suitable letter for circulation which you feel will attract donations and sponsors.

Leafleting

Door-to-door leafleting and free samples can be a cheap and effective way of communicating with prospects. Leaflets can be distributed by the GPO or inserted in free newspapers. Alternatively people can be hired to deliver leaflets on foot at a low cost.

Research seems to indicate that leaflets are in fact read by recipients and often considered to be interesting. Free samples delivered through the letter box are also well received.

Exhibitions

Exhibitions are used to show and demonstrate the facts and features relating to a product or service to the public. They can be staffed or unstaffed. Staffed exhibitions obviously have the advantage of being able to bring trained and experienced sales personnel into contact with potential buyers. They also make technical experts available to the customer. Exhibitions are widely used by producers of industrial products and also by suppliers of a wide range of consumer durable goods. Travelling exhibitions or roadshows have been used by a number of different marketers. They

Free samples through the letter box are well received

'I think we'll have to leave this one on the doorstep, Bert.'

have the benefits of static exhibitions but can bring them to a variety of locations.

Sponsorship

Sponsorship involves a company or individual supporting or subsidising an activity with hard cash in return for publicity and/or free exposure in the media. Sporting events and sporting personalities predominate in the kind of activities that receive sponsorship, for example, ADT sponsors the London Marathon.

From the sponsor's point of view, the company name is kept in the public eye. From the marketer's point of view, the effectiveness of the target marketing is less obvious.

Forms of sponsorship

A company selling natural mineral water, Abbey Well, supported the Pop Art Show at London's Royal Academy in 1991 with an on-pack promotion. An offer printed on over three million bottles offered exhibition-goers priority admission.

Radio Rentals indicated (1991) it was going to sponsor the British Olympic Association . Cash will go to British competitors in the winter and summer games.

► Total expenditure on sports sponsorship was estimated to be £230 m in 1990 (Source: *The Marketing Pocket Book*, 1992), with horse racing £17.0 m. receiving the largest amount. Total expenditure on the Arts in 1990 was £35 m. (more than double the amount in 1984), with 32% going to classical music.

CHAPTER SUMMARY

1 Marketing communications makes use of the basic elements of communications theory. Various models for the communication process have been suggested including the stepwise models which relate to general communications, selling and to advertising.

2 Since the process of marketing communications is a multi-stage one, objectives can be set for marketing communications which relate to each stage in the process. For example, to create awareness or to evoke interest.

3 Marketing communications have to be designed carefully. Matters relating to the format and structure of the message and the credibility of the information source require special attention.

4 There are advantages and disadvantages to using different types of media – newspapers, magazines, televisions, commercial radio, outdoor advertising, cinema advertising. Marketers have to choose appropriate media, assess the cost effectiveness of media vehicles and, in conjunction with agencies, schedule advertising.

5 Because advertising can have a number of objectives there are

► Now that you have reached the end of the chapter, turn back to the objectives and make sure you have achieved each of them.

different ways of measuring advertising effectiveness – including its relationship to sales.

6 There are many different forms of marketing communication, each one of which has its own specific usefulness . The range involves sales promotion, public relations, direct marketing, direct mail, leafleting, exhibitions and sponsorship.

Selling

Chapter objectives

By the end of this chapter you should:

▮ understand the role of selling within the marketing communications mix

▮ be able to describe the different roles of the salesperson

▮ be able to describe the different kinds of selling situation that are to be found

▮ know the different kinds of selling skills and strategies that are required

▮ be able to describe the various ways of motivating sales staff

▮ know how sales managers can determine the size of the sales force required and organize it in the most effective manner, particularly with respect to assigning people to territories

▮ be familiar with the following terms as used by marketers: order takers, missionary salespeople, technical sales representatives, creative selling, sales territories, telemarketing.

Introduction

In this chapter we look at the importance of selling within the communications mix and how the emphasis on selling varies with the type of product concerned. The task of the salesperson is a complex one and there are many different roles for a person to fill. There is a broad variety of different selling situations to be found in practice. The different situations require different kinds of selling skills and there are some guidelines for people who are involved in selling activities.

The chapter also considers the subject of sales management and attention is given to the ways in which a sales manager can try to provide a framework within which sales staff can become motivated in their work. The manager's job extends to organizing the sales force in an efficient manner and this is explored in some detail.

IMPORTANCE OF SELLING IN THE MARKETING MIX

Selling involves:

● influencing attitudes towards a product or service

- moving people towards a desire to purchase a product or service
- convincing people that it is the right decision to make
- actually getting them to take the purchasing step
- reassuring the person after purchase that he or she has made the right decision.

Expenditure on personal selling varies according to the types of goods and services that are on offer. This often reflects the nature of the target market which is being addressed, though there are exceptions to the rule. Industrial goods manufacturers put a greater financial emphasis on selling in the marketing mix whereas large consumer goods producers tend to spend more on other forms of promotion.

The role of the salesperson

In the case of fast-moving consumer goods, the salesperson often has to negotiate with professional buyers who have responsibility for a large number of sales outlets. In conjunction with the buyer, the sales-person has to ensure that the product is stocked and displayed in an eye-catching manner at the point of sale.

▶ To be able to sell something one needs to know not only the product but also the customer.

The industrial goods salesperson faces a somewhat different task. Here the task is to identify the persons who make the purchase decisions and then to find ways of influencing them. Sometimes the decision making may be influenced by recommendations made by outside consultants such as engineers and architects. Salespeople need to have the skills and the knowledge to negotiate with these kinds of specialists.

Selling is also important in marketing services either to industrial or consumer markets. Some people take the view that it is more difficult to sell services. Products are tangible and the benefits can be readily demonstrated. This is not the case with services and persuading people that they need or want a particular service is a hard task. If people do not attach a high personal priority to something they may well put off the decision to purchase even if they recognize that it is a service which they need. Moreover from the salesperson's point of view it may be difficult to relate long-term benefits to the cost of the service.

TYPES OF SELLING SITUATION

Order takers and those who respond to requests

▶ The amount of persuasion that has to be exerted here is at the lowest end of the spectrum. Relatively little knowledge of the customer or his or her business is required.

The task of personal selling varies considerably with the situation. Some salespeople do little more than take orders or respond to requests. Sales assistants in shops, van salespeople and manufacturer's salespeople calling on the retail trade usually fall into this

Selling life assurance

In general terms everyone will recognize the benefits of life assurance but actually getting people to apply the need to themselves may be an extremely difficult task. It is an intangible and so it is difficult to demonstrate its benefits. Perhaps the biggest problem is the relatively low priority which people attach to it. Younger people have many other commitments and attach a lower probability to the fact that it will be necessary to lodge a claim in the foreseeable future. Older people may have had the opportunity to build up substantial financial reserves and feel that it is no longer a necessity. How can one get round these kind of difficulties?

One way is to sell life assurance as an investment – a way of saving for the future. In other words, the 'insurance' benefit of a policy is less important than the 'assurance' part. This may appeal to older people who are looking for ways of saving surplus income or capital and can see that there are other benefits to be had as well as financial ones. However, such an approach may not always convince the younger person who may not have any spare money to invest. Here the approach might be to link life assurance with other benefits such as making it easier to obtain a mortgage on a house.

The stages in the family life cycle (see page 109) provide a useful framework within which to consider the various benefits attached to the service provided and how these benefits might be perceived by consumer groups. The above examples are illustrative of this approach.

category. These latter two categories often represent food, confectionery or soft drinks manufacturers. The salespeople check shops for their stock levels. One should not confuse this kind of sales job with that of key account managers who negotiate with retail managers at a very high level discussing large quantities, and very competitive terms and promotions. There is an expectation on the part of the retailer that the account manager will be familiar with the retailer's operations. Large retailers, such as multiples ,expect to be consulted in advance about manufacturer's new product plans, including pack and package design and expect cooperation!

▶ Account managers need to be persuasive and highly conversant with the customer's business.

Missionary salespeople

There are missionary salespeople who take a low-key approach and whose prime purpose is to provide information and advice about a product, for example pharmaceutical salespeople who call on general practitioners. These people cannot usually take orders but try to create a level of awareness whereby the benefits of a specific product or service will be favourably considered when the need arises.

► There is much debate over whether one should train salespeople in technology or train technologists to sell.

Technical salespeople

There are technical sales representatives who have technical training as well as selling skills. They offer technical advice to clients as well as trying to supply goods or services to meet the customers' wants and needs. These kinds of salespeople abound in industrial marketing where technical knowledge regarding the product and the purposes for which it is to be used are of paramount importance.

Creative salespeople

► There is a variety of selling situations and each one requires a different degree of persuasability.

There are also creative selling jobs, which can be found in tangible and intangible goods and services. In a creative selling role, the salesperson has to persuade people to purchase products or services which they have not heard about before, or for which they have not previously seen a need, or where they have to be persuaded that the new product can satisfy their needs better than others already available.

Selling skills and strategies

A salesperson is expected to do many things as part of his or her job. In addition to clinching actual sales, salespeople also have to collect information on what competitors are doing in the field and identify any unfulfilled wants and needs that customers may have. The task of selling itself is divided into a number of stages:

► The selling task comprises many different activities.

- getting together a list of prospects
- finding out as much as possible about the potential buyer/customer
- identifying the benefits which are likely to be of most interest to the customer
- examining and evaluating what the competitors are offering
- determining what benefits the user would derive from using the product or service
- planning out the sales interview
- making arrangements to visit the prospect's premises
- travelling to the prospects premises
- conducting the sales interview
- recording an order
- progressing the order back at the firm
- reassuring the customer the order will be delivered on time
- checking up to make sure that when the order is delivered everything is as it should be
- checking up some time later to ensure that no problems have arisen since the order was delivered.

Sales interviews

The focus of selling activities must be on the sales interview. This is the point where the salesperson meets the potential customer, often referred to as the prospect and tries to sell the product or service to him or her.

Various writers have tried to suggest how one should conduct a sales interview. This, however, is a very personal thing and much depends on the people and the situational factors which surround the sales interview. Personalities, experience and knowledge of the people involved exert considerable influence over the outcome of the encounter. Getting the prospect to pay attention to what one has to say, promoting interest and then desire and finally obtaining action are key elements of the process.

There are a number of guidelines which might be followed. Firstly, sales interviews have the best chance of success if sales interview objectives are established for each call and a plan of how to achieve these objectives is laid down. As with other forms of communication the AIDA model (see page 242) clearly has applicability in this case. The salesperson has to get the prospect's attention, arouse interest in what he or she has to say and then move on to desire and action with respect to buying or ordering the product.

The key thing to remember in a selling situation is that it is not a product or service that is being offered for sale but a **set of benefits**. It is these benefits which are of interest to the customer and not the features of the product or service itself. Knowledge of how the product will benefit the customer is extremely important. Three types of benefits can be demonstrated:

1 Those that arise from the product itself.
2 Those that arise from it being offered by the salesperson's company.
3 Those that differentiate it from competitors' products.

Benefits will satisfy felt needs and the salesperson has to identify the felt needs and show the prospect how the product or service will satisfy them. For example, a prospective purchaser of a car may have a felt need for 'low cost of running the car'. If the car has low fuel consumption then the salesperson can stress that the product can meet with the prospect's requirements because it has a small, fuel efficient engine. If the same concern exists where a larger car is being sold, the salesperson can stress the efficient engine design or point to other low cost running features of the car such as the fact it only requires a service every 12,000 miles.

Dealing with objections raised in sales interviews

During a sales interview it is very common for a prospect to raise objections when he or she cannot perceive a need for the product

► The 'born salesperson' probably does not exist. But experience of other walks of life can be readily transferred into the selling situation.

► The AIDA model: attracting **attention**, maintaining **interest**, arousing **desire**, getting **attention**.

► A sales promoter on the cosmetics counter of a department store is not selling make-up but confidence. A salesman in a used-car showroom is not selling cars but freedom. A funeral parlour is not selling burials or cremations but help and empathy at a sad time. A football club is not selling football matches to its fans but an identity to belong to.

Selling foodstuffs to farmers – getting attention and arousing interest

Bill Maddocks parks his car in the lane outside the farm. Donning his rubber boots and grasping his sales manual and free samples, he makes his way over to the cowshed where he knows Farmer Jones is always to be found, regular as clockwork at this time of the day.

'Good Morning Mr Jones, how is Sally this morning?'

'Good Day, Mr Maddocks. She's recovering well from the infection. The vet says we've just got to be a bit careful how we handle her. I reckon she'll soon be back to normal again.'

'I'm glad to hear that because I did hear there was a nasty virus knocking around these parts. But your herd doesn't wander off the pasture.'

'No. I keep a close eye on them. But the pigs, now that is a different problem altogether. You know I like free ranging the animals but they're a handful they are'

'Talking of pigs, I have something which might speed up the fattening process and take them off your hands a couple of weeks earlier than your used to.'

'Well, I don't know about that. I don't go in for those chemical additives you know. They can cause nasty side effects, I am told.'

'No chemicals, I assure you. Everything in the mix is natural, the company spent millions developing it and I have heard that the Duke of Sussex is trying it on his latest breed.'

'That so? Can't be bad then. Tell me more. What is in it and how does it work?'

---

or service on offer. Objections may relate to price, delivery schedule or certain products or company characteristics. Objections are overcome by:

- maintaining a positive approach
- asking the prospect to clarify the objection
- questioning the prospect in a way that the prospect has to answer his or her own objections
- denying the validity of the objection
- turning the objection into a reason for buying.

A sale is 'closed' when the salesperson gets the prospect to place an order. Perhaps the best way to do this is to attempt trial closures throughout the length of the sales interview. Positive cues denoting interest or desire on the part of the prospect should be followed up with an attempt to close the sale. An example of how this might done is given below:

Handling objections

'I really have no need for that kind of product.'
'Of course, and that is what many of our clients says until they appreciate what it can do for them. Would you like a demonstration?'

'Timber, you say. No, they just do not work properly.'
'I see. Perhaps you could give me some examples so that I can refer them back to our technical people for their advice.'

'I've tried them before and I couldn't get them to work.'
'You'd better tell me exactly what you did and then perhaps we can see what went wrong.'

'I can't believe that it really will do what you say it will do.'
'Look here are reports of it being used by the Duke of Sussex on his Friesians. What more is there to say?'

'I really think the price is much too high.'
'A high price? Well that of course is what distinguishes it from inferior imitations.'

'Many executives like yourself are now wearing this particular model'
'Yes its so thin and fits well on my wrist and I do like the blue stone on top of the crown. It's very elegant'
'All these watches have specials clasps as well. Did you notice?'
'Yes, I suppose that is why it is such a good fit on my wrist.'
'We can offer it to you on terms if you would like, sir. Would you like me to get you a form.'

The key thing to remember is that a salesperson will only achieve a final sale if he or she asks for an order.

Imagine you are selling umbrellas. Use the directories in your local library to get a list of prospects and retailers who might be interested to stock umbrellas. Find out as much as possible about the retailers whose names you have selected.

Think up the kind of benefits that these retailers would be likely to expect from the products you are selling. Examine what other competitors are offering to retailers in the area in the way of umbrellas. Determine the benefits the users would derive from using the umbrellas you are selling and plan out the sales interviews with prospective retailers.

Some common reasons why a sales interview may not produce results

1 Too many interruptions so that both the salesperson and the prospect tend to lose their track of what the sales argument is all about.

2 The salesperson talks about features of the product and not the benefits of the product.

3 The sales argument has nothing new in it – the prospect has heard it all before. To get the interest of a prospect it is important to inject something new into the sales argument.

4 The prospect is not given the opportunity to say whether he or she fully understands the sales argument.

5 The sales pitch is over the prospect's head – usually this means it is too technical.

6 The sales presentation lacks enthusiasm. If the salesperson does not show some enthusiasm for the product or service he or she is selling then it is difficult to expect the prospect to show any enthusiasm.

7 The prospect's objections to the sales argument are problems, but the salesperson does not treat them as such and gives rather superficial answers. These leave the prospect's objections unanswered.

8 The salesperson annoys the prospect by disagreeing with him or her personally instead of citing the opinions or the experiences of third parties.

9 The salesperson is unable to distinguish phoney objections from genuine ones.

10 The salesperson may fail to identify the true decision maker and may present the sales argument to a person who cannot make or even influence the decision.

11 A lack of knowledge, on the part of the salesperson, regarding how the benefits of the product or service would meet the needs of the prospect.

12 Failure to ask for a sale.

13 Giving up after the first 'no'. A prospect may say 'no' but really mean 'maybe'. The salesperson has to try more than once to ascertain if this in fact is the case.

14 The salesperson may talk too much and fail, in so doing, to gain the correct impression of the prospect's attitudes.

15 A lack of confidence on the part of the salesperson – not believing that a sale could be achieved from the outset.

 Role play a sales situation with a friend. Allow adequate time for both of you to consider how to play the roles.
Try to get the role play to bring out some of the points made above.

THE TASK OF SALES MANAGERS

Sales managers have to manage. They have to plan, coordinate, organize and control the activities of a sales force. They have to agree targets for the sales force to achieve and have to manage the resources which will support the sales force in pursuing these targets. Additionally, it is important to note that sales managers can only be successful if they recognize that they are no longer salespersons but teachers of other salespersons. The sales manager has to develop the selling skills of sales staff.

► A sales manager's job is to get other people to sell. It is not primarily the sales manager's job to sell.

Sales compensation and motivation

The picture concerning what people consider to be most important in a job is relative difficult to unravel. In a recent survey 29.5% of people said that 'interesting work making use of one's own skills' was the most important, 18.1 % considered 'job security' to be the most important, 15.2% considered 'convenient working hours' to be the most important and 13.9% considered 'good pay' to be the most important.

► Source *The British Social Attitudes Report*, Social & Community Planning Research, 1989.

Most important points in a job

	Most important
Interesting work	29.5%
Job security	18.1%
Convenient working hours	15.2%
Good pay	13.9%
Other	23.3%

However, when asked what was the second most important point, 'good pay topped' the list.

Second most important point in a job

	2nd most important
Good pay	22.0%
Interesting work	14.9%
Job security	11.7%
Convenient working hours	8.1%
Other	43.3%

There are a number of **motivational factors** to be considered, these include:

1 Financial rewards

Motivating salespeople to do their work is a prime task of sales management. In some cases firms pay their sales staff on a **salary only** basis. This usually occurs where there is not a lot of persuasion involved in the sales job, e.g. order taking. Such a system does not offer any positive reinforcements to really good salespeople since they are not provided with better benefits than the weaker salespeople.

At the other extreme salespeople may be paid on a **commission-only** basis. This is the approach used most widely where there is a lot of creative selling involved. Here financial rewards are related directly to sales achieved. Clearly this sort of approach is most useful where the entire selling role is to achieve a sale and nothing more than that. If the customers do require technical advice and assistance then this approach will have its limitations since the salesperson, having clinched a sale, is really only motivated to move on to the next prospect.

In between these extremes there is a whole range of selling situations where a combination of commission and salary is more appropriate. This is particularly the case in industrial products where a technical salesperson is employed who can provide a great deal of advice to the customer in terms of using the product.

► See also Maslow's hierarchy of needs in Chapter 7.

2 **Opportunity for advancement**

It is advantageous to have some sort of promotion policy which motivates salespeople to do a good job. Not everyone wants to be promoted but for some people promotion prospects are a very important factor.

3 **Personal status**

Giving a person a special job title may well affect the way he or she performs. Many people, for example, relish holding manager status. Some organizations use the titles executive and manager profusely so that the meaning of the terms have different meanings to what is customarily associated with them. The genuine value of such organizational nomenclature within the firm is doubtful, since everyone knows their relative importance but it certainly enhances the status of the individual with customers and clients.

4 **Job security**

Marketing jobs are not traditionally associated with job security. However the advantage of job security in motivating personnel is obvious. A person always performs better when he or she is not immediately concerned with the fear of losing his or her job.

5 **A worthwhile job**

Convincing a salesperson that he or she is doing a worthwhile job is important. The job of a salesperson can involve a lot of rejection by potential customers on whom unsuccessful calls have been made. Continual refusals and rejections can be demoralizing and a great deal of support from the sales manager is required.

Other positive incentives include such things as giving salespeople some personal authority when it comes to dealing with customers and allowing staff some degree of self determination. People resent being told what they should do and how they should do it. In addition people like to feel that they are receiving fair and personal treatment.

There are also **negative incentives**

A range of negative incentives that can be used to provide a basis for motivation. These are not as commonly practised today as they have been in the past. It has to be borne in mind, however, that it is not possible to manage an organization without some form of **discipline**. In principle, discipline amounts to setting minimum standards of performance and establishing appropriate penalties for failure to achieve them. Penalties may range from private warnings to public reprimands and penalties. The ultimate penalty for breaking an organizational rule is termination of employment.

Discipline in selling tends to be the exception rather than the rule but it is advisable to establish the managerial prerogative of using negative incentives when necessary. Discipline is necessary for good morale and failure to enforce it can jeopardize an entire marketing operation.

▶ An important point to bear in mind is that one should first look for the causes of sub-standard performance and not just try to treat the symptoms. After all, prevention, is better than cure.

 Look in the *Daily Telegraph* at the sales appointments Make a list of the type of sales jobs, the salary/compensation offered and any other perks that go with the job.

Determining the size of the sales force

Here we will be looking as a sales force which makes contact with other organizations. We are not concerned with sales staff who are catergorized as sales assistants in shops.

Sales forces are expensive to maintain because high salaries are paid and salespeople tend to have sizeable expense accounts. There are many approaches to determining the best size of sales force to keep. One approach is to estimate the extent of the selling task and divide this task by the amount of it that a single salesperson might handle. Let us assume that an industrial firm sells to two classes of customers, end-users and retailers. Imagine there are 1000 end-users and 200 retailers. The requirement is for the necessary number of salespeople to make 12 calls on each of the end-users and 24 calls on each of the retailers in the course of a single year. We also need to have some idea of the number of calls that an 'average' salesperson can make in a single year. Suppose we estimate from past experience that this amounts to 600 calls per year. We can then use a simple formula to find the optimum number of salespersons:

$$N = \frac{1}{K} \times [F_1(C_1) + F_2(C_2)]$$

Where
N = desired number of salespeople
F_n = call frequency required for a given customer class
C = number of customers in a given class
K = average number of calls a salesperson can make during a year

In this case it works out to be:

$$N = \frac{1}{600} \times [12(1000) + 24(200)]$$
$$= 0.0016 \times [12,000 + 4800]$$
$$= 28$$

Therefore , the optimum number of salespeople in this case is 28.

Altering the size of the sales force

► The approach adopted here assumes that all new sales staff are likely to be equally productive.

Most sales managers are faced with the problem of making adjustments to the size of an existing sales force. The general principle is that if one decides to do without a salesperson then the total sales will diminish as will selling expenses. If a manager decides to hire an additional salesperson then the salesperson has to contribute more in gross margin than he or she will cost. Of course, if a salesperson is not replaced and the cost that is saved exceeds the gross margin then the company is better off with fewer salespeople.

Suppose a firm employs twenty salespeople and its selling costs are £600,000. Suppose also that its salespeople produce £1,000,000 in gross profit contribution. Imagine that one of the sales staff has decided to leave the company.

The sales manager has a number of options. He or she can:

- decide not to replace the salesperson who is leaving (this reduces the sales force to nineteen)
- hire one person to replace the one who is leaving (keeping the sales force size at twenty)
- hire more than one person (increasing the size of the sales force to more than twenty staff)

Marginal approach to changing the size of the sales force

No. of sales people	Profit Contribution		Selling Cost	
	Total	Marginal	Total	Marginal
19	940,000		570,000	
		60,000		30,000
20	1,000,000		600,000	
		50,000		30,000
21	1,050,000		630,000	
		30,000		30,000
22	1,080,000		660,000	
		20,000		30,000
23	1,100,000		690,000	

The table indicates that hiring three people is the most desirable course to follow. If a replacement is not made then gross margin will drop by £60,000 while a saving of only £30,000 will be achieved. Hiring additional people over and above the replacement is worthwhile. It is not worthwhile hiring more than two

additional salespeople as well as the replacement. Hiring two people including the replacement will increase profit by £20,000. The
hiring of the next person will **not** increase total profit but it will
enable the firm to increase sales. The cost of hiring additional staff
beyond that point will not be profitable.

Sales force organization

A sales organization can be drawn up along one of several lines. It
can be based on product lines whereby some salespeople and their
respective managers are responsible for one part of the product line.
Another group of salespeople may be in charge of other products.
This is a method of organization commonly encountered when a
company serves two or more types of customers, for example consumer and industrial markets.

► See also pages 13 and 14 where
different kinds of marketing
organization are examined.

Another way of organizing the sales force is along geographic
lines. Here the sales manager manages a territory. This works well
in companies with short or homogeneous product lines and in
cases where extreme market segmentation is not encountered.
However, where a territory contains several different types of
industries it may not be possible for the salesperson to be familiar
with the special needs of each. This often leads to the assignment of
salespeople on a customer or market basis. One group of people
deal with one type of client while another group handles others.
Customers may even be divided on the basis of size. Large and
small customers tend to demand different services. Another basis
for assignment can be the level or type of customer. Different salespeople may be calling on manufacturing wholesale and retail
accounts.

It is not uncommon to find various combinations of these methods
of sales organization.

Fitting salespeople to sales territories

Assuming a firm possesses a sales force of a certain size and ability
it can choose to develop its territories around these people. This is
often done when there is a limited sales force. Let us assume that a
firm has thirty salespeople. The manager can proceed in one of two
ways:

1 The manager first determines approximately how many territories the sales force can handle effectively (based on geographic size
of the territory and the number of potential customers in the territory). Let us assume this to be thirty territories. The manager then
divides the total market into this number of geographical areas, i.e.
thirty areas.

2 The manager determines the optimum size of territory for a single salesperson (based on geographic size of the territory and the
number of potential customers in the territory). The manager then
divides the total market by the optimum size of territory for a single
salesperson. This may produce more territories than there are
salespeople say thirty-five territories. The manager then sets out the

territories in the order of attractiveness to the firm and assigns people to the territories at the head of the list.

The first approach results in a thin coverage of the market and the second may leave a number of markets uncovered. This is a dilemma faced by all sales managers. Assigning too large an area to a sales representative means that fewer calls can be made. On the other hand not covering some markets will lose sales but it may then be possible to develop the others intensively. Not covering part of a market, however, may allow competitors to establish a foothold with serious long-term consequences.

Size of territories

It is desirable that territories are approximately equal both in terms of sales potential and in terms of difficulty of servicing. This makes it easier to compare sales performance and at the same time improves the morale of sales staff since bickering or negotiating over territorial assignments is minimized.

Difficulties arise when one has to design territories which are equal both in terms of potential and workload. Since customers are not evenly distributed it is inevitable to find pockets of high potential concentration. A single customer in Greater London may have as much business potential for a product or service as the whole of Wales. There is no ready solution to this problem it has to be solved by compromise. For example a single large customer may be handled by the sales manager as a 'house account'. Alternatively, someone who is asked to cover a very large area may be paid a more attractive salary.

Imagine that you are the district manager of an insurance office in a large town. You employ nineteen agents to call on people in the town to collect insurance and assurance premiums. Some premiums are collected weekly while others are collected at larger intervals.

Each agent covers a different area of the town. The agents vary in ability: some have a lot of experience and produce good results in terms of new business while others have the same amount of experience but do not do as well. Less experienced staff usually do not do well in producing new business sales for a considerable period of time. There is a high staff turnover in the business and it is difficult to get good agents. The really good ones tend to go on to different jobs while the poorer ones stay only for a short time.

The town contains a mixture of different types of urban dwellings ranging from better quality terraced housing to much poorer quality terraced housing. There are three large council estates in the town and one better off suburb which contains up-market housing. Unemployment in the town is currently running at eleven per cent of the population.

Twenty per cent of the population is known to be over the age of sixty-five.

What steps would you take to try to ensure that territories are allocated to agents in such a manner that overall, and in the longer term the opportunities for generating new business are maximized?

Setting objectives for sales staff

In essence the quantitative sales objective which are set for salespeople should be derived from the sales plan which is a sub-plan of the marketing plan. This will stipulate such things as:

- how much to sell of each product – quantity, value and profit-wise
- what to sell – the mix of unit sales
- where to sell – the markets and the individual customers to sell to
- if possible the desired profit contribution
- a desired level of sales expenses which it is expected sales staff will keep within.

It has to be stressed to sales staff that they should try hard to keep to the targets which have been set and not to oversell on one product at the expense of another. If this were not to happen then it could well be that the firm is unable to meet the demand for particular products and yet will carry unsold stocks of other products. To exceed target on a particular product may create as many problems as underselling on another.

There are also other kinds of quantitative objectives which can be set for sales staff, where they are appropriate. These include:

- number of point of sale displays to organize
- number of letters written to prospects
- number of telephone calls to prospects
- number of sales reports produced
- number of trade meetings attended

► Sales management is concerned with planning, organizing and controlling the sales force. Teaching and providing the means for motivating staff are important tasks.

Not all objectives that are set are necessarily quantitative. Qualitative objectives might be set though it might be more difficult to assess these. Even the assessment of how well a sales representative conducts a sales interview is not that easy to assess because of the many situational variables involved. Product knowledge and work planning are however easier to evaluate.

Sales support staff

This chapter has indicated that the task of the sales representative goes beyond selling and involves such activities as drawing up a list of contacts. However, there is no doubt that there are considerable benefits to be had from having marketing staff and sales office staff working alongside the sales team. Indeed, lists of possible contacts and sales leads can easily be identified by the back-up team and this can increase the effectiveness of the sales operation.

Telemarketing

In addition to selling in a face-to-face situation there is also selling from a distance. Telephone selling has been around for may years. Originally it tended to be used by sellers of financial services and insurance. Now it is used by providers of a large variety of products and services. While it is a more economical way of approaching prospects than personal selling the telephone as a means of inter-personal communication suffers from several limitations. People are often influenced by non-verbal cues when interacting with others. These are clearly absent when using the telephone. Nevertheless, the proof of the usefulness of a selling method is to be found in its take-up rate amongst users. At the present time this still appears to be increasing. A recent innovation in telemarketing has been the advent of the Freephone service. Here, instead of firms making personal calls to prospects, the latter are encouraged through advertising to find out more about a product or service by using the Freephone service. This method at least goes part way to reducing the wastage rate in unsuccessful sales calls, since by and large it will only be used by interested people. It is however open to abuse and a potential target for commercial vandalism. Commercial vandalism could involve making deliberately time-wasting or misleading calls without the intent or interest in making a purchase.

▶ People are influenced by many factors when listening to a message some of which may reinforce the message and others which may detract from the message. Visual cues about the speaker often tell us something about their personality and attitudes. The absence of visual cues can have an effect on how people respond to telephone calls.

CHAPTER SUMMARY

1 Selling plays an important role within the marketing communications mix. It influences attitudes towards a product or service, moves people towards a desire to purchase a product or service and tries to convince people that it is the right decision to make. Selling is concerned with actually getting people to take the purchasing step and reassuring the person that he or she has made the right decision.

2 The role played by a salesperson varies according to the type of products being sold and the kind of selling situation. Some products and situations, require a good deal of technical knowledge as well as persuasive skills. In some cases, in dealing with retail buyers, knowledge of the buyers' business activities and the problems it encounters are essential.

3 There are no clear cut ways concerning how best to hold a sales interview but there are guidelines which can help in developing different kinds of selling skills and strategies.

4 Selling involves getting marketing communications across to an audience with the aid of people. People have to be motivated to do well. Sales managers have to be aware of the ways in which staff can become motivated.

5 Sales managers have certain other functions to carry out. These include determining the best size of sales force to maintain and organizing it in the most effective manner, particularly with respect to assigning people to territories.

6 Telemarketing is an area which despite apparent limitations is increasing in importance as an element within the communications mix.

▶ Now that you have reached the end of the chapter, turn back to the objectives and make sure you have achieved each of them.

17 Marketing for non-commercial organizations

Chapter objectives

By the end of the chapter you should:

▌ know how profit and non-profit-making organizations differ in terms of the kinds of objectives they pursue

▌ know what kind of benefits non-commercial organizations (NCOs) and their customers expect to obtain during the exchange process

▌ know how NCOs can identify customer wants and needs and match their services to meet them

▌ be able to describe the kind of promotional methods that NCOs employ

▌ know how NCOs treat the question of pricing their services to customers

Introduction

In this chapter we examine what marketing means to a variety of **non-commercial organizations (NCOs)**. Attention is given to the kind of benefits the organizations and their customers expect as a result of the exchange process. In the case of commercial organizations, goods and services are exchanged for profit. In the case of non-commercial organizations and their clients, the exchange process has different benefits.

Of considerable importance is how such non-commercial organizations identify customer wants and needs given the limited resources that most of these organizations have at their disposal. The same constraint also applies to promoting the services of non-commercial organizations. Given the non-profit making nature of such organizations the area of pricing is also examined.

TYPES OF NON-COMMERCIAL ORGANIZATIONS

Types of non-commercial organizations include:

● local authorities and publicly owned institutions such as schools, colleges, universities, libraries, museums and the National Health Service

- churches
- learned societies and charities
- political organizations – such as the Labour and Conservative Parties, their local organizations and political candidates
- charitable organizations.

Such organizations do not have a profit objective as their prime purpose. Indeed the establishments may be simply trying to balance their books between what they have to spend and what they receive in terms of grants from the government or from other sources. Not all of these bodies operate in the public sector. Private charities come into this category.

Despite the fact that such organizations are not profit oriented they are still organizations with aims, objectives and goals. The aims and objectives may be quite varied in nature and are related to the kind of benefits the organizations expect to obtain as a result of the exchange process.

Differences between NCOs and profit-making organizations

Commercial organizations have a prime objective to make a profit. This is one of the **benefits** which such organizations expect to obtain from the exchange process – that is exchanging goods with customers for money. In the same exchange process the customer expects various benefits from using the purchased goods or services.

In the case of non-commercial organizations the basis of the exchange process can take different forms. For example it can take the form of votes in return for better government in the case of electing a political candidate. We will look in more detail at the benefits of the exchange process as far as non-commercial organizations are concerned in a later section.

Objectives of non-commercial organizations are more complex than their profit-making counterparts and success or failure cannot be measured in strictly financial terms. The objectives of NCOs are linked to the benefits which they expect to obtain from the exchange process.

► There may be several objectives and there is a tendency for non-financial ones to dominate.

The benefits provided by non-profit services are often not related to consumer payments, for example only a small part of the population use museums and art galleries. This is in stark contrast to the situation encountered in the case of profit-making organizations where all the benefits are related to payments made by the consumers.

There are two other major differences between the non-commercial and the profit-making sectors. The first of these is that non-profit organizations may be expected or be required to serve economically unattractive market segments. The second is that non-profit organizations usually have two constituencies – clients and donors.

► Clients pose the problem of resource allocation: donors of resource attraction.

Lack of financial resources

A major problem for many of these enterprises is the lack of financial resources. Problems occur if NCOs are unable to charge higher prices for their services and at the same time cannot receive sufficient grants or donations to enable them to pursue all their identified objectives. For example local authorities raise money from local residents through taxes and also receive grants from central government. The latter may reduce the grant given and prevent the local authority from increasing the rate of tax levied on the local population. NCOs have to select feasible objectives that are constrained by the amount of resources they can muster.

Application of the marketing concept enables such organizations to identify and prioritize the needs and wants of the users of their services. The organization then has to provide the means of matching services to needs.

The exchange process and non-commercial organizations

We can look at the exchange process as it applies to the marketing of organizations, people, places and ideas for non-commercial purposes. Let us consider each one of these in turn.

Organizations

An example of a non-commercial profit organization is a **professional association**. A professional association is a body to which people can make subscriptions and enjoy a variety of benefits as a result of their membership. The benefits to members include the social experience resulting from attending meetings and sharing knowledge with other professionals. The benefits to the association include membership fees which can produce improved facilities and attract more professionals to join the association.

People

Political candidates are elected by people to serve the interests of a community at either national or local level. From the point of view of the voters their choice of candidate will offer benefits such as efficient government, better services, and similar views on key issues. The benefits to candidates include prestige and power.

Places

Major cities may be marketd as sites for conventions. The benefits to those attending conventions will be central locations, cultural facilities, superior accommodation and transportation. For the cities the benefits will include additional revenues, prestige, and the lessening of tax burdens for residents.

Ideas

An example of the promotion of ideas is a government sponsored campaign against smoking. The benefits to smokers include improved health, financial savings, a better self-image, and increased social acceptance. The benefits to society (whom the government represents) include a cleaner environment, a longer life span for loved ones, and lower costs for the health service.

 Draw up a list of non-commercial organizations.

Indicate in every case whether the NCO is concerned with organizations, people, places, ideas, products or services. Consider also:

- the basis of the exchange process
- the objectives of the organizations
- the benefits provided by the NCO – stating who are the main beneficiaries.

 Bill Proops is the prospective Labour Party candidate at a forthcoming general election. At the last election the Conservative candidate was elected by a majority of five votes and the previous Labour candidate came second. Assuming that the date of the election is the present time, draw up a list of benefits which you think Bill can offer to the electorate if he is elected. Do you think that any sectors of the electorate will not receive certain benefits if they vote for Bill?

What benefits do you think Bill would derive from becoming a Member of Parliament?

Establishing the needs of users of NCO's

Clearly the exact nature of the needs and wants of users of services will vary with the kind of organization involved. Moreover, given the amount of money available to discover what the wants and needs of customers are, the task can become quite a challenging one.

In 1991 a specialized surgical unit in a health authority in the north west of England wanted to gather evidence of the potential demand for its service to justify the acquisition of resources from the central funding body. By and large most of its business would come through referrals made by GPs. It decided that it would like to ask the opinions of some 500 GPs residing within the region in which it was operating. The services of an MBA student at a local university were acquired and the latter produced a suitable questionnaire, sent it out by post to each one of the sample of GPs and provided a detailed analysis of the results. The cost of acquiring this information was minimal and the unit was provided with ample evidence to support its case. Sometimes, of course, the

► Limited resources mean that NCOs have not much money to spend on market research. Innovative ways have to be found to identify market needs.

information required may be very technical in nature or be difficult or inappropriate for collection by mail survey. Making use of the knowledge assimilated by all members of the organization and through contacts with user groups on a formal or informal basis can provide a means of gathering data without incurring expensive surveys.

 St James Cathedral is looking for ways of attracting more visitors to the building during the winter months. There are many visitors during the summer and the Cathedral has a shop which it operates over the summer months. Volunteers run it and all proceedings from its activities over and above the costs of the items sold in the shop go directly into the Cathedral maintenance funds.

However, there are relatively few visitors in the winter. At a recent meeting of the senior clerics the Bishop argued that there was a need to market the Cathedral to locals inhabitants. 'What we need to do', he argued, ' is to find out how the cathedral can reach out to the local people during the cold winter months and best serve their needs.'

Suggest practical ways in which the Cathedral might be able to find out the kind of information which the Bishop indicates is necessary.

Matching services to needs

The major constraint on an organization's ability to match a service to needs is, of course, the amount of resources it has available. There simply may not be enough money available to have staff on hand to provide the services required. Moreover, even if sufficient funds are available there are still difficulties in recruiting suitably qualified staff to provide such services.

Excess demand

In cases where demand exceeds supply for services some form of rationing has to be introduced. This usually means prioritizing among requests according to the urgency and neediness – for example, a local authority allocating housing to families in need. An alternative approach is to look for other ways of satisfying the need.

Promotion of non-commercial services

Non-commercial services vary considerably in terms of their use of marketing communications. Some services, such as local government social security departments, do not communicate their services to potential users in the conventional sense. They rely on other organizations which may refer cases to them, such as GPs, solicitors, the police, etc.

Matching services to needs

Meals on wheels

Charity promotion

The publication *Marketing* (3 October 1991 p. 21) reported on the activities of a cancer research organization. Marketing breast cancer research to individuals and especially to corporate donors poses a real challenges. Break Through, the organization concerned, aimed to broaden the target donor group from the domain of large scale companies to that of the everyday consumer and smaller corporate donors. Break Through followed the lead of the most advanced charity marketers in making giving money easier.

The advice of the 'marketing-sharp' charities is not just to present a potential donor with an open request which demands heart searching and heavy arithmetic but to give them a commercially attractive offer which they understand. The suggestion of the experts is to go for their marketing budget , not for their heart-strings.

Break Through interpreted this in terms of their '£1000 challenge ' to encourage 15,000 large organizations, individuals and corporate donors to raise £1000 each, to reach a target of £15 million. Participants have a specific cash target to reach and they gain a sense of 'ownership'; each £1000 fund raiser would have its name displayed at Break Through's new centre.

As in the case of gathering information on user's wants and needs non-commercial services are usually restricted in terms of the cash they have available for marketing communications purposes. Museums and libraries make use of leaflets and posters in the foyers of their own buildings and publicize their activities through leaflets distributed to the general public by local information centres and tourist offices.

Innovative marketing programmes to attract people to public libraries

1 **General population**

- musical instrument practice room
- afternoon callisthenics/eurythmics sessions
- exchange discount coupon room
- lend-out prints of paintings or reproduction of sculptures
- poll tax rebate help by students
- home delivery of books
- extension of library hours

2 Children

- borrow a hamster (for a week)
- lend-out toys, jigsaws and videos
- dial library for a three minute recorded story
- karate/judo instruction
- road safety/bicycle safety programmes
- creche for shoppers

3 Other population

- tool lending for workmen
- instruction in basic English for immigrants
- interview techniques for the unemployed
- handling requests for transportation for physically handicapped persons
- bookmobile service to hospitals, nursing homes and institutions
- exercise programmes for senior citizens

Pricing and charging for non-commercial services

A large proportion of non-commercial organizations do not charge for their services since their operating costs are financed from local or central government. Other organizations, colleges, universities and even some schools and hospitals do charge for some of their services.

Moral pricing is a term which is often given to the kind of pricing approaches adopted by NCOs. Charity organizations may price their products and functions at a low level. But when they put on a special event to attract the wealthy then they price their tickets to their 'all star' attractions at a very high level indeed. This is because in this case they are in fact appealing to wealthy people who can afford to pay. Pricing is therefore related to ability to pay.

 A local primary school is organizing a fete to raise money to provide additional school equipment for its scholars. Parents have contributed items to the school which are to be sold on the day of the fete. Some of the items comprise home-made jams and cakes, knitted toys and embroidered clothes. Others items have been bought by the parents at some time in the past but are now surplus to their requirements. These include books, records, toys, crockery and paintings. There are also some items which have been bought especially by parents for the occasion and donated for sale at the fete. In this last category are various bottles of wines and spirits.

The head teacher has to come up with a pricing policy for the items which are to be sold. What sort of things do you think she should consider when setting the various prices? How would you price the various items mentioned above?

CHAPTER SUMMARY

1 Non-commercial organizations differ from profit-making organizations in terms of the kinds of objectives they pursue.

2 Non-commercial organizations are largely constrained in the amount of marketing activities they can pursue because they have less money to spend. Nevertheless, there are effective communication channels which they can use and economical ways of finding out about customer wants and needs.

▶ Now that you have reached the end of the chapter, turn back to the objectives and make sure you have achieved each of them.

18 *International marketing*

Chapter objectives

By the end of this chapter you should:

▌ know what motivates firms to become involved in international marketing

▌ be able to describe the various ways in which firms can become involved in international marketing activities

▌ be able to describe the various factors that firms should take into account when screening potential international marketing opportunities

▌ know what factors firms have to take into account when pricing their goods in international markets

▌ be able to describe the difference between global and international marketing

▌ be familiar with the following terms used by marketers; tariffs, quotas, confirming house, licensing, joint ventures, global marketing.

Introduction

Not all firms engage in international marketing activities. There are various reasons for this which we will explore below. There are several ways in which firms can get involved in international marketing. These range from simply supplying goods to intermediaries who then look after the shipping of the goods to various overseas markets, to actually setting up in business in the countries themselves.

Motivation for firms to become involved in international marketing

International economic theory puts forward a good case for countries to become involved in international trade. It argues that some countries can produce certain goods, extract certain raw materials or provide certain services more economically than others. In the case of producing goods, this may be because they have access to cheap labour or have automated manufacturing processes . With respect to raw materials, these may be readily accessible and cheap to obtain. Over the years, some countries will have developed efficient service industries such as banking and insurance. By countries specializing in producing those goods, materials and services and then engaging in trade, the global economy, it is argued, will benefit.

One does not need to be an expert on international economics to recognize some obvious truths in this. For example, countries which are rich in natural resources such as oil and metals, but have no means of producing consumer products, can supply other countries which do not have these natural resources and they in turn can supply consumer goods to the former countries. As a result, all should benefit.

The benefits of international trade are well documented in the economics literature. However a number of barriers stand in the way of encouraging international trade. These are:

1 Financial

- **shipping costs** – which add to the cost of imported goods
- **tariffs** – government taxes imposed to discourage the import of certain kinds of goods
- **limited mass communication systems** – these make it difficult for firms wanting to advertise their wares
- **limited transportation systems** – these make it difficult to implement physical distribution
- **cost of adapting goods** to the needs of individual countries – even where goods are standardized they may need some minor modification
- **credit risks** – credit worthiness is relatively easy to ascertain in most western, developed countries. In underdeveloped or developing nations it may not be so easy
- **currency risks** – in some countries there are high rates of inflation. This makes it harder to actually get the agreed price for goods supplied. If inflation is running at three hundred per cent per annum, which is not unknown, then this is nearly one per cent each day. If goods to the value of £100 are supplied then every day's delay in the payment for those goods reduces the amount actually received by £1.

2 Legal

- **protectionism** – in addition to tariffs there may also be quotas on the kind of goods which can be imported. This again is to protect domestic industries and/or to save scarce foreign currency
- **foreign legal restraints** – there may laws in force which govern and restrict what foreign companies can do
- **foreign government interference**
- **required foreign government participation**

▶ In October 1991 Littlewoods unveiled shops in St Petersburg. It claimed that it was the first mainstream western retailer to launch in Russia.

Some countries encourage foreign companies to invest and do business in those countries. However, they sometimes insist on a joint venture operation.

3 Cultural

- **nationalism** – in some countries there is a strong preference for home produced products which makes it difficult for would-be exporters to break into those markets
- **cultural differences** – this creates particular problems for all aspects of marketing. Custom and practice in different countries have developed a preference for certain kinds of food which have to be prepared in a specific way. There are certain expectations about what would be considered an acceptable meal. While many foods and dishes are accepted internationally there are many others which would not be considered palatable in certain countries. English pork or beef sausages, for example, are viewed with disdain by people in other European countries
- **different business relationships and practices.**

4 Psychological

- **racial and ethnic prejudice** – in some countries there is a definite prejudice against imported goods from certain countries. Prejudices arise for many different reasons
- **risk** – this particularly applies to machines and other mechanical and electrical goods. Goods of this kind which are produced at home can be supplied with spare parts and readily be repaired. This does not always apply to foreign imported goods.

The reasons given for countries to engage in international trade do not explain why firms should engage in international trade. It would seem simpler for firms to concentrate their efforts in the domestic market rather than having to deal on international markets. There are three main reasons why firms become involved in international marketing:

1 To sustain growth

Relying on a single market in some instances can be risky. If agricultural tractor manufacturers, for example, were to rely solely on their domestic markets they would experience some variation in demand from year to year and no overall growth in the market. Moreover all the producers of agricultural tractors would have much smaller sales volumes if they did not engage in selling to overseas markets. Indeed, where the domestic market is static or showing only a slow rate of growth, or is highly competitive, then international marketing may be used to gain expansion. The only thing a firm must ask itself is whether it could achieve growth in a less risky and/or more profitable way.

 Obtain a copy of *The Times 1000 UK firms* (Times Books, London: HarperCollins) which you will find in the reference section of your local library. Take a random sample of twenty firms from the list. From the figures in the book estimate the percentage of export business each one of the twenty firms undertakes.

Can you account for any large difference between firms in terms of the percentage of goods they export?

2 To achieve economies of scale

A competitive advantage can be gained from economies of scale resulting from the increased volume of output and lower unit costs. Additional sales generated from export opportunities enable firms to obtain this advantage

3 Competition

Pressure of competition from other operators in the marketplace may make it necessary to supply to international markets. If all other firms in the industry develop international status then those that do not follow suit risk loss of status in the eyes of the customer/industry and then market share in the domestic market.

There are also indications to show that it is becoming easier for firms to consider entering international markets. Many countries now have large retail chains, TV advertising and credit cards and tariff barriers are falling. Advances in technology have reshaped industries and shifted product leadership to new countries thereby stimulating the need for international trade. Improvements in communications have overcome geographically imposed barriers to trade and made buyers increasingly aware of global markets.

▶ Despite the many barriers to international trade many firms engage in marketing in foreign countries. Growth, taking up capacity, and pressure of demand at home are reasons for this.

APPROACHES TO INTERNATIONAL MARKETING

Choice of international marketing strategy depends upon the amount of resources firms command and the amount of control they wish to exert over the international marketing of their goods and services.

Checklist for export markets

- the approximate size of the market (production/imports exports)
- the politial/economic stability of the market (British Overseas Trade Board, hints to exporters booklets are a good source)
- the growth trends in the market (production and apparent consumption)

▶ Before deciding to enter a foreign market a firm should check that it will meet with its requirements.

- the products which are currently available (how well they satisfy tastes, habits, etc.)
- the leading competitors, their market shares, promotion methods, services and facilities offered)
- the channels and costs of distribution
- the legal requirements, standards, etc.
- tariffs, quotas, import licenses (British Overseas Trade Board give details)
- ease of transportation (speed/frequency/costs)

Exporting through intermediaries in the domestic market

Goods can be sold through export houses in the domestic markets. These are rather like wholesalers but specialize in supplying goods to foreign markets. This is sometimes a first step taken by firms wanting to increase sales by selling to international markets. Firms adopting this approach, of course, usually do not know what happens to the goods after they have been supplied to the export house and hence are not in a position to adjust the product to market needs. In effect it is an extension of the domestic market but without the advantage of being able to assess customers' responses to the product.

Confirming Houses

Another approach involves making use of a **confirming house**. These are organizations which place orders with manufacturers on behalf of an overseas buyer, such as a department store, take care of the shipping arrangements and pay cash for the goods supplied. These firms also act as export houses and obtain orders for manufacturers. A set fee or a percentage of each invoice is payable as commission.

Present distributors in the domestic market

Sometimes a firm's distributors in the home market operate on an international basis so that it may be possible for a producer to make use of existing intermediaries to get into some international markets.

Other manufacturers in the domestic market

Other manufacturers with whom the firm is on friendly terms and not in direct competition may be used. They may be prepared to carry products which complement their own product lines.

Import houses

In the same way that there are organizations in the country of origin who specialize in exporting there are also specialist importing houses in the countries of destination as well. Producers can sup-

▶ The UK publication, *Trident*, carries advertisements of opportunites for importers and exporters.

ply certain goods direct to import houses. The producers lose control of the marketing of the goods but at least they do know where the goods are going and can research the market for themselves to get some idea of customers wants and needs in the country of destination.

Soviet Trade Fair

The November/December 1991 edition of *Export Today* (p. 33) reported that some 100 Soviet industrial organizations were due to take part in an exhibition at the Business Design Centre in London called 'Russia and the Republics Soviet Trade Exhibition'. These organizations were from sectors as diverse as raw materials, electronics and consumer goods. It had been indicated that they would be exhibiting their services and products. The 300 Soviet business people present would be seeking to discuss cooperation deals, joint ventures and business in the Soviet Union.

Direct export

This involves the exporting company having its own sales staff who obtain orders in overseas markets. Products are then supplied directly to the customer. It may or may not include the establishment of a local office in the country of destination to handle paperwork and other matters. This method does have considerable advantages in so far as it enables the suppplying firm to exercise complete control over the marketing of its goods and services. Local tariffs and import restrictions, on the other hand, may make it difficult for the company to compete price-wise.

Supplying through local agents

This approach is similar to direct export with the exception that the expense of setting up a local office is spared and at the same time local agents are used who have an expert knowledge of the market, its practices and customs. Clearly, while there are benefits there are also limitations since much depends on how easy it is to obtain motivated and effective agents.

Local assembly

Tariff and quota restrictions on finished products can reduce the competitive effectiveness of products in international markets. In many instances if it can be shown that there is a 'local manufactured content' in goods supplied by foreign firms then tariffs may be lowered. If products can be assembled in the country of destination then a natural development from marketing direct and having a sales office in the country concerned is to have local assembly facilities. More investment on the company's behalf is required but it can lead to a more effective means of marketing

► Ways of serving foreign markets range from supplying goods to importers, in much the same way as firms supply agents at home, to setting up foreign subsidiaries to manufacture and market the products or services.

the goods. Of course, availability of suitable premises and personnel are important factors to take into consideration.

Nissan's Sunderland venture

On September 8th 1986 the Japanese car manufacturer Nissan opened a new plant near Sunderland. It aimed to increase its British output to 100,000 cars a year. Despite worries about the effect on the British motor industry, several areas of Britain had tried to get the Japanese firm to set up in their region.

The British Government had agreed to provide £100 m. in regional aid towards Nissan's expenditure of £380 m. Setting up the factory in Sunderland was expected to provide 2,000 jobs.

Local manufacture

Setting up a full-scale manufacturing plant rather than just an assembly operation in the country where a firm wants to market its goods can be an attractive proposition. This is particularly the case when the country concerned enjoys political stability and offers good tax incentives to foreign firms to make such an investment. Japanese firms have been encouraged to do just this in the UK. The countries themselves benefit as well as the companies since it provides jobs for people.

Licensing

Licensing involves arranging for the product to be assembled, manufactured or even marketed by local companies based in a foreign market. In return the supplying company may obtain periodic or once and for all payments called **royalties**. Such agreements usually restrict the supply of goods to the domestic markets in the countries concerned. Licensing arrangements may be the only realistic way of marketing to some countries or parts of the world.

Franchising

Franchising allows a distributor to be independent and control the business to his or her own liking. It usually requires an investment and a commitment to buy the franchiser's product and in return the distributor receives advice or assistance in managing or promoting the business. Franchising is discussed elsewhere in the book but it is mentioned again here since it can apply to international marketing.

▶ See Chapter 14

Joint ventures

This is an arrangement whereby manufacturing and/or distribution is undertaken by a company established and jointly owned by the exporting company and local shareholders or the government of the country of destination. Such a strategy may be imposed on the exporter by the government of the country concerned as the only way of gaining access to the market.

► This is the only way to get into the Japanese home market.

ANALYSING INTERNATIONAL MARKETING OPPORTUNITIES

With the exception of marketing through export houses in the domestic market producers know where their goods are going. The need to understand the export marketplace in the same way as they understand the domestic marketplace is therefore very important.

More specifically a company should establish what are the stated foreign government policies about the range and type of imports that will be accepted into a country and the extent to which the foreign government imposes tariffs and quotas to protect industry at home. International marketing is a complex business and there are legal and financial regulations to get to grips with. In addition, the marketing and commercial infrastructures of countries differ considerably and it is important to understand these.

We have examined the need to understand consumer behaviour elsewhere, and in the case of foreign markets it becomes very important. What we assume to be true of the home market does not necessarily remain the same when we consider different foreign markets. Life cycle patterns, bases of motivation, cultural values and life styles may be very different from what we are used to and require an entirely different marketing approach.

Marketing communication channels need to be explored to identify how effectively information regarding products and services can be brought to the attention of the consumer. Literacy and language are often difficult barriers that have to be overcome.

Most important of all as far as the firm is concerned is the capacity of the market to pay for the goods and services supplied. This will be influenced by such factors as personal disposable income and government restrictions on the expenditure of foreign currency reserves. For larger items and industrial projects loan terms, interest and capital requirements are also key factors.

Movements towards a free market

All the points above paint the picture of a complex world for the international marketer. International markets in which there are no trade barriers, a common currency and economic equality in terms of development between countries would help the international marketer's case.

In many areas of the world steps have been taken to create common markets, that is markets shared by different countries with a long-term view of working toward the reduction of trade barriers and even economic union. One such market is the **European Economic Community** (EEC).

► In 1991 Volkswagen was granted an injunction from a Paris court forbidding its French rival Renault to continue its current advertising campaign. Volkswagen argued that the press advertisement saying 'Renault is selling twice as many automobiles in Germany as VW in France' constituted comparative advertising which is prohibited in France.

> ### Market research reports
> Metra Martech, in their 1991 publication *Supplying to the German Building Market,* reported that 5.3 million new homes will be needed in Germany by the year 2000. The report also indicated that the the commercial and industrial sectors were developing fast and as construction output grows so will the demand for building materials and components.
>
> Germany is the largest buildings materials and components market in the EC and is currently enjoying boom conditions. The report shows how companies can profit from these opportunites. It highlighted local market views, market experience and entry methods and what the Germans expect from UK manufacturers.

1992 was the year set to have goods, services, capital and people moving freely between EEC countries. It required the elimination of physical, technical and fiscal barriers making international trade much easier and cheaper. At the same time, however, it made the market more competitive in the sense that what were formerly national markets enjoying varying degrees of protection were opened to greatly increased competition. The competition emanates not just from within the EEC countries but also from other countries outside the common market such as those in the Far East.

Increased competition is a threat to those businesses which operate in undifferentiated markets.

PRICING ON THE INTERNATIONAL SCENE

Firms should not underprice their products in foreign markets. This is particularly applicable to new entrants. It is much more difficult to raise prices from an unduly low level than it is to reduce prices from a comfortable margin in response to competition or to achieve some expansion. Entry to a new market at a low price will be seen in an unfavourable light by competitors and they will respond accordingly. Prices should always be related to what the market will bear.

In European Community countries the following are expected to take place in the 1990s:

- a drop in costs generally
- the opening up of public purchasing contracts to broader competition
- extra foreign investment in the European Community leading to in additional production capacity
- more rigourous enforcement of competition policy

- general increase in competiton.

All of these should create a downward pressure on prices in the EEC. Amongst the changes probable are:

- more price rivalry on airway routes after deregulation
- the prospect of selling financial services internationally with a consequent drop in the average price for banking, insurance and securities
- advancements in freight capacity as a consequence of more efficient border crossings leading to enhanced price competition among carriers
- at the time of writing there are substantial differentials in the price of drugs across the EEC. It is expected that this will diminish somewhat in the 1990s.

It is likely that price cutting will be used as a short-term strategy to gain market share. However, at the present time it is uncertain whether pricing will play a more prominent role in competition than the non-price elements of the marketing mix.

At the beginning of the 1990s there are clearly wide differences in prices for similar products throughout EEC countries. Often differences indicate calculated manufacturer strategies to vary product positioning based on the stage of economic development in each country. Variations may also be ascribed to different taxation policies and distributor margins in the particular countries. With the beginning of the 1992 regulations to improve market integration it is expected that this may lead to smaller price variations in individual countries for similar products.

Amongst the pricing implications of these changes for manufacturers is the need to understand the price elasticity of consumer demand for each product in each country in the EEC. It is also necessary to identify product substitution effects at different price points.

▶ See pages 202–3 for further information on price elasticity.

Global versus international marketing

There is a school of thought which differentiates international marketing from **global marketing**. It is argued that international marketing involves the marketer in adapting products, services, and methods of marketing to meet the needs of individual countries. In the case of global marketing, identical products, services and methods of marketing are standardized for every country.

The case for international as opposed to global marketing rests upon the belief that the marketing concept is only really satisfied by interpreting the different wants and needs of different countries individually. Global marketing rests on the idea of having standardized products and methods of marketing. It argues that through rising standards many of the differences between coun-

▶ Baker (1991) argues that globalization is production-oriented in the sense that it seeks to 'drive' the wants and wishes of potential users toward commonality rather than modify the supply to match a varying demand. Baker, M. J. (1991), *Marketing: An introductory text*. London: Macmillan, 5th edn, p. 541.

tries at a similar stage in economic development have become eroded – their wants and needs are similar. On this assumption it is possible to market the same product and use the same methods of marketing communication in differe nt countries. McDonalds is an example of an organization which uses global marketing.

 Indicate whether the following products are most suitable for international marketing or global marketing:

- confectionery items
- cigarettes
- microcomputers
- washing machines
- ice-cream
- clothes

- machine tools
- fast food outlets
- cars
- cinema films
- TV soap operas
- shoes

Selecting markets

It is often the case that opportunities in foreign markets may present themselves to would-be exporters and international marketing firms from time to time. If a firm is actively searching for such opportunities, the following points are useful to bear in mind

- there has to be enough potential in the market to justify a firm's marketing efforts
- the firm's products should stand out well against competitors' offerings when it comes to quality performance and price
- where pricing is very keen one should look for opportunities where price is not all-important and where profit margins will not easily be eroded
- there should be some indication of growth in the sector or sectors of interest (five to ten per cent growth per annum at the least)
- It is better to avoid countries where there are likely to be problems in obtaining money for goods supplied and/or transfer of currency back to the country supplying the goods.

 Take each one of the following products/services and each one of the countries indicated and consider what kind of market there will be for the product or service in each case.

| Product | Country | | | | |
	Japan	Brazil	France	Australia	Egypt
Whisky					
Cars					
Insurance					
Shoes					
Washing machines					

CHAPTER SUMMARY

1 Firms get involved in international marketing to sustain growth, match competition and to achieve economies of scale.

2 There are many ways in which firms can get involved in international marketing activities. Supplying to confirming houses in the home market is perhaps the easiest way to start but eventually firms may set up their own manufacturing facilities and retail outlets in foreign countries.

3 Before firms get involved in international marketing they need to establish a variety of facts. These include the stated government policies about the range and type of imports that will be accepted into the country and the extent to which the government imposes tariffs and quotas to protect industry at home.

4 The marketing and commercial infrastructure of countries differ considerably and it is important to understand these. Firms also need to understand consumer behaviour since what we assume to be true of the home market is not necessarily true of different foreign markets.

5 Life cycle patterns, bases of motivation, cultural values and life styles may be very different from country to country and may require an entirely different marketing approach. Marketing communication channels need to be explored to identify how effectively information regarding products and services can be brought to the attention of the consumer. Most important of all as far as the firm is concerned is the capacity of the market to pay for the goods and services supplied.

6 Pricing goods in international markets has to be handled with care. Firms have to study the various factors that influence prices and ensure that they do not underprice their goods.

7 A distinction is made between global and international marketing. Global marketing is an attempt to achieve some degree of standardization in terms of the products and services which are offered in different countries. On the other hand, international marketing stresses that the needs and wants of consumers in different countries will always be different and that as a consequence it is necessary to meet their specific requirements.

▶ Now that you have reached the end of the chapter, turn back to the objectives and make sure you have achieved each of them.

Appendix 1 A Case study

This is a case study exercise which will allow you to apply a wide range of knowledge you have learned from this book.

Gribbles

Gribbles was founded in 1878 when Josiah Gribble set up in business as a stone mason outside the cemetery gates at Cloudburn, East Lancashire. Stone masons were skilled craftsmen who could, among other things, produce the most grandiose, baroque or elegant effigies to mark the final resting places of loved ones. Poorer people were buried in unmarked graves but for the more prosperous individuals and families, the ornaments of the graveyard were a symbol of their status in local society. In addition to memorials in graveyards there was also other business to be won in the town. Firms, the town council and even local individuals often wanted work carried out on buildings and monuments.

Cloudburn was a medium-sized industrial town situated in the industrial heartland of the north-west of England. Nestling in the shadows of the bleak Pennine moorlands it supported a prosperous middle class which could easily afford the services of Josiah Gribble. In the course of the next twenty years Josiah Gribble's apprentices became well known as real craftsmen all over the North of England. To have worked at Gribble's was a commendation that was difficult to surpass and was a passport to permanent employment.

At the turn of the twentieth century, Gribble acquired a mill close to the centre of Cloudburn and began to cut stone into blocks which could be used by other masons throughout the industrial North of England. Orders flooded in and at the outbreak of war in 1914, Gribble employed twenty men in the mill in addition to his stone masons and their apprentices.

After the First World War fashions began to change. Although war memorials provided a boost to post-war business immediately after the war, work outside of memorials in cemeteries and churchyards began to decline. Even on the cemetery and churchyard side of the business simple gravestones became fashionable and the demand for elaborate carvings on cemetery memorials diminished. People were more conscious of status symbols of a different order and there was less emphasis on having symbols to commemorate oneself after death. There was, however, a demand for simple gravestones of different sizes and cost.

The economic recession of the late 1920s made its mark on the town and these were lean years for Gribbles. Josiah Gribble died in 1931 and he was succeeded in the business by his son Joshua. Joshua was a man who was content to get by with a modest standard of living and sought only to ensure that the business would support himself and his family. He had an eye for cost savings from an early age and implemented them with fervour throughout the fifty years that he directed and managed the business.

Between 1931 and 1981 the business did not expand in terms of volume of business undertaken. Taking inflation into account receipts in 1981 were only forty-five per cent of what they had been in 1931 and the labour force had been reduced from thirty-five employees to just eleven.

In the intervening period the population of Cloudburn had quadrupled in size and the annual number of deaths had also quadrupled. There was only one stone mason in the town throughout this period and this was Gribble. Two trends had been apparent during this period of time. Fewer families were interested in marking graves with gravestones and there was a marked shift to cremations rather than burials.

In 1982 John Gribble, the present owner of the business, inherited Gribbles. John is not a stone mason but a solicitor in Cloudburn. John's father had decided that the business did not really represent the best opportunity for his son and encouraged him to seek a professional career.

In the last ten years the labour force at the mill has been reduced to five workers and the firm now employs a semi-retired part-time stone mason. Business is now at an all time low and John would really like to get along without the business altogther. The mill is valued at around £750,000 but it is unlikely that he would find a buyer at anything like this price. The premises outside the cemetery present a similar problem with regard to saleablity. The value of these premises is under £50,000.

The five men working at the mill are all aged under forty. Work in the town for semi-skilled and unskilled workers is scarce. Since the business makes a small profit and keeps the five men in jobs, John feels some pressure to keep the business going as it is, at least for a little while longer. John feels that it would be virtually impossible to find a buyer for the business. He thinks that it offers little in the way of profits and offers no scope for development as a viable business. Moreover, the machinery in the mill is more than thirty years old and has only scrap value.

His view is that in the longer term the business must eventually fold – this he feels is inevitable. However, he does think there is another possibility. The council have offered to buy the cemetery site for forty per cent of the value he has put on it and he has thoughts of turning the mill into a night club.

John feels he can raise the necessary financial backing for such a venture provided that he can demonstrate that the project is a viable one. The mill would have to be stripped of its fittings, furnishings and machinery and completely refurbished to provide the kind of facilities that are associated with night clubs in big cities such as Manchester some thirty miles away.

Questions

1 Stone masons in the 1870s could cater for different market segments. Market niching was obviously a possible strategy in those days. Identify possible market segments and suggest what kinds of wants and needs have to be satisfied in each case.

2 How do you think stone masons would have marketed themselves at the turn of the century?

3 Why do you think simple gravestones became more fashionable after the First World War?

4 Why do you think that Joshua Gribble emphasized cost savings rather than diversification over the years 1931 to 1982?

5 What kind of product-market strategies (e.g. diversification) do you think that Joshua Gribble could have pursued over the years 1931 to 1982? Try to be specific.

6 John Gribble is now faced with the problem of what he should do with the business in the 1990s. What kind of problems do you think he would encounter if he were to pursue the project of turning the mill into a night club?

7 Do you think that the night club venture is the best option open to John Gribble at the present time? Why or why not?

8 Assuming that John had to justify the night club venture to a group of financial backers what kind of information and evidence do you think he would need to produce?

9 What other options do you think John Gribble could pursue?

Appendix 2 Assessment and examination

WRITTEN ASSIGNMENTS

Get briefed

The requirements for written assignments vary from subject to subject, course to course, examination board to examination board. If you are asked to complete a written assignment without being given a detailed guidance on how it should be presented, you have every right to complain. This is not something you should be left to guess about.

Understanding the brief

Study the brief carefully. You can solve a lot of problems at this stage. It might be something as short as an essay title, or a long briefing for a marketing project. Right from the start try to imagine what the finished product will look like. This may well raise questions of interpretation. Make a list of these and ask for guidance from a tutor. If this is not forthcoming, discuss the problem with someone else. You will often find that simply putting your problem into words makes the problem disappear.

Organizing your time

For large pieces of work, especially those which require research, it is essential to make a plan showing what you are going to do and by when. All kinds of contingencies may cause problems for you: the book you require is on loan to someone else, the person you want to interview is on holiday, some data you require isn't published until after your deadline, etc. The better you plan, the easier you will find it to adjust to changing circumstances.

Organizing your mind

Many people find that the best way for them to organize their mind is to use a spider diagram like the one shown overleaf. Many of the spider's legs will turn out to be irrelevant, but at least you will know which ones are there to be cut off.

When you have thought around the assignment in this way and as you think further about it, you can start to assemble materials. Look at your lecture notes, activity responses and file cards. Check reading lists. Look at the contents pages and indexes of your textbooks. By the time you have done this you will probably have to draw another spider diagram.

WHY?
(1) Enables firms to provide products/services that fit consumer/industrial requirements.
(2) Enables Marketers to target users.
(3) Determines which are the best segments to target and how many.
(4) Identifies needs wants, gaps in market, etc.

SEGMENTATION OF INDUSTRIAL MARKETS

SEGMENTATION OF CONSUMER MARKETS

SIC
(Standard Industrial Classification)
(1) By industry/type of business.
(2) By size of company.
(3) Geographical location
(4) Distribution, etc.

MARKET SEGMENTATION

LIFE STYLE
(Plummer)
(1) Activities.
(2) Interests.
(3) Opinions.
(4) Demographics.

ACORN SAGACITY, etc.

HOW?
By assessing the variables which distinguish consumers/industries from each other.
Variables include:
(1) Geographic: rural/urban, pop. density, etc.
(2) Demographics: age, sex, income, education, etc.
(3) Psychographic: social class, life style, etc.
(4) Behavioural: user status, attitude to product, etc.

LIFE CYCLE
(1) Young, single.
(2) Married, no kids.
(4) Married, kids left home.
(5) Retired couple.
(6) Solitary survivor.

Start drafting

Unless you are a very skilled writer, you simply won't be able to start writing an assignment at the beginning to reach a successful conclusion at the end. Before it reaches this point, your work will have to go through several drafts. Either keep your early drafts in note form, or if you write them more fully, be prepared to cut them, and reassemble them in a different order. If you use a word processor this is easy.

If you get stuck

If you get stuck, the first thing to do is to try to make a list of your difficulties. Say to yourself 'I can't do this because . . . '. A lot of the confusion surrounding your difficulties will then disappear and the real problems should emerge. If you have any left, take the list of difficulties to a tutor or some other source of help. The worse things to do if you get stuck are to stay up night after night getting nowhere, or to give up without seeking advice.

Check before you finalize

When you have a draft, check it against the brief. Be tough with yourself. Will this draft, when written up, really meet the requirements? If it doesn't then make a list of the ways in which it fails. Use the list to redraft and repeat.

Sleep on it

If you possibly can, leave the work alone for a few days. When you come back to it you will see its strengths and weaknesses more clearly.

The final version

This may be the second or third version. It should be clearly written and correctly spelled and punctuated. Leave wide margins on the page for tutor's comments. Make sure you follow any local requirements for length, line-spacing and structure. It may well require a bibliography. Failing any local advice, references quoted in the text should take one of the following forms:

Either '(Proctor, 1992)' or 'as Proctor says (1992)'. Then at the end list the references in alphabetical order according to author name. For book references the references are: second name, initial or first name, publication date, publisher. For articles: second name, first name or initial, date, title, periodical title, volume, part or part number, page. And where your reference appears in a book edited by someone else: author's second name, initial or first name, date, title, editor's second name, initial or first name, title of book, publisher.

Check the final version and hand it in on time.

REVISION

In an ideal world you would be reviewing your work from the second day of your course. But we don't live in an ideal world and most people leave revision until the last few weeks before the examination. Nevertheless, if you have taken some of the advice offered earlier, you will have been maintaining good, easily-retrievable notes and file cards throughout your course and so be off to a flying start when revision time comes.

Work out a revision timetable, with realistic learning objectives at each stage – you will find many of the chapter objectives in this book useful, but you will have to make some up for yourself. Use past papers, but NOT to question spot. Question-spotting is a bad mistake. Use past papers to identify which broad topics and themes the examiner usually asks about and revise them carefully. Analyse past papers for their commands. Make sure you know the differences between 'describe', 'account for', 'analyse', and so on. What you must not do is to revise actual questions and prepare model answers. Model questions rarely come up!

► Make sure you know how you will be examined. How many exams? How long? What choice of questions? Will there be compulsory questions, essay questions, data-response questions, short answer questions? These all require different skills and different ways of revising.

► Establish how much of your syllabus you should revise.

► Check the assessment objectives which are printed in the syllabus document produced by your board.

Ask yourself questions and answer them. Try to think like an examiner. As you approach different topics ask yourself, what questions could the examiner ask me about this.

Revise actively

Make notes and summaries all the time. Make notes of notes, summaries of notes and notes of summaries. Annotate your notes with notes from a textbook and then produce a tidy version. Convert notes in continuous text into notes in diagram or table format, or vice versa.

As your revision proceeds, try to reduce the whole course to a series of trigger words and phrases – just enough to jog your memory. Practise writing your answers under the pressure of time. How much can you get down in the time available? Practise writing answers of that length.

Work in regular sessions with breaks every hour, but get used to working for three hours at a time before taking a longer break.

THE EXAMINATION

Think of the examination as an opportunity for you to give a performance, with an audience of one – the examiner. You are displaying your knowledge, understanding and skills to someone who wants to applaud you.

Here are some key points to bear in mind:

- make sure you know when and where the examination will be held. If it is an unfamiliar place, try to visit it beforehand and check your travel arrangements
- the evening before the exam, make sure you have all the pens, pencils and other equipment you will need
- arrive in good time, but don't stand around chatting. Go for a walk to loosen up and get the oxygen flowing to the brain
- when the exam starts, read through the whole paper (or those parts which relate to your options)
- do NOT start writing immediately, but settle down, get the feel of the paper, check the instructions and find the questions you feel ok about. Take a few minutes to double check that you are following the rubric correctly
- choose your probable questions, but don't firm up your choice at this early stage
- the marks allocated to each question, or parts of each question are a rough guide to how much you should write on each. If two marks are allocated, make two good points and stop. You won't get more than two marks however many brilliant points you make
- draw up a rough timetable for yourself – 'by 10.35 I should have finished the first question', etc.

▶ Read the Chief Examiner's reports for previous years. Note well what these reports say. Not only does the Chief Examiner have experience of the mistakes of thousands of students, he/she actually decides what is mistaken and what is correct.

▶ Taking an active approach to revision is essential. Passive revising, i.e. sitting reading through notes and textbooks is both boring and ineffective.

▶ Revise with friends, discussing questions and trying to explain things to each other.

▶ Give yourself time off, especially on the day before the examinations start.

▶ Examiners want you to do well. They are instructed to mark your work by giving you credit for everything you do properly, not to penalize you for your mistakes. Your marks start at zero and go on up whenever you do something right. The examiner is looking for opportunities to reward positive achievements, so supply plenty of these and make it easy for the examiner to find them. Examination answers are vehicles for you to display your achievement.

▶ If you suffer badly from nerves, learn to relax through the use of deep breathing techniques. Don't take pills, except under medical supervision. Don't drink alcohol before an exam. It relaxes the wrong part of your brain.

► The most common reason for candidates failing to get the marks they should is not lack of knowledge or skill, but failure to observe the golden rule. Make sure you do what the examiner asks you to do.

► Presentation and layout are important, because they should help the examiner to find your good points easily. Use short sentences and paragraphs to make your points clearly and concisely.

► GOOD LUCK!

● start your first question. Now for the golden rule of exams

> ANSWER THE QUESTION SET:
> DO WHAT THE EXAMINER TELLS YOU TO DO

● For all but very short answers, make a plan
● think all the time. Don't just try to remember things, but think about how to apply what you know to the question set
● don't overrun your time on a particular question. It takes much longer to get a few more marks at the end of an answer than at the beginning of another
● take rests during your exams. Loosen up physically; breathe, stretch, shut your eyes while you are thinking
● leave enough time for checking and polishing your answers. A single additional mark could mean a higher grade.

Index